THE GLOBE ENCOMPASSED

Connections: Key Themes in World History

THE GLOBE ENCOMPASSED

The Age of European Discovery, 1500–1700

Glenn J. Ames
The University of Toledo

PEARSON

Prentice
Hall

Upper Saddle River, New Jersey 07458

Library of Congress Cataloging-in-Publication Data

Ames, Glenn Joseph.
  The globe encompassed / Glenn J. Ames.
    p. cm.
  Includes bibliographical references and index.
  ISBN 0-13-193388-4
  1. Discoveries in geography—European. I. Title.

  G95.A53 2008
  910.94'09031—dc22

                                    2007001935

Editorial Director: Charlyce Jones Owen
Executive Editor: Charles Cavaliere
Editorial Assistant: Maureen Diana
Marketing Manager: Kate Mitchell
Senior Marketing Assistant: Jennifer Lang
Production Liaison: Marianne
  Peters-Riordan
Manufacturing Buyer: Ben Smith
Cover Art Director: Jayne Conte
Cover Design: Bruce Kenselaar
Cover Illustration: Courtesy of the Library
  of Congress
Director, Image Resource Center:
  Melinda Patelli

Manager, Rights and Permissions:
  Zina Arabia
Manager, Visual Research: Beth Brenzel
Manager, Cover Visual Research &
  Permissions: Karen Sanatar
Image Permission Coordinator:
Composition/Full-Service Project
  Management: Shiny Rajesh/Integra
  Software Services, Inc.

Credits and acknowledgments borrowed from other sources and reproduced, with permission, in this textbook appear on appropriate page within text.

Pearson Education LTD.
Pearson Education Singapore, Pte. Ltd
Pearson Education, Canada, Ltd
Pearson Education–Japan
Pearson Education Australia PTY, Limited

Pearson Education North Asia Ltd
Pearson Educación de Mexico, S.A. de C.V.
Pearson Education Malaysia, Pte. Ltd
Pearson Education, Upper Saddle River,
  New Jersey

ISBN-13: 978-0-13-193388-0
ISBN-10:   0-13-193388-4

For my mother,
Janet Elizabeth Wescott Ames

Contents

reword

Connections: Key Themes in World History focuses on specific issues of world historical significance from antiquity to the present by employing a combination of explanatory narrative, primary sources, questions relating to those sources, a summary analysis ("Making Connections"), and further points to ponder, all of which combine to enable readers to discover some of the most important driving forces in world history.

The increasingly rapid pace and specialization of historical inquiry has created an ever-widening gap between professional publications and general surveys, especially surveys of world history. The purpose of *Connections* is to bridge that gap by placing the latest research and debates on selected topics of global historical significance, as well as some of the evidence upon which historians base their insights, into a form and context that is comprehensible to students and general readers alike.

Two pedagogical principles infuse this series. First, students master world history most easily if allowed to focus on specific themes and issues. Such themes, by their very specificity, as well as because of their general application, enable students to perceive and understand the overall patterns and meaning of our shared global past more clearly than is possible through reading, by itself, a massive world history textbook. Second, students learn best when asked to think critically about what they are studying. So far as the study of history is concerned, critical thinking necessarily involves analysis of primary sources.

To that end, we offer a series of brief, tightly focused books that embrace a radical simplicity and a provocative format. Each book goes to the heart of a key theme, phenomenon, or issue in world history—something that has connected humans across cultures, continents, and time spans. By actively engaging with this material, the reader comes to understand in a nuanced and meaningful manner how often distantly located human cultures have been connected to one another as key actors in the epic story of world history.

Alfred J. Andrea
Series Editor
Professor Emeritus of History
The University of Vermont

Series Editor's Preface

The Franciscan missionary friar Toribo de Motolinía noted in his *History of the Indians of New Spain* that during the week of the Feast of Corpus Christi, in June 1539, the recently baptized Indians of Tlaxcala put on a play entitled *The Conquest of Jerusalem*. Some 1500 Indians took part in the six-act extravaganza, in which the new converts crafted the play's script and its elaborate staging, with probable help from Franciscan friars. Whatever the role of their Spanish Franciscan mentors, surely it was Indian playwrights who ironically transformed Hernan Cortés into the infidel "Great Sultan of Babylon [Cairo] and Tetrarch of Jerusalem," who illegitimately ruled over the Holy City. In like manner, Pedro de Alvarado, conqueror of the Yucatán and Ecuador, became the "captain-general of the Moors." Of course, both villainous roles were played by Indians posing as Sultan Cortés and Captain-general Alvarado. After a series of staged battles, in which the combined armies of Spain, France, and Hungary-Bohemia prove incapable of capturing Jerusalem, the "newcomers to the faith," "the Nahuales or people of New Spain," take the field, led by St. Hippolytus, on whose feast day (13 August 1521) the city of Tenochtitlán had fallen to the Spaniards and their Tlaxcalan allies. Reinforced by these "new Christians," the allied crusader army storms the city. In the midst of ferocious fighting, St. Michael appears and convinces the Moors to surrender, and Sultan Cortés accepts baptism and Emperor Charles V's overlordship. The play then ended with the real-life baptism of large numbers of adult Indians.

What an extraordinary play, with layer upon layer of meaning! It is clear that this lavish production gave voice to the Tlaxcalan sense of ethnic pride, their commitment to their new religion, and their ambivalent attitude toward Spanish rule. Their world had been turned upside down fewer than 20 years earlier, but they could and did hope that these events would usher in a new age in which they would play a preeminent role. Equally, it displays Catholic Spain's aspirations for the role that the Indians of New Spain would play in the grand scheme of God's plan for the universe. Jerusalem, Christendom's holiest city, had fallen to the armies of the First Crusade in 1099 but was recovered by Saladin in 1187. Regained briefly by Emperor Frederick II in 1229, it was again lost to Islam in 1244. The last crusader bastion on the continent of Southwest Asia fell in 1291, but the Christian West continued in the centuries that followed to hatch detailed plans and often less-than-well-planned expeditions to defeat the Muslim enemy and recover the Holy Land. Despite these efforts, Islam kept advancing at the expense of Christendom. In 1516–1517 Ottoman Turkish forces had wrested control of the entire coast of Syria-Palestine, including Jerusalem, from the Mamluks, and under the leadership of Suleyman the Magnificent (1520–1566) were threatening to overrun all of the Mediterranean, as well as Eastern and Central Europe. In this time of crisis, a time that many saw as the Age of Antichrist as foretold in the New Testament's Book of Revelation, there was the promise of Catholic Christendom's ultimate triumph, and perhaps, just perhaps, that triumph would be secured through the human and material wealth of the New World and the Asian spice trade.

The Catholic powers of Europe, led by Portugal and Spain, never did recover Jerusalem nor did they overturn Islam, but arguably the silver and gold of the Americas enabled Spain and its allies to destroy an Ottoman fleet at Lepanto in 1571 and, at least momentarily, blunt the Turkish advance. Similarly, Vasco da Gama and his Portuguese successors succeeded in outflanking Islam and defeating Muslim naval power in the Indian Ocean as part of this same crusade, a crusade that, by the way, the author of the present book has already detailed in his *Vasco da Gama: Renaissance Crusader* (2005).

The *Conquest of Jerusalem* is but one small example of the impact of Europe's early global explorations and colonial ventures on the psyches, histories, and cultures of what had once been widely scattered and, in many cases, unconnected peoples around the world. Glenn J. Ames opens *The Globe Encompassed* with the bold statement, "The age and process of European discovery from ca. 1500 to 1700 constitute one of the great revolutions in the history of humankind," and no historian would contest the validity of that judgment. In essence, the modern, interconnected world, the so-called global village, had its origins in Western Europe's transoceanic voyages that began in the late 15th century and culminated in the early Portuguese, Spanish, Dutch, French, and English overseas empires whose rise and vicissitudes of fortune Ames so ably traces and analyzes in these pages. No student of world history can ignore these events and the people behind them. To do so would be to deny world history's special qualities and perspectives.

As is true of its *Connections* predecessors, *The Globe Encompassed* lays out in clear narrative form a series of connected stories that simultaneously instruct and fascinate the reader. Beyond that, our authorguide provides carefully chosen excerpts from primary sources that enable the reader to enter the mindsets of such notable personalities (and driving forces in Europe's profound impact on the early modern world) as Vasco da Gama, Hernan Cortés, and Samuel de Champlain, and to see first-hand such widely separated and profoundly different colonial enterprises as Dutch-held Batavia (Jakarta) and Puritan New England. In so doing, Ames allows the reader to encompass the globe as it existed between 1500 and 1700.

Alfred J. Andrea
Series Editor

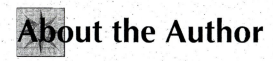About the Author

Glenn J. Ames is Professor of Portuguese and French History at the University of Toledo. His books include: *Colbert, Mercantilism, and the French Quest for Asian Trade* (1996), *Renascent Empire?: The House of Braganza and the Quest for Stability in Portuguese Monsoon Asia* (2000), and *Vasco da Gama: Renaissance Crusader* (2005). He has held fellowships from the Leverhulme Trust, the Calouste Gulbenkian Foundation, the Portuguese Ministry of Education, the National Endowment for the Humanities, and the American Institute of Indian Studies.

knowledgments

The genesis of this book can be traced back to a query several years ago to Prentice Hall's regional representative Michael Morley regarding books to use in a course on European expansion. Since not much had appeared in the field recently that could be used in undergraduate courses, I thought the time might be right for a new concise overview of the topic. Michael graciously put me in touch with Charles Cavaliere in New Jersey, who then put me in touch with Alfred J. Andrea, who was then in the process of putting together what has become the *Connections: Key Issues in World History* series. Well, as the cliché goes, the rest is history. So, I will begin by thanking Michael for helping me make a fortuitous 'connection,' Charles for his encouraging words and help over the past few years, and particularly to Al for his encouragement and meticulous editing of the manuscript.

The first half of this book was largely completed while I was on research leave with my family during the first half of 2005 in Goa, India. Being surrounded by the lush tropical landscape of Goa, and the architectural, cultural, religious, and culinary legacies of the

Portuguese presence there, no doubt infused the project with more energy than would otherwise have been the case. I would therefore like to thank the American Institute of Indian Studies, the National Endowment for the Humanities, and the University of Toledo for helping to make that semester in India a very pleasant reality. In particular, I would like to thank Elise Auerbach, Purnima Mehta, and David Stern for their assistance in facilitating the trip. In Goa, Sergio and Mafalda Mascarenhas, Sudip and Shyamalee Chakravarti, Xavier and Sonali Furtado, Desmond Nazareth, Dilip Barreto, Oscar Noronha, Mangesh Kankonkar, and the rest of our neighbors in "Latino Splendor" all made our time there truly memorable.

Since my own research interests focus on European expansion to Asia, I have received assistance with the Atlantic-world material from various colleagues and friends over the past year. Accordingly, I would like to acknowledge and thank Charles Beatty Medina, Ruth Wallis Herndon, Ronald S. Love, Michael N. Pearson, Francis A. Dutra, Artur Teodoro de Matos, Luiz Filipe R. Thomaz, and Malyn Newitt. Finally, I would like thank my wife, Beth, and children, Miranda and Ethan, for making life both enjoyable and interesting in the United States and abroad.

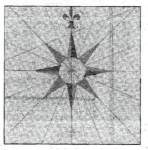

Introduction

The age and process of European discovery from ca. 1500 to 1700 constitute one of the great revolutions in the history of humankind. At the beginning of this period, contacts among many civilizations of the world were generally sporadic and superficial in nature. The disparate civilizations that had developed since the Neolithic revolution, including the Ming dynasty in China, the Aztecs and Incas in the Americas, the Swahili city states of East Africa, the Islamic dynasties in the Middle and Near East, and the Western European monarchies, operated in a fashion that was largely distinct from each other. Moreover, the flora, fauna, and trading products, as well as the theological and intellectual traditions of these civilizations, were shrouded by the mists of intermittent and indirect interchange. There were exceptions to this rule: the travels of Marco Polo in the late 13th century and the voyages of Zheng He in the early 15th century were important precursors to the great explosion of interchange and exchange that Europeans initiated in the early decades of the 15th century and continued unabated for the following two centuries. The result of this process of European expansion was the creation of the sinews of the global economy and society in which we live today. By 1700, thanks to the age of European discovery, the globe had indeed been encompassed. In doing so, the major European states had carved out empires around the globe and, in doing so, initiated an exchange of goods and ideas that set the stage for the advances as well as the struggles of the modern age. To understand the genesis of these seminal events, it is necessary to begin with some brief background on the motivation and the means for accomplishing this daunting task. After all, it was one thing to want to reach the riches of China and India, and quite another to develop the ability to do so.

MOTIVATION: "CHRISTIANS, SPICES, AND MORE?"

It should come as no surprise that there were a myriad of reasons that prompted the major European states of the late medieval and early modern periods to undertake the process of expansion, discovery, and conquest overseas. The well-worn adage, "money makes the world go around," has validity, and economic factors certainly played a role. The money at stake related to the lucrative trading products of Africa (gold, ivory, and slaves), the Middle East (silver, myrrh, frankincense, horses), India (pepper, cinnamon, gemstones, textiles), the islands of Southeast Asia (cloves, nutmeg, mace), and China (silk, porcelain, lacquer ware). Royalty, nobility, and well-heeled merchants in Europe all craved these products as a demonstration of their wealth and power. Asian spices were sought after as tokens of prosperity and to season otherwise bland food. The main problem for the Europeans of the 14th century was that these goods were exorbitantly expensive. This was due to the huge distances and transportation costs involved and the accompanying profits of middlemen. As we all know, cutting out the middlemen in any commercial transaction is always a desirable goal. Therefore, the attraction of finding a way to obtain such products in a more economical manner, ideally at their source, was a strong motivating factor. This attraction fueled the imaginations of Europeans and tested the limits of their knowledge and technology in much the same way as did the Space Race of the 1950s and 1960s waged between the United States and the Soviet Union. In the end, this modern quest culminated in

Neil Armstrong walking on the barren landscape of the moon. In the late 15th century, this quest culminated with Vasco da Gama walking on the tropical beaches of India. Ironically, the image of both historic walks would have prompted an equal degree of incredulity among people who lived only a generation before these men.

Geo-political competition also served to motivate expansion overseas. As in the days of the Roman empire, or any other period in history, overseas possessions and the wealth they produced were viewed as tangible signs of a kingdom's power. The expansion of Europe also played an important social and political role for the monarchies of Europe. The two groups that traditionally posed the greatest threat to the power of the king were the nobility and the Roman Catholic Church. These institutions had the wealth, education, and cultural power to undermine the standing of the kings who, during this period of the New Monarchies, were striving for greater powers over all facets of their kingdoms. One effective means of keeping the nobles and the church happy had been to bestow royal largesse on them. Overseas expansion offered the monarchs of Europe the promise of new lands, titles, offices, and converts that would demonstrably increase the wealth of the nobles and the church. These activities would also be based thousands of miles away, thus keeping potentially destructive forces away from the king's seat of power. Additionally, the king himself did not have to do any of the fighting in these distant lands. His nobles and his subjects would take care of that for him. None of the major monarchs of Europe traveled to either Asia or the Americas between 1500 and 1700. Their retainers would stake their claims to distant corners of the globe for them in a classic *quid pro quo* for wealth and social advancement.

Religiously, the struggle between Christianity and Islam had been waged for centuries. This struggle had focused during the crusades of the Middle Ages around the religious shrines of the Holy Land, particularly in Jerusalem. Militarily, however, the crusades made little impact on the dominance of Islam. Despite the best efforts of various popes, dynastic rivalries and logistical difficulties prevented an effective counterattack by European Christians in the Holy Land. Moreover, the schism in Christianity between the Latin and Greek churches also undermined the quest to reclaim Jerusalem on a permanent basis. During the Fourth Crusade, this rivalry was showcased when the crusaders attacked, sacked, and occupied Constantinople (1204–1261). This fiasco for the Christian world set the stage for the final collapse of the Byzantine Empire in 1453, when the

Ottoman Turks, a people originally from Central Asia, captured and looted Constantinople and transformed it into the capital of an Islamic empire that now threatened to overrun Christian Europe. While the Europeans had largely lost the Middle Eastern Crusade by the mid-15th century, they had better success in reclaiming lands in southern Europe that had earlier been lost to Islam. From the 8th century onward, an Islamic vanguard of Arab and Berber dynasties had spread over most of North Africa and across the straits of Gibraltar, to cover much of the Iberian Peninsula. Sicily and other Mediterranean islands had also been taken. By the mid-15th century, the so-called *Reconquista,* or Reconquest, had expelled the Moors from Portugal and most of Spain. But this struggle was far from over in the Mediterranean Basin, and this rivalry would furnish a powerful motive for expansion. If a way could be found to outflank the Muslims, this struggle could perhaps finally be won.

One of the most important figures in the Age of Discovery was Prince Henrique of Portugal, usually known to us as Prince Henry the "Navigator." From 1418 until his death in 1460, Henry was instrumental in organizing and funding voyages of discovery along the western coast of Africa. According to his chronicler, Gomes Eannes de Azurara, six factors motivated the prince in these endeavors: (1) to learn what lay beyond the Canaries and Cape Bojador; (2) to open profitable new trade with Christian peoples; (3) to investigate the extent of Islamic power; (4) to win converts for the "true faith"; (5) to make alliances with any Christian peoples who might be found, particularly the Prester John, a mythical Christian king who reigned somewhere in the Indies; and (6) to fulfill his horoscope, which compelled him to engage in "great and noble" conquests and to seek "the discovery of things hidden from other men." Henry's motivations, therefore, combined elements of the major structures and issues inherent in the late medieval world in which he lived.

Another key figure in the Age of Discovery was the Portuguese nobleman Vasco da Gama, who from 1497 to 1499 would complete the first successful voyage between Europe and Asia. In late May 1498, da Gama reached the tropical coast of Calicut, India, the center of the coveted pepper trade. He had sailed across 10,000 miles of ocean, much of it hitherto unexplored by Europeans. Da Gama and his men had overcome fierce storms in the South Atlantic, a hostile reception on the Muslim Swahili Coast of East Africa, the ravages of scurvy, and the mind-numbing boredom of endless sailing at an average of less than 10 miles an hour. When they landed on the beach, they were met by two Castilian speaking Muslims from Tunis who demanded to know why they had come. The Portuguese replied, "We come in search of Christians and spices." Da Gama in much more concise and common language had echoed the sentiments originally stated by Azurara. For the Portuguese, the century of conquest and colonization in Asia which followed would indeed combine the twin motivations of seeking wealth and converts for the Christian faith.

THE MEANS: "MAPS, MONEY, AND SHIPS"

It undoubtedly came as a surprise to many educated people that it was the European kingdoms that ultimately succeeded in encompassing the globe during the 15th and 16th centuries. After all, in 1400 Europe was far from the most powerful or civilized region of the globe. In many spheres, Europe was far behind the level of sophistication of China, India, and the Arab world. In fact, Europe had benefited intellectually from the interaction and interchange with Islam over the centuries. But there was little doubt that it had been on the defensive for a century or more. Islam was in the ascendance in many regions from 1400 to 1550. In the Middle East, the power of the Ottoman Turks had grown substantially, and Mehmed II's conquest of Constantinople heralded further advances into the Balkans. Arab traders, meanwhile, had spread Islam from the Red Sea and Persian Gulf ports to the Indian Ocean Basin. Muslim merchants and communities were thus entrenched along the Swahili Coast of East Africa, Arabia, India, and the islands of Southeast Asia (see Map I.1).

Ottoman and other Muslim powers in Central Asia had also effectively blocked European merchants and missionaries from direct overland access to China, an access that Western travelers had enjoyed for about a century (ca. 1260–1368) known as the *Pax Mongolica*, or Mongol Peace. Under successors of Chinggis Khan (1167?–1227), the Mongols had controlled not only China but Mongolia, Korea, Turkistan, Iran, Iraq, and parts of Anatolia, Syria, Ukraine, and Russia, an empire that stretched from the Pacific to Eastern Europe and the Eastern Mediterranean. Once the Mongols had turned from conquest to ruling this empire, they presented Eurasia with a vast and somewhat well-policed land bridge linking China with the West, and provided numerous European merchants and missionaries with new Asian

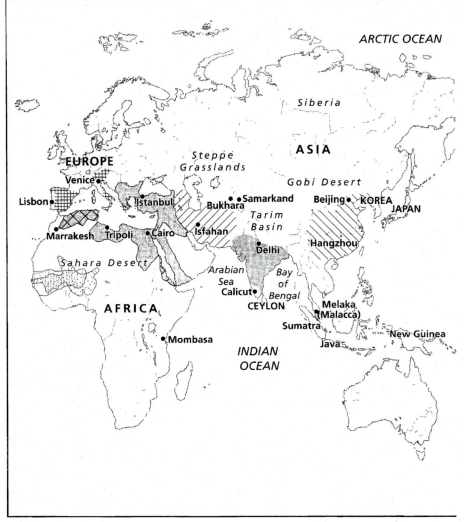

MAP I.1   The World in 1450.

markets and new souls to convert. The Mongol khans had demonstrated broad religious toleration and an interest in Christianity. Franciscan missionaries had been allowed to preach in their domains and
Marco Polo had been employed by Kublai Khan (r. 1260–1294). But
this all changed when the Chinese overthrew the Mongol dynasty in
1368 and established the Ming dynasty (1368–1644). This act, combined with the rise of strong Islamic powers in Central and Southwest
Asia, as well as an Eurasia-wide pandemic of bubonic plague, ended

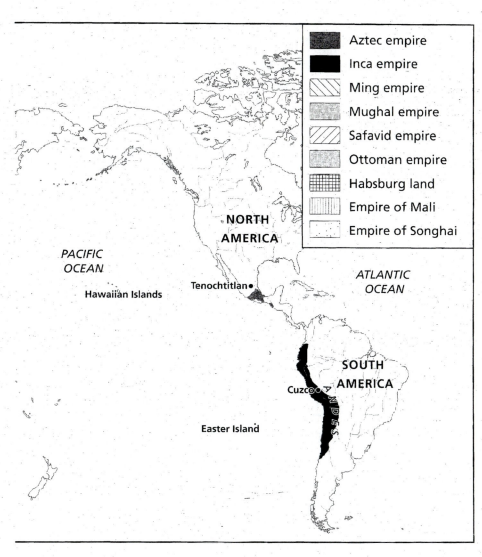

Legend:
- Aztec empire
- Inca empire
- Ming empire
- Mughal empire
- Safavid empire
- Ottoman empire
- Habsburg land
- Empire of Mali
- Empire of Songhai

NORTH AMERICA

PACIFIC OCEAN

Hawaiian Islands

Tenochtitlan●

ATLANTIC OCEAN

SOUTH AMERICA

Cuzco

ANDES

Easter Island

this direct interchange between Western Europe and East Asia. Having, however, once enjoyed such access to China and the rest of the Indies, Europeans were not about to forget these markets and peoples.

So, the obvious question is, Why was it Europe and particularly the kingdom of Portugal that initiated the process of overseas expansion in 1415, a process that would encompass the globe by 1700? Why is it that as I write these words sitting on the tropical western coast of India in Goa, I can communicate with ease in both Portuguese and

English? And why, a few minutes away, is there perhaps the most impressive collection of Christian churches east of Rome? The answer is that the kingdoms of Western Europe alone harnessed the physical, intellectual, technological, economic, and military resources at their disposal through the efforts of individuals at all levels of society. The old cliché about European society in the medieval period was that it was composed of "those who fought, those who prayed, and those who toiled." All of these groups would contribute and profit from the process of expansion. Yet, it was not only kings, nobles, clergy, and peasants who embraced the challenges of the Age of Discovery. The burgeoning merchant class in Europe played a vital role as well.

It was no coincidence that the Age of Discovery coincided with the maturation of a new type of economic system in Europe during the late 15th century. This new economic system was mercantilism, and its basic tenets facilitated the voyages of discovery in the Age of the New Monarchies. Mercantilism was not characterized by blind adherence to a single, precisely defined economic theorem, but rather its adherents embraced parts of a set of commonly held theoretical beliefs that were best suited to the needs of a particular time and state. The underlying principles of mercantilism included (1) the belief that the amount of wealth in the world is relatively static; (2) the belief that a country's wealth can best be judged by the amount of precious metals, or bullion, it possesses; (3) the need to encourage exports over imports as a means of obtaining a favorable balance of foreign trade that would yield such metals; (4) the value of a large population as a key to self-sufficiency and state power; and (5) the belief that the Crown or State should exercise a dominant role in assisting and directing the national and international economies to these ends. As such, mercantilism developed logically from the changes inherent in the decline of feudalism, the rise of strong national states, and the development of a world market economy. But shifts in economic theory alone were not sufficient to bring about the Age of Discovery. There also had to be practical advances in map-making, navigation, and shipbuilding before the challenges of over-coming thousands of miles of unknown oceans and coastlines could be attempted. Advances in metallurgy and the casting and mounting of artillery aboard ships also had to take place before the Europeans could not only protect themselves on such voyages but utilize such weapons in conquest. The period from 1400 to 1550 in Europe witnessed significant advances in all of these fields.

WAS THE WORLD FLAT OR ROUND?

Contrary to the cliché of elementary school, most educated people in 15th-century Europe did not think the earth was flat. Most knew it was round, thanks to the combined knowledge of the mathematicians, astronomers, and geographers of Antiquity, such as Hipparchus of Rhodes (190–120 BCE), Eratosthenes (ca. 276–194 BCE), Theon of Smyrna (70–135 CE), and Strabo (64 BCE–25 CE). Eratosthenes calculated the earth's circumference in a fairly accurate manner. Theon of Smyrna argued that the earth was spherical. Hipparchus's work on the precession of equinoxes, the position of stars in the night sky, and the rising and setting of constellations held great potential importance for navigation. Yet, by far the most influential scholar of the Hellenistic World was Claudius Ptolemy (85–165 CE). Two of Ptolemy's major works survived the ravages of time, his treatise on astronomy, usually called by its Arabic title, the *Almagest*, and his *Geography* of the known world of the 2nd century. These works synthesized much of the astronomical and geographical knowledge of the classical age and postulated a geocentric universe, a view that would formally survive until the work of Copernicus and others in the scientific revolution of the 16th and 17th centuries in Europe.

Ironically, most of this classical knowledge would have been lost to the Europeans of the late Middle Ages had it not been for the indirect assistance of their archenemies of the period: the Arabs. Arab scholars had a great interest in both astronomy and astrology. They had translated and used Ptolemy's *Almagest* extensively. His *Geography*, however, had received less attention. Nevertheless, Arab geographers had contributed theoretical knowledge to the academic mix especially regarding the symmetrical position of continents around the center of the known world. But during the mercurial spread of Islam beginning in the 7th century, the Arabs had added little practical knowledge to world geography as presented by Ptolemy. This dearth resulted from the fact that Islam had spread to areas already well known to classical scholars: the Mediterranean Basin, the Near East, and the countries around the northern Indian Ocean Basin. Arab scholars had also shunned the Atlantic as not navigable and they created a series of foreboding myths about the "green sea of darkness" which influenced medieval views of the Atlantic in Europe. But the key factor for the age of European expansion was that the Arabs had preserved this body of work, and this knowledge would make its way, sometimes through Jewish scholars, to medieval Europe in Latin translation.

In this academic dissemination, the work of Cardinal Pierre d'Ailly, called the *Imago Mundi* (*Image of the World*) published in 1410, was one of the most notable. It was a great synthetic work combining the works of Latin, Greek, and Arab scholars with biblical scriptures. That same year witnessed the publication of Ptolemy's *Geography* in Latin. For the first time, educated Europeans could mine the powerful mix of classical and medieval geographical knowledge together. But a little knowledge can be a dangerous thing—or in this case, a discouraging thing, at least for Europeans such as Prince Henry, who were hoping to expand down the western coast of Africa. For one thing, Ptolemy had declared that it was impossible to sail in the whole southern hemisphere; it was simply too hot. Arab geographers and

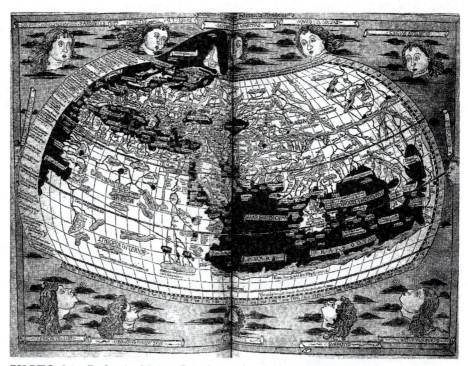

PHOTO I.1 Ptolemic Map. Based on the 2nd-century *Geography* of Claudius Ptolemy, this 1482 map attempted to recreate his description of the world. Note the landlocked Indian Ocean, a psychological obstacle for the Portuguese to overcome in their quest to reach India.

the popular 14th-century travel writer Sir John Mandeville had disputed this view, arguing that the region south of the equator, known as the antipodes, was inhabited and could be reached safely. But Ptolemy was considered a more reliable authority, and his famous map of the world included a vast southern continent that stretched from Africa to China, making the Indian Ocean landlocked, and thus difficult to reach by sea, as some Portuguese were hoping to do. More encouraging was the fact that Ptolemy had declared that Eratosthenes's estimate on the circumference of the earth was too large and gave his own, which underestimated the actual size by one-sixth. It is indisputable that Ptolemy's *Geography* enjoyed an immense reputation in the 15th and 16th centuries. Nevertheless, Prince Henry of Portugal and his seamen were eminently practical men. Henry probably surmised that while Ptolemy's map was probably accurate for the areas controlled by the Roman Empire of the 2nd century CE, the rest of Ptolemy's *mappa-mundi* (world map) was far more suspect. The attempt to revise the academic theories of Ptolemy's *Geography* by practical sailors would dominate the century from 1410 to 1510.

To accomplish this revision, it was necessary to possess more practical tools than a copy of Ptolemy's *Geography* or d'Ailly's *Imago Mundi.* Reading and discussing such works at the royal courts of Europe would no doubt impress one's noble and academic friends, but they would certainly not help one sail from Lisbon to the Cape of Good Hope. For the substantial rigors of long ocean voyages, the intrepid mariners of the 15th century needed practical charts and the ability to calculate their position along a coastline and the open sea. While trade and navigation in the Mediterranean had yielded much information for academics, it had also resulted in more practical tools for sailors by ca. 1410. Practical sailing charts called *portolani* had developed. Originally pilot books containing maps and information on coastlines, harbors, and rivers mouths along the Mediterranean basin, these guides had evolved by the 15th century into practical coastal navigation charts. In English they were known as *rutters*, in Portuguese as *roteiros*. The techniques adopted in these charts were eventually extended to the coast of Africa and beyond by the Portuguese. Yet, one problem with the portolani charts was that they were of little assistance once a sailor was out of sight of land. To fix one's position in the open sea was a fundamental precondition for long-range ocean discovery.

By the early 15th century, Europeans possessed the means to accomplish this challenging task. The compass, astrolabe, quadrant, and cross-staff were all known to European mariners of the day. There had been references to the compass (a Chinese discovery) as early as the 12th century in Europe, with most wrongly crediting its invention to the Italians. The compass cards of Vasco da Gama's day were vastly different from today. Given high illiteracy rates, the points were given in different shapes or colors radiating from the pivot point in the center, instead of in numbers and letters. The Portuguese called these cards the *rosa dos ventos,* or 'rose of the winds.' The astrolabe (Arabic *asthar-lab,* or 'to take a star') also proved of

PHOTO I.2 Syrian Astrolabe. The advanced state of Islamic astronomy and science is revealed in this early 13th-century Syrian astrolabe crafted by al-Sarraj. Astrolabes were crucial for determining latitude and sailing out of sight of land for long distances. The Portuguese would also use them to great effect during their voyages.

great value to the Portuguese on their voyages of discovery. This instrument was essentially a flat wooden or brass circle etched along the edges in degrees and minutes, with two sights for reading celestial bodies. Used in conjunction with tables of declination provided in works like Abraham Zacuto's *Almanach Perpetuum Celestium* (*Perpetual Almanac of the Heavens*), the astrolabe could provide fairly accurate readings of latitude. By the 1490s, the Portuguese had added a single meridian, usually at Cape Vincent, along traditional portolani charts marked with degrees of latitude to facilitate navigation. To compensate for the loss of the Polestar and a lower sun closer to the equator, King D. João II's Mathematical Council in 1484 had recommended a calculation of latitude with a sun sighting at midday using the table of declination. These sightings were taken using either the astrolabe or quadrant. By the final decade of the 15th century, therefore, Europeans possessed the motivation and requisite nautical skills for long ocean passages. All that remained was the need to construct ships that could withstand the punishment of thousands of miles of pounding waves and heavy winds.

CARAVELS, *NAUS*, AND CARRACKS

The need to design and build such seaworthy ships was one of the greatest challenges confronting the Europeans in the quest for overseas expansion. To complicate matters, at the beginning of the 15th century, European ships were generally inferior in design and construction to vessels in most parts of Asia. During the next hundred years a minor revolution took place in shipbuilding theory and techniques, especially in southwestern Europe. These developments yielded new types of hybrid sailing vessels called the caravel, the *nau*, the carrack, and finally the galleon. The caravel proved to be the ideal vessel for exploration and discovery and was used by both Vasco da Gama and Christopher Columbus. The square-rigged *nau* and even larger full-rigged carrack became the preferred vessel for transporting the goods of Asia and the Americas during the initial decades of the 16th century. The more powerful galleon served to protect such fleets and would come to symbolize the imperial power of Portugal and Spain by 1550.

The caravel, *nau*, and carrack all combined elements of Atlantic and Mediterranean ships, as well as of Arab vessels sailing in the Indian Ocean. These ships possessed three masts (Mediterranean), a

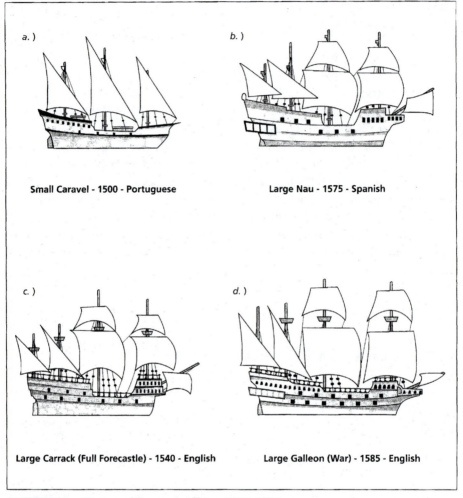

a.) Small Caravel - 1500 - Portuguese

b.) Large Nau - 1575 - Spanish

c.) Large Carrack (Full Forecastle) - 1540 - English

d.) Large Galleon (War) - 1585 - English

FIGURE I.1   Design of European Ships, 1500–1585.

square main sail (Atlantic) and a lateen (Arabic), or triangular, mizzen, or rear sail. Of the three, the Portuguese initially concentrated on the caravel. The flush-planked hulls of these ships, built skeleton first, made them very durable, while a length-to-breadth ratio of about 5:1 made them very seaworthy. Caravels were not particularly large, perhaps 65–80 feet in length and with a shallow draft which displaced between 80 and 130 tons of water. Caravels were far from comfortable; they were generally open to the elements with perhaps one small cabin aft, and they could not carry many men, supplies, or weapons. Yet, these vessels were ideally suited to the main work that was required in the Age of Discovery—exploring frequently fickle and unknown coastlines and handling close to the wind. From about 1420 onward, caravels had been used to great effect by the Portuguese exploring islands in the Atlantic, such as Madeira. Nevertheless, while the caravel represented an ideal craft for exploration, it was not well suited for the demands of maintaining and protecting an empire. As *naus* and the larger carracks began to carry increasing numbers of guns, especially below deck, caravels found themselves increasingly supplanted by these more powerful, if initially less seaworthy, ships.

Between 1450 and 1500, caravels and *naus* co-existed on the voyages of discovery. Columbus's fleet, for example, consisted of a *nau*, the *Santa Maria*, and two caravels, the *Niña* and *Pinta*, while many Portuguese fleets, including that of Vasco da Gama, consisted of both *naus* and caravels. On these voyages, the caravels carried dispatches between ships and explored rivers and coastlines, while the *naus* hauled most of the fleet's manpower, firepower, and supplies. By the early 1500s, however, these voyages of discovery were giving way to the needs of the growing empires of the Europeans in Asia and the Americas. For ships, this meant the need for more cargo space and artillery mounted below deck, which in turn mandated larger and broader ships. Despite the fact that artillery pieces had been mounted on caravels by the Portuguese since the 1450s, there were serious problems with adapting the caravel to large-scale naval combat. Above all, their relatively small size placed definite limits on the effective firepower of such vessels. As the need for larger, heavier, and more powerful ship-borne cannon became more acute, first the full-rigged *naus* and then the carracks had clear advantages. *Naus* could carry more cargo than the caravel, and for the Portuguese and Spaniards, the larger the cargoes, the better. In the early 16th century *naus* became more seaworthy, and this development spelled the death knell for the caravel. At the same time, the allure of rich Iberian cargoes to pirates and European rivals created the need to combine cargo-carrying and military capabilities. The carrack developed to fulfill this task; possessing huge storage capacity, these ships were designed to overawe any and all attackers by presenting a formidable defensive front. Carracks were built with extremely high castles fore and to a lesser degree aft. These ships also were probably the first sailing ships to mount heavy guns low in the hull behind watertight gun ports, and weapons were also manned from the crow's nests at the tops of the masts. The carrack projected a menacing appearance to all approaching ships.

By the late 16th century, the allure of even larger cargoes resulted in the construction of huge, unwieldy monster carracks. As opposed to a menacing appearance, such vessels became easy pickings for the smaller, well-armed, and more maneuverable galleon-type vessels that had also developed. The Portuguese carrack *Madre de Deus* (*Mother of God*), for example, when captured by the English in 1592 with a huge cargo from Asia, was estimated at 1600 tons. As the carrack became a floating dinosaur, the galleon replaced it and dominated in naval encounters around the globe involving the European powers from 1600 to 1700. Galleons evolved to overcome the defensive advantages that the carrack possessed. They were specialized fighting ships. Unlike the taller and less stable carracks, galleons had relatively low fore and aft castles, and were longer, narrower, and thus more seaworthy. These ships averaged about 600 tons during the 16th and 17th centuries. Their solid hulls were designed mainly to mount large number of artillery pieces below decks. Galleons were not designed for the transportation of bulk cargoes. The only product they were expected to carry was the gold and silver bullion of the New World. Like contemporary armored cars, galleons were designed to protect their valuable cargoes from attack. Both the Portuguese and Spaniards also used galleons to protect their annual fleets of cargo ships that sailed from Asia and the Americas to Lisbon and Seville.

THE IBERIAN CENTURY, CA. 1490–1600

In this book, Chapters 1 and 2 will examine the background and structures of the Portuguese spice empire in Monsoon Asia and Brazil, and the New World empire of the Spaniards. As we will see, exploiting all of these nautical, geographic, and economic advantages, the Portuguese and Spanish from ca. 1490 to 1525 would explore and connect most regions of the world. Cartographically, this revolution was admirably reflected in the increasingly accurate maps of Henricus Martellus (ca. 1490), Juan de la Cosa (1500), Antonio Cantino (1502), and Diogo Ribeiro (1529). As opposed to the landlocked Indian Ocean of Ptolemy, Martellus's map, based on the discoveries of Bartolomeu Dias (1487–1488), depicted a fairly accurate western Africa and Cape region. His map also reinforced the fundamental idea that the Indian Ocean was reachable by sea from Europe via the Cape of Good Hope. De la Cosa, who sailed with Columbus, not only reiterated this point, but his map following the voyage of Vasco da Gama depicted a fairly accurate east coast of Africa and India. Moreover, details of the islands and mainland of the New World had begun to emerge. Cantino, an agent of the Italian duke of Ferrara, purchased an illegal copy of the closely guarded world maps of the Portuguese Crown in 1502. On his map, the Caribbean islands and the coast of South America were accurately depicted. In Asia, the Portuguese had extended their voyages to Malaysia and the western islands of Indonesia. In 1529, Diogo Ribeiro, with a good deal of justification, claimed that his map contained details of "all the world that had been discovered up to this time." Perhaps most importantly, the remnants of Magellan's fleet had returned to Seville in 1522 providing additional information on the west coast of South America, the Pacific, and the islands of Indonesia. With the

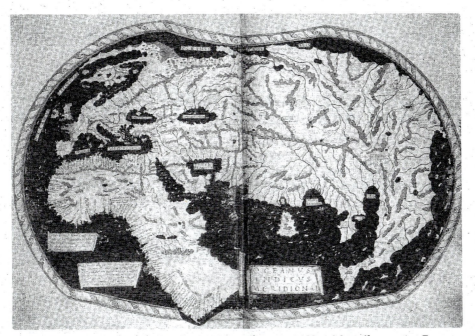

PHOTO I.3 World Map of Henricus Martellus, ca. 1489. Martellus was a German cartographer who worked in Florence. His 1489 map represented a significant improvement on earlier maps based on Ptolemy. These revisions were based on the travels of Marco Polo, Portuguese voyages along the west African coast, and the voyage of Dias around the Cape of Good Hope.

exception of the interior of North America, Ribeiro's map provided a geographical depiction of the world that would be generally recognizable today.

The cartographical advances reflected by the ink on these pages of parchment, however, in some sense belie the huge human sacrifices and triumphs, suffering and celebrations, victors and vanquished that were part and parcel of these amazing decades. This cultural interaction between the Iberian powers of Portugal and Spain and the indigenous societies they encountered in the New World, Africa, and Asia had political, social, economic, and military aspects to it. At times, these relations would reflect the best aspects of human nature, at others, the worst. The names of the European "conquerors" in this process are reasonably well known: Dias, da Gama, Albuquerque, Columbus, Cortés, and Pizarro to mention a few. The men who struggled against them are generally less well known—Montezuma, Adil Shah of Bijapur, and the Zamorim of Calicut, for example. While this book will focus primarily on the process of European expansion, it will also examine the indigenous structures the explorers encountered and the indigenous responses to their arrival. By 1525, both the Portuguese and Spaniards had begun to build huge and potentially lucrative empires in Asia and the New World. One of the fundamental questions to examine in these chapters is how the Iberians had managed to create these empires successfully and in doing so subjugate entire populations. Both these kingdoms also began the process of spreading the Roman Catholic faith around the globe. In return, a grateful papacy issued a series of bulls in essence sanctioning the division of the world these discoveries had created among them. As a result, in Asia the Portuguese would dominate the trade in spices and other luxury goods to Europe. Millions of pounds of pepper would make the voyage from India to Portugal and profits of perhaps 200% would be made. In the New World, the relative meager monetary returns of Columbus's voyages were being supplanted by windfalls of gold and silver that accompanied the Age of the Conquistadors. As a result, the Spanish Habsburgs would receive millions of ducats in bullion over the course of the 16th century, as well. The century from 1500 to 1600 can accurately be called the Iberian century. During these years, the rest of Europe looked enviously to the southwest. The kingdoms of Portugal and Spain had not only created global empires based on this wealth, but they were able to maintain them largely unchallenged for a hundred years (see Map I.2).

THE FIRST CENTURY OF GLOBAL CONFLICT, 1600–1700

Chapters 3 and 4 will examine the entrance of the Dutch, English, and French into this overseas competition in the New World and Asia and the global power struggle that resulted during the 17th century. By the last decade of the 16th century, serious rivals at last began to challenge the dominance and near monopoly of the Iberians overseas. In 1580, Philip II of Spain had successfully staked his claim to the Portuguese throne, thus uniting the Iberian Crowns and to a degree their overseas empires. Yet, problems had already begun to undermine the dominance of the Iberians. The two kingdoms possessed reasonably small populations, and they had thus experienced problems populating such huge global empires. The easy money from Asia and the New World also allowed the Iberians to neglect internal developments and improvements in their domestic economies. This weakness had been exacerbated by a generally arid climate and poor soil, as well as a continued adherence to an aristocratic lifestyle, which by definition generally shunned trade and manufacturing in favor of agrarian rents and overseas appointments. In northern Europe, the Protestant Reformation had begun. This event not only undermined the traditional claims of the Iberians to overseas monopoly sanctioned by the papacy, it also witnessed the rise of merchant capitalism, which had been embraced by the burghers of Amsterdam and the merchants of London. It was thus no surprise that England and the United Provinces of the Netherlands led this offensive against the combined kingdoms of Philip II and his less worthy successors. Philip, of course, had done his best to preempt this challenge to his European and overseas power by continuing the struggle in the Low Countries against the Dutch and launching his famed Armada against Elizabeth I of England in 1588. His failure in both quests had not only served to energize his Protestant opponents, it had also encouraged the French to rejoin the fray.

By 1601, both the Dutch and the English formed joint-stock proto-capitalist trading companies for the Asian trade, the VOC and the EIC. A similar strategy and challenge would soon be followed in the New World as well. Catholic France after halting for a half century of civil war would also find the allure of such overseas wealth too much to resist. In the first decade of the 17th century, Henry IV, the first Bourbon king, also sanctioned the formation of an East India Company, and French expeditions were also sent to the New World. Predictably, all of these rivals initially sought to attack the Iberian edifice at its weakest

MAP I.2   The World in 1600.

points. In Asia, this meant Indonesia, where the Portuguese presence had never been particularly strong. In the New World, the weakest link was judged to be the North Atlantic coastline of America. From 1601 to 1625, the Dutch, English, and French would seek to establish themselves in precisely those places. From 1625 to 1665, following initial successes, these rival powers would extend their offensive to other more central parts of the Iberian overseas world: the west African coast, India, Ceylon, Malaysia, Brazil, the Caribbean, and the Spanish

Legend:
- Ming Empire
- Ottoman Empire
- ◆ Spain and possessions
- ◆ Portugal and possesions (ruled by Kings of Spain 1580-1640)
- England and possessions
- France
- Songhay to 1590

Main, comprised of Central America and northern South America, would all be attacked. Interestingly, these rivals would also fight each other for overseas spoils, as the cases of Pulo Rum in Indonesia and New Amsterdam in the New World attest.

It is interesting to compare the methods and structures of the empires of the Dutch, English, and French with those of the Iberian powers. The traditional view long held that in this struggle the monarchical monopolism of the Portuguese and Spanish was no match for the capitalism of the Protestant Dutch and English. But is this view still

MAP I.3 The World in 1700.

viable? One crucial point is to detail the response of the Portuguese and Spaniards to these threats during the 17th century. Were the Iberians simply doomed to decadence, or were their monarchies and empires more resilient than has traditionally been assumed? Moreover, were the relationships between the Dutch and the English and the indigenous powers and cultures they encountered in Asia and the New World fundamentally different from those pursued by the Catholic

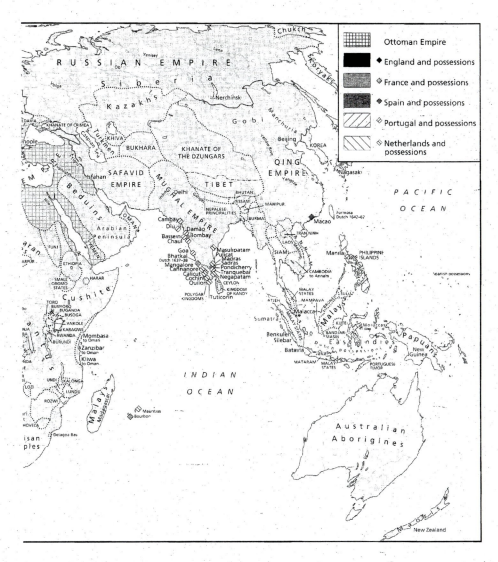

Legend:
- Ottoman Empire
- ◆ England and possessions
- ◇ France and possessions
- ◆ Spain and possessions
- ◇ Portugal and possessions
- ◇ Netherlands and possessions

powers a century earlier? By 1700, not only had the Age of Discovery linked the oceans of the globe, but an interchange of products, populations, disease pools, and ideas had been initiated that continues to the present day (see Map I.3). The origins of the contemporary world market economy, as well as many of the issues that dominate our own time, can be traced to the intellectual, cultural, and economic fallout of the seminal process of European expansion during these centuries.

CHAPTER

1

The Portuguese Empire in Asia and Brazil, ca.1500–1700

PORTUGAL AND PRINCE HENRY THE NAVIGATOR

To the surprise of many, it was the small kingdom of Portugal that was the first power to harness Europe's advances in cartography, navigation, finance, and shipbuilding and launch the Age of Discovery. By 1460, Portugal was poised to build on an already impressive record of discovery it had achieved along the west coast of Africa. What factors had initially motivated the Portuguese Crown in this process? Certainly the search for wealth and trade was a crucial factor. The Portuguese wanted to exploit the rich interchange of products like gold, slaves, and ivory that they knew flourished along the African Coast. As far as religious politics were concerned, the Portuguese had expelled the Moors by the late 13th century, but there was a strong impetus to continue the *Reconquista* against Islam. Socially, expansion overseas offered an avenue for advancement for the restless nobility. This expansion campaign began in 1415 when the first king of the Aviz dynasty, D. João I (r. 1385–1433), took an army to North Africa and conquered the strategic trading town of Ceuta. This victory began a search for the sources of African gold, ivory, and slaves that continued for decades, and with notable results for both Portugal and Europe.

The most influential figure in the early years of Portuguese exploration was D. João's third son, Prince Henry the Navigator. Many obstacles confronted Prince Henry in his quest: centuries of daunting myths, nautical difficulties inherent in unknown coastlines, and jealous European rivals. Moreover, Portugal possessed a relatively small population of about 1.5 million compared with ca. 18 million for France and ca. 10 million for neighboring Spain. It was also a relatively mountainous and arid country with poor soil ill-suited to an age when agriculture was overwhelmingly the basis of wealth. Nevertheless, Henry exploited the advantages the kingdom possessed—a long Atlantic seaboard, fine ports, excellent seamen, and a rich seafaring tradition—to overcome these problems. He also provided the logistical, financial, and emotional leadership necessary to co-ordinate this great enterprise. As noted in the Introduction, economic, religious, and personal factors motivated the prince in these endeavors.

Henry established himself at Sagres in the Algarve and attracted sailors, cartographers, astronomers, and shipbuilders to his enterprise. In 1420, he became Grand Master of the rich crusading military Order of Christ. Using revenues from this order to underwrite his expeditions, his caravels henceforth bore the order's red cross on their sails and had as an ancillary object the conversion of pagans to the Christian faith. Prince Henry sent out scores of vessels from the nearby port of Lagos. His squires Zarco and Teixeira discovered the Atlantic islands of Porto Santo and Madeira between 1418 and 1420. During the 1420s, the Prince's expeditions explored the Azores Islands and the Canaries. In 1434, Gil Eannes doubled the daunting Cape Bojador. By 1441, Antão Goncalves had returned from the coast of West Africa with gold and slaves, sold at the market in Lagos. Nuno Tristão and Dinis Dias reached the mouth of the Senegal and Cape Verde in 1445, and Alvaro Fernandes pushed on to Sierra Leone the following year. In 1448, Henry ordered a fort built on the island of Arguin to exploit the new Guinea (West African) trade. The Venetian explorer, Cadamosto, in the prince's employ, explored the Senegal and Gambia from 1455 to 1456. Although Henry died in 1460, his skill and determination had made Portugal the preeminent power in

Europe with respect to maritime technology and skills and overseas exploration. The African coast was quickly yielding its secrets, and the quest for gold, slaves, and ivory had become intertwined with the quest for the spices and riches of India.

ROUNDING THE CAPE OF GOOD HOPE: THE REIGN OF D. JOÃO II

D. João II (r. 1481–1495), the "Perfect Prince," strove to culminate this quest. A Machiavellian, he established a more absolutist regime in Portugal by crushing the longstanding threat from the nobility. His father, Afonso V had concentrated his energies warring with Castile and the Moors, while leasing out the Guinea trade to entrepreneurs. D. João II, however, restored royal control over the trade and actively encouraged the process of discovery. In 1482, he built the fortress at São Jorge da Mina near the island of São Thome in the Gulf of Guinea, where the Portuguese had earlier established a sugar plantation. His purpose was to defend Portuguese pretensions along the West African coast. By the mid-1480s, Diogo Cao reached Cape Cross at 22 degrees south latitude. In 1487–1488, Bartolomeu Dias finally rounded what he called the Cape of Storms. This voyage opened up navigation in the Indian Ocean for the Europeans via the South African Cape, a cape that D. João renamed 'Good Hope.' The king, wanting to gain as much knowledge as possible about the trading system that awaited the Portuguese in the Indian Ocean, had meanwhile dispatched two Arab-speaking agents to that region via the Levantine, or eastern Mediterranean, route in 1487. These men had traversed much of the Middle East, East Africa, and India and sent the king a vital report from Cairo in 1490. D. João had already begun preparations for the culminating voyage in the search for Indian spices by ordering ships and other preparations before his death in October 1495.

THE FIRST VOYAGE OF VASCO DA GAMA (1497–1499)

In January 1497, the new king D. Manuel I appointed Vasco da Gama to command the long awaited voyage to India. Da Gama came from a provincial noble family with longstanding service ties to the Crown. Not much is known about his early years, although he received a solid education in nautical and military matters. Da Gama's fleet did not sail for India until 1497, nine years after the return of Dias. Why the long delay? First, D. João II waited for intelligence from his Arab-speaking agents. The king also dealt with pressing military matters in Morocco, and the fallout from the arrival of large numbers of Jews who came to Portugal following their expulsion from Spain in 1492. Moreover, Columbus reached Lisbon in March 1493 claiming to have reached the Indies by sailing west. Pope Alexander VI, a native of Aragon, had issued a series of bulls granting Spain control over the lands Columbus had discovered. The papal bull *Inter Caetera* drew an imaginary boundary line from north to south a hundred leagues west of the Azores, defining all land and sea to the west as an exclusively Spanish sphere of exploration. Realizing that his chances for a fair hearing in Rome were slim, D. João spent the next few years negotiating directly with Ferdinand and Isabella. In 1494, in a diplomatic triumph for Portugal, the Treaty of Tordesillas was signed. This agreement fixed the line of demarcation at 270 leagues farther west than *Inter Caetera*. In doing so, it assured Portuguese control over the ocean passage to India, most of the South Atlantic, and Brazil. D. João's death and questions on the succession also delayed the first India voyage.

Da Gama's fleet consisted of four ships: the *São Gabriel*, the *São Rafael*, the *Berrio*, and a store ship. It departed from Lisbon in July 1497 with about 170 men aboard. After stopping in the Cape Verde Islands, the fleet headed out into the Atlantic to exploit the prevailing winds. On 22 November, the Cape of Good Hope was rounded. In the Indian Ocean, da Gama confronted the entrenched economic power of the Arabs. This religious and economic hostility complicated his task along the East African coast during a stay at Mozambique (March 1498) and especially at Mombassa (April 1498), where the local sultan sought to storm the fleet in a midnight raid. Da Gama received a more favorable reception at Malindi, obtaining a skilled pilot who guided the Portuguese fleet across the Arabian Sea to the pepper-rich Malabar Coast of India by May 1498. Da Gama's mission of arranging both a treaty and pepper trade in the key port city of Calicut was complicated by the intrigues of Arab merchants with the local Hindu ruler, the Zamorin (*Samudri Raja*), and his rather paltry gifts. His resolve overcame these problems, and he departed in August with a respectable cargo of spices. The *Berrio* and *São Gabriel* reached Lisbon in July and August 1499. Da Gama, after burying his brother Paulo on Terceira in the Azores, reached home in September.

He received the aristocratic title Dom, a hefty annual pension, and other rewards, including the title Admiral of the Indian Seas.

BUILDING A SPICE EMPIRE IN ASIA, CA. 1500–1520

D. Manuel quickly exploited the opportunities presented by da Gama's success. Although some of his councilors argued against creating an Asian empire, given the kingdom's relatively meager resources and the power of Islam, the king brushed aside such doubts. In D. Manuel's opinion, God had guided da Gama to India and back; he wanted Portugal to rule over parts of Asia and spread the Catholic faith. The king realized that da Gama's success served as a call to action for the Muslims who then controlled the trade, as well as to the Italians who had grown rich as middlemen on the traditional Levantine caravan route. It was vital to send a large expedition to establish a Portuguese presence at key points along the East African Coast and in India before the Muslims and Italians could mount an effective response. To lead this expedition, D. Manuel selected Pedro Álvares (de Gouveia) Cabral. Cabral's powerful fleet included 13 ships. D. Manuel provided Cabral with precise sailing instructions, a large cargo for trade, as well as more suitable presents for indigenous rulers. He also gave Cabral a letter for the Zamorin of Calicut that offered friendship and trade, but also contained a threat that the fleet's firepower could enforce. "Our set purpose is to follow the will of God rather than of men, and not to fail through any opposition to prosecute this enterprise and continue our navigation, trade, and intercourse in these lands which the Lord God desires to be served newly by our hands, not wishing that our labors to serve Him be in vain." Overall, the second India fleet carried close to 1,500 men.

Cabral's fleet departed in March 1500. By 22 April, the coast of Brazil had been sighted and claimed for D. Manuel. Cabral sent a ship back to Lisbon announcing this discovery and remained on that lush coast until early May. One of his officers, Pêro Vaz de Caminha, also sent the king a detailed description of his new discovery. According to Caminha, "the vastness of the treeline and foliage [was] incalculable" and the soil incredibly fertile. These attributes would encourage later settlement. Meanwhile, the passage across the Atlantic for Cabral's remaining 11 ships was difficult. A comet sighted on 12 May was judged as an ill-omen, and a fierce storm soon scattered the fleet.

Four ships were lost, including that of the great explorer Bartolomeu Dias. After refitting in Mozambique, the fleet made for Kilwa. There, the powerful sultan refused to sign a treaty, and Cabral headed for the friendly confines of Malindi, reached in early August 1500. After taking on supplies and capable pilots, the ships traversed the Arabian Sea and anchored off Calicut in September. Cabral learned that the old Samudri had died and a new more dynamic Zamorin had taken power eager to develop his domains and trade at the expense of rival Hindu petty coastal kingdoms, such as Cochin.

Cabral's stay in Calicut was anything but productive. Mutual suspicions and mistrust characterized the visit. Initially, a warehouse was provided for the Portuguese, but events soon turned ugly. Ayres Correira, the factor ashore, awoke on the night of 16 December 1500 to find the Portuguese under attack from Arabs, Moplahs (the local Muslims), and Hindus. The compound was abandoned, but of the 80 men ashore, at least 40 were killed within and another 14 on the retreat to the beach. Fewer than 30 Portuguese reached Cabral's ships. This unfortunate massacre, for which the Samudri Raja offered no explanation, ended any hope for peaceful relations with Calicut. In revenge, Cabral seized and burned at least 10 Arab ships anchored before the town and bombarded Calicut. He then sailed for Cochin.

The ruler of Cochin, Unni Goda Varma, anxious for an ally against the Samudri, was more gracious to Cabral. He sold him a large cargo of pepper, cinnamon, porcelain, and cotton textiles and allowed the Portuguese to set up a factory (trading center). In January 1501, Cabral stopped in Cannanur, where he was well received by the Kolattiri Raja. By July 1501, Cabral's ships had returned to Lisbon carrying some 4,000 *cantari* of goods, mainly pepper. The sale of this cargo not only reimbursed D. Manuel for his investment, but returned close to a 100 percent profit! The king boasted that the Venetians should consider sending their vessels to Lisbon for spices.

Yet, Cabral's voyage still left many questions unanswered. Relations with the Zamorin were terrible, the factory at Cochin tenuous, and the Arabs and Muslims were still in control of the trade. How could this monopoly be broken? By the late summer of 1501, the Portuguese had decided to embrace open warfare to break Muslim dominance over the Indian Ocean trade. Preparations began for a powerful expedition that would break the stranglehold of the Arabs and Mamluk rulers of Egypt over this trade, and divert it from the Levantine routes to Lisbon via the Cape of Good Hope.

This powerful 1502 expedition commanded by Vasco da Gama totaled 20 ships. Da Gama used this formidable force to make the sultan of Kilwa on the East African Coast cower into fealty (July 1502), to intercept Muslim shipping arriving on the Indian Coast, and to inflict a decisive defeat on an Arab fleet in the service of the Zamorin of Calicut (February 1503). He returned to Lisbon in October 1503. Da Gama's ruthless nature was revealed on this voyage when he burned to death several hundred Muslim pilgrims aboard a captured ship in September 1502. Following da Gama's departure from India, his kinsmen, Vicente and Braz Sodré, embarked on a voyage to the Red Sea and Persian Gulf from India to disrupt Arab shipping. As the Arabian chronicler Muhammad bin Umar al-Taiyab Ba Faqih noted, "In this year (Rajab 908/1503) the vessels of the Frank appeared at sea en route for India, Hormuz, and those parts. They took about seven vessels, killing those on board and making some prisoner. This was their first action, may God curse them." Although a storm battered the Portuguese fleet and both Sodré brothers died, Pêro de Ataíde, brought three of the ships back to India. In the meantime, the Zamorin had attacked Cochin and forced the Portuguese factors there to flee. This temporary setback was overcome beginning in late August 1503, as Portuguese naval power grew on the Malabar Coast. First, Ataíde returned with the remnants of Vicente Sodré's fleet, and Francisco Albuquerque and Nicolau Coelho arrived with a squadron of three ships from Lisbon. This firepower forced the Zamorin to withdraw, and Albuquerque constructed a strong wooden fortress in Cochin. The Portuguese position was further reinforced with the September arrival of another three ships under the command of Afonso de Albuquerque. In September 1504, Lope Soares de Albergaria arrived with 14 ships and more than 1,000 soldiers. The Portuguese were clearly determined to remain in India.

To prevent this unwelcome development, the Islamic powers in the trade needed to mount a swift counterattack. By 1505, rumors had reached Cairo that the Iberians would soon attack Jeddah, the port for the holy city of Mecca. In November, Emir Husain Mushrif al-Kurdi was sent from Cairo to the Red Sea to prevent such an attack. Overall, however, the Islamic response to the escalating Portuguese presence in the Indian Ocean trade was lethargic. This lethargy was due in part to a succession struggle in Egypt at the end of the reign of Sultan Qait Bay (r. 1468–1496) that was only resolved with the accession to power of the mercurial Qansawh al-Ghawri (r. 1501–1516). Christian pressure in the eastern Mediterranean was also a concern, as were the difficulties inherent in coordinating an effective response in Constantinople, Cairo, and the Indian Muslim sultanates. The Venetians, by downplaying Portuguese naval power, also contributed to these delays. Finally in the summer of 1507, a Muslim champion set out to engage the unwanted Christians who had shown themselves to be little more than uncouth corsairs. Emir Husain Mushrif al-Kurdi sailed out of the Red Sea with a fleet of at least 12 ships and 1500 men-at-arms to defend Muslim dominance over the Indian Ocean trade. According to the Hadrami sources, he was a "holy warrior sent to engage the Franks who had appeared in the Ocean and cut the Muslim trade routes."

By that time, D. Manuel had appointed a viceroy for his new Asian possessions. This Crown official would govern for three years and was expected to bring order and structure to what had been a de facto empire. For this post, the king selected the well-connected and powerful nobleman D. Francisco de Almeida. Almeida's fleet comprised some 22 ships and over 2,500 men. After capturing and fortifying Kilwa (July 1505), Almeida sacked Mombassa before heading to India. The viceroy then fortified the island of Anjedive near Goa, Cannanur, and finally Cochin, where he established his seat of power. Almeida did much to establish Portuguese power in the Indian Ocean spice trade. He signed an advantageous commercial treaty with the sultan of Melaka (Malacca), an important entrepôt for the Indonesian and South China Sea trade, while his only son, D. Lourenco de Almeida, opened up a trade for cinnamon on the island of Ceylon. D. Manuel's first viceroy also formalized a pass (*cartaz*) system whereby indigenous captains needed to procure signed passes from the Portuguese in order to pursue trade in the Indian Ocean. Armed fleets would patrol the main shipping routes, and ships without such a pass were deemed fair prizes.

By 1508, the Portuguese were clearly gaining the upper hand in their struggle with Islam for the trade. Between 1497 and 1500, the Crown sent some 17 ships to India. From 1501 until 1510, more than 150 left Lisbon for the Indian Ocean. In tonnage, the figures climbed from 2,665 tons to 42,775 tons. In terms of cargoes sent back to Lisbon, the Portuguese were also in a period of rapid proliferation. The fleet of 1505 returning under Lopo Soares de Albergaria, for example, carried more than 1,121,000 kg in spices and other goods, including over 1,000,000 kg in pepper. During this same period, the Portuguese were also effective in shutting off the traditional flow of spices through the Levant that had previously made the Italians, and particularly the

Venetians, rich. At Alexandria, the average annual cargo in pepper had ranged from ca. 480 to 630 tons between 1496 and 1498. That figure had dropped to only 135 tons for the years 1501 to 1506. At Beruit, the story was much the same. For these same years, the average amount of pepper had fallen from ca. 90 to 240 tons to only 10 tons.

To reverse this trend, Emir Husain Mushrif al-Kurdi's fleet reached the Indian coast in late 1507 and joined with the forces of Malik Ayaz, the governor of the port of Diu for the sultan of Gujarat, who provided some 60 small ships for the Muslim armada. In March 1508, the D. Lourenço de Almeida engaged this powerful fleet with a force of 12 ships and 600 men. In a three-day battle, the superiority of Portuguese ship-borne artillery was reconfirmed. But the overwhelming numbers of Emir Husain and Malik Ayaz and tactical mistakes by D. Lourenco, resulted in the defeat of the Portuguese. During the final stages of the battle, the younger Almeida, after having his thigh broken by a ball, had himself tied to the mast of his flagship to continue to lead his troops. There, he was struck in the back by another ball, which ended his life. In this engagement, Portuguese losses were 140 killed and 124 wounded; the Muslim losses were perhaps 400. News of Emir Husain's victory in this battle touched off three days of celebration in Cairo. Yet these celebrations were premature.

The death of his beloved son only hardened Almeida's antipathy toward Islam. Afonso de Albuquerque reached Cochin in late 1508 with secret orders from the king naming him governor of Portuguese India. Yet, Almeida refused to hand over power until he had exacted revenge against Emir Husain and Malik Ayaz. The viceroy sailed north in December 1508 with 18 ships and 1,200 men. On 2 February 1509, the fleet reached Diu. There, Emir Husain's fleet of 12 Egyptian ships supported by another 100 Muslim ships waited at anchor. On 3 February, in one of the seminal naval battles of the 16th century, the Portuguese viceroy advanced into the harbor and engaged the Muslim fleet. In this battle, Almeida's triumph was complete. Emir Husain was wounded and his fleet badly mauled. Most of the Muslim ships were plundered and then set aflame; the colors of both the sultan of Egypt and Emir Husain were captured and sent to Lisbon. Muslim naval power in the Indian Ocean was destroyed, thus opening even greater possibilities for Portuguese pretensions in Asia. On his return voyage to Cochin, the viceroy executed some of his captives and then fired their limbs toward the main Muslim towns he passed in a gruesome demonstration of revenge for his son.

The superiority of Portuguese naval power and the foundations of a trading empire in Asia were confirmed during the governorship of Afonso de Albuquerque. Albuquerque was single-minded and relentless in his quest for Portuguese power in the Indian Ocean Basin. He was extremely literate, and his letters to D. Manuel reveal brilliance of both language and strategy. Albuquerque's strategy for commercial dominance called for the Portuguese to control key points on the traditional trading routes. These points included strategic cities near the mouth of the Persian Gulf and Red Sea, the traditional routes for the Levant trade to Europe, as well as a position at the nexus of the Indonesian and Malaysian trades, and a base in India. Strong fortresses would be established at these points. In turn, these fortresses would serve as the loci for Portuguese fleets sent out to enforce the *cartaz* system, as well as collection and embarkation points for the trade with Europe and elsewhere. Obviously, this aggressive and dynamic strategy not only involved a sizable investment on the part of the Crown, it also engendered a good deal of debate in Lisbon and Cochin.

Albuquerque began his second voyage to India in April 1506 commanding 5 ships in a 16-ship fleet under Tristão da Cunha. After bombarding several cities along the East African Coast, he reduced several towns along the Omani coast, cutting the ears and noses off the inhabitants of entire towns who betrayed him. Albuquerque then began to implement his grand strategy by attacking the rich entrepôt of Hormuz at the mouth of the Persian Gulf. Albuquerque reached India in December 1508, where his imbroglio with Almeida dragged on for nearly a year. Only the arrival of the marshal of Portugal, D. Fernando Coutinho, with a fleet of 18 ships and 1,600 soldiers in October 1509 broke this stalemate. Coutinho carried orders reconfirming Albuquerque's succession as governor. The marshal had also been instructed to use this force to destroy the power of the Zamorin of Calicut. Coutinho ensured that Albuquerque took power. Yet, the limitations of the marshal as a warrior were soon revealed in his bungled sacking of Calicut in January 1510. Coutinho spent much more energy setting fire to a mosque and to the palace of the Samudri than in defeating enemy troops. This tactical mistake cost the marshal his life during a wild retreat to the beach. Although Albuquerque received two wounds as well, he at least now had a free hand to undertake his grand plans for further establishing Portuguese power in the Indian Ocean and a large fleet of some 23 ships to assist him.

The new governor originally prepared an expedition for the Red Sea, but on the advice of the Hindu corsair Timoja, he instead turned his attention to the rich city of Goa on the Konkan coast, then under the control of the Muslim Adil Shah dynasty of Bijapur. Albuquerque first captured Goa in March 1510, but he was forced to abandon the city in May when Yusuf Adil Shah, launched a counterattack. Albuquerque definitively recaptured Goa on St. Catherine's Day (25 November) 1510. As he informed D. Manuel, "In the capture of Goa the Turks lost over 300 men . . . Many were also drowned whilst crossing the river. I afterwards sacked the city in which for four days the carnage was fearful, as no quarter was given to anyone. The agricultural laborers and the Hindus were spared, but of the Moors killed the number was at least 6000. It was indeed a great deed, and well carried out."

Albuquerque's capture of Goa provided the Portuguese with a capital for their Asian empire for the next four centuries. To provide them with a strategic fortress to influence the rich Malaysian and Indonesian trade, Albuquerque then captured and fortified the important entrepôt city of Melaka (Malacca) in August 1511. On the return voyage to India, his flagship was shipwrecked, and the governor barely survived. Reaching Goa in September 1512, he prepared an expedition to reduce Aden near the mouth of the Red Sea.

PHOTO 1.1 View of Goa, ca. 1590. This view of Goa from Linschoten's work highlights the vivid street life and rich trade of the capital of Portuguese Asia. Goa was famous for its slave market and for the importation and shipment of horses to the inland Hindu empire of Vijaynagar. On the left, note the sale of a female slave.

Yet, Albuquerque's March 1513 attack on Aden failed. The governor at least partially atoned for this setback in May 1515 when he again captured Hormuz a vital possession for controlling the Persian Gulf trade and in particular the lucrative horse trade from Persia to India. The Portuguese controlled Hormuz until 1622. The difficult climate and work of fortifying this conquest, however, took a toll on Albuquerque's health. He managed to complete the fortress, but died off the coast of Goa on 16 December 1515, having established the basis for Portuguese dominance over the European share of the Indian Ocean trade for the next century. As Albuquerque informed D. Manuel shortly before his death: "Sire, I do not write to your Highness in my own hand because it trembles greatly when I do so, and this forecasts death . . . As for the affairs of India . . . everything is settled."

THE *ESTADO DA INDIA,* 1520–1600

For the next eight decades, the Portuguese dominated the Asian spice trade with Europe. This empire, called the *Estado da India* (State of India), was administered from Goa. It extended geographically over 10,000 miles from Mozambique in the west to Macao in China in the east. The list of Portuguese fortresses in the *Estado* included Sofala, Mombassa, Maskat, Hormuz, Diu, Damão, Bombay, Cochin, Ceylon, São Thome near Madras, Melaka, and Timor, to name but a few. These fortified settlements were located at the crossroads of local trading routes. They were multicultural enclaves that witnessed a mixture of European, African, and Asian peoples, laws, customs, and traditions. The structure of this empire reflected the power realities of the period. The ship-borne artillery of the Portuguese made them virtually invincible at sea. This string of fortified outposts could thus be constantly reinforced and managed to resist a long list of indigenous enemies and besiegers. Economically, the empire was based on the *Carriera da India* (The Indies Route) and the *cartaz* (pass) system. The *Carriera* embodied the yearly roundtrip journey between Lisbon and Goa that was the very lifeline of the empire. Each year fleets loaded with European trading goods, soldiers, nobles, priests, and royal dispatches from the king departed from Lisbon, ideally by Easter. The fleet would then reach South Africa in time to profit from the favorable winds of the southwest monsoon (June–September), which would carry them to Goa by September or October. In January or February of the following year, ships loaded with pepper, cinnamon, precious stones, China goods, textiles, and the viceroy's replies would leave from Goa to profit from the favorable winds of the northeast monsoon (January–March), which would ideally carry the ships to Lisbon by July or August. During the 16th century, these fleets were generally made up of 6–7 ships on the outward passage and 4–5 on the return voyage. Thousands of men and women made this perilous journey.

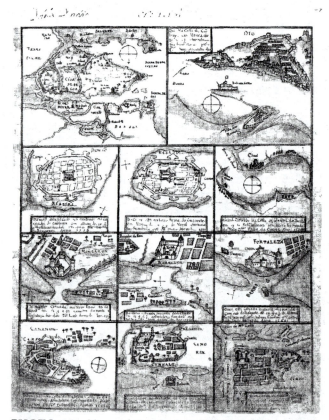

PHOTO 1.2   View of *Estado da India*, 1630. This depiction of the Portuguese possessions in India demonstrates that these cities were usually highly fortified coastal enclaves. Important civic and religious buildings were constructed within the city walls. Goa and Damão, however, also exerted control over significant rural areas.

And by 1550, perhaps 40,000 quintals (1=ca. 122 lb) of pepper were sent back to Lisbon each year, roughly 2,440 tons of the spice.[1] Given the military strength of the indigenous powers on land in India, the Portuguese never attempted to control the production areas of the spices they coveted. They were content to purchase pepper, cinnamon, and other spices from local middlemen and then passed the costs on to their consumers in Europe. After all, during the heyday of the empire in the mid-16th century, profits of 150 percent or more were made on the sale of these spices in Europe.

The *cartaz* system had originated in the early days of the empire. The Portuguese Crown claimed a monopoly over all the seaborne traffic in the Indian Ocean. Thus, each indigenous ship sailing these waters had to purchase a *cartaz* at one of the main Portuguese fortresses. Each year, fleets were sent out from Goa, Hormuz, Ceylon, and Melaka that would intercept any craft they encountered. Those possessing a valid pass were allowed to continue; those that did not were confiscated as legitimate prizes, with the crews placed at the disposal of the Portuguese. Sometimes they were killed; other times they were sold into slavery. The prizes of the *cartaz* system not only furnished additional revenue for the Crown, it also provided ready cash to pay the sailors and soldiers of these fleets, thus relieving the king's overhead expenses. Throughout these decades, the Portuguese never controlled large expanses of indigenous territory. At Goa, their control extended for perhaps 20 miles north to south and 15 or so from west to east. In the so-called Province of the North near Bombay, they controlled perhaps 20 leagues (60 miles) inland around Baçaim and Damão. The Crown used these territories to reward loyal nobles and soldiers, who received the rents and use of these lands for up to three generations.

When Vasco da Gama first reached Calicut, he declared that the Portuguese had come "in search of Christians and spices." From that time on, the twin motivations of economic gain and the desire to spread Christianity were at the heart of the Portuguese empire. As the chronicler Diogo do Couto noted in 1612 on the symbiotic relationship between these two goals, "The Kings of Portugal always aimed in this conquest of the East at so uniting the two powers spiritual and

---

[1] See Chapter 1 of the Connections Series book, *Trading Tastes: Commodity and Cultural Exchange to 1750* (2006) by Erik Gilbert and Jonathan Reynolds.

temporal, that one should never be exercised without the other." This merging of geopolitical, economic, and religious motivation was exemplified best in the *Padroado Real* or "royal patronage," over the missionary activities of the Roman Catholic Church in Asia, Africa, and Brazil that had been bestowed on the kings of Portugal by Rome. In the initial decades after 1500, however, the quest for spices had dominated over the quest for souls. Goa became the first bishopric in Asia only in 1534, and the site of an archbishopric in 1560. The first missionary priests came out with the first fleets, but these Franciscans, Dominicans, and others numbered only 100 by 1540. Some of these priests were ignorant of the native languages "and most interested in their trade and their concubines." They were thus hardly effective agents for the introduction of the new religion into a region of Hindus and Muslims. This laxity in early missionary zeal had been matched by flexibility in dealing with the religious practices of the Hindus. In seeking allies against Islam, it was logical that the early Portuguese adventurers would give the inhabitants of these lands every opportunity to demonstrate that they were indeed practicing the religion of some strange or lapsed Christian sect. Da Gama after viewing the temples and icons of Malabar for three months was still willing to consider the inhabitants Christian.

This initial laxity came to an abrupt end in the 1540s with the arrival of the Counter-Reformation Church and its talented shock troops, the Order of Jesus, better known as the Jesuits. In 1540, all Hindu temples on the island of Goa were destroyed. In 1542, the great Jesuit missionary Francisco Xavier reached India and gave a strong impetus to missionary efforts. During the next decade, Xavier made mass conversions in India, Ceylon, Melaka, Indonesia, and Japan. To facilitate this work, Xavier wrote to D. João III (r. 1521–1557) in 1545 calling for the establishment of the Inquisition in Goa. In 1560, the Regent of Portugal, Cardinal Henrique, ordered the establishment of the Holy Office in Portugal's Asian empire. The final step in entrenching this Counter-Reformation mentality came in 1567 with the first Ecclesiastical Council at Goa. This council declared that all religions other than the orthodox Roman Catholic faith were "intrinsically wrong and harmful in themselves," that the Portuguese Crown had the "inescapable duty of spreading the faith and should use the secular power of the Church to do so," but, that conversions "must not be made by force or threats of force."

The following decades witnessed the rapid proliferation of the numbers and power of the religious orders in the *Estado da India*. By 1600, the Jesuits, Dominicans, Franciscans, and Augustinians were all well entrenched both ecclesiastically and financially. The city of Goa had at least seven parish churches, with another 60 or so scattered in the surrounding provinces. The College of St. Paul was the largest Jesuit educational institution in Asia, with "70 priests and, in theory, 2000 students." The most impressive shrine to Christendom in Goa was the *Sé*, or Cathedral of St. Catherine (1562–1652). With a length of nearly 250 feet, this Portuguese-Gothic masterwork has eight chapels and six altars in the transept. By the early 17th century, the Portuguese Crown was paying perhaps 60,000 *xerafins* (silver coins) per year for the upkeep of the 900 *religiosos* in Goa alone. The period from 1560 to 1600 also witnessed the enactment and attempted enforcement of strict anti-Hindu laws in the campaign to achieve religious conformity. These laws banished Brahmin priests from Portuguese-held territories, forbade open Hindu marriages, forced Hindus to listen to Catholic dogma, prevented Brahmins from wearing their sacred thread, and excluded them from public offices. Conversely, those Hindus who converted to the Roman Catholic faith enjoyed a wide array of inheritance, tax, and employment benefits. Of course, once they had converted, these men and women were liable to the rigors of the Goa Inquisition.

Spearheading this religious assault was the *Pai dos Christãos*, or Father of Christians, charged with the overall welfare of the converts in Goa. According to the Frenchman François Pyrard, who visited Goa in the early 17th century, "There [was] another house . . . called Cathecumenos and it is for catechizing and teaching the new Christians; they are fed and supplied with clothing there, until such time as they are instructed and baptized: over these the Father of the Christians has charge of the whole house." The *Pai dos Christãos* monitored infractions of anti-Hindu laws; he kept records on the times and dates of the main Hindu festivals and noted and punished those who attended; he sought to prevent pilgrimages to neighboring temples and to prevent the celebration of Hindu marriages. His most controversial duty was to enforce a 1559 decree on the forcible conversion of Hindu orphans. According to this law, children of Hindus who were left "without, a father, mother, grandfather, grandmother, or other ascendant lineals and are not of an age at which they can have understanding and judgment, as soon as the last of such relatives is dead" were to be put in the care of the Judge of the Orphans and handed over to the Jesuit College of St. Paul. There they would be "baptized, educated, and indoctrinated" in the Catholic faith. As time went on, interpretation of this 1559 law became increasingly flexible, causing a great deal of controversy. Besides the cultural affront inherent in this law, there were many cases where Hindu children were taken and forcibly converted after the death of their father alone, with the family's property confiscated to defray expenses. Not surprisingly, increasing numbers of Hindu merchants sought asylum in the lands of the *Reis Vizinhos* (neighboring kings) instead of risking the harsh religious and financial penalties inflicted with enforcement of this law.

Overall the success of this concerted conversion campaign was limited. By 1600, there were perhaps 175,000 Christians in all of India out of a total population of some 140 million. Of this number, perhaps 100,000 "were the low-caste fishers and pearl divers on the Manar Coast," where Xavier and later Jesuits had been successful. On the island of Goa, there were perhaps 50,000 Christians, or 25 percent of the population of approximately 200,000 in 1600. In the city of Goa perhaps two-thirds of the population was Christian. The resiliency of the indigenous religion can be attributed to several factors: the strong opposition of the Hindus to this foreign faith and the ease with which indigenous religious temples and icons could be relocated to the lands of the neighboring kings. The local business acumen and capital of Hindu merchants in Goa also tempered the zeal of the campaign. It was also inevitable that a de facto tolerance and intermingling between the two religions and communities occurred. Many viceroys and other secular officials, as well as archbishops and clerics, for example, used Hindu doctors. Nevertheless, this religious campaign and the mission of the *Padroado Real* ensured that the *religiosos* played a vital role in the social, economic, cultural, and political life of the *Estado da India*.

BUILDING A LAND EMPIRE IN BRAZIL, 1500–1600

In Brazil, exploration and settlement took place in a more gradual fashion. Cabral's fleet landed near Bahia at Porto Seguro. He found these lands populated by indigenous tribes (estimated at from 1 to 8 million before 1500), who may have spoken as many as 100 dialects.

The Andes and the mountain ranges in northern South America had created a natural and cultural boundary between the settled, agrarian-based urban civilizations to the west, such as the Incas, and the less settled tribes to the east. These semi-nomadic Tupi tribes subsisted thanks to a mix of hunting, fishing, gathering, and some agriculture. Although they had no written languages, archeological remains suggest that periodic tribal federations had existed. The indigenous inhabitants of Brazil initially demonstrated curiosity and hospitality toward the Portuguese. However, these indigenous structures could not withstand the combination of European military technology and the ravages of hitherto unknown diseases. Hundreds of thousands soon died from smallpox, measles, tuberculosis, typhoid, dysentery, and influenza.[2] Down to the early 1530s, while the Crown was concentrating on building an African and Asian empire, not much was done to develop a permanent presence in the Americas. Some expeditions were sent to guard the coastline and to enforce Portugal's claim, but no fortresses or towns were established. Unlike the Spaniards in the valley of Mexico or the highlands of Peru, the Portuguese did not find rich deposits of gold or silver at this time. Nor did they encounter rich civilizations to plunder. Instead, exploiting Indian labor, they concentrated on cutting and exporting the red-colored *pau-brasil*, or brazilwood, that was used in dying fabrics in Europe.

It was the arrival of French expeditions on the coast of Brazil that prompted D. João III to seek a more forceful presence in South America. In 1532, using the essentially medieval system of conquest that had begun on the Atlantic islands, 15 hereditary captaincies were set up and granted to a dozen *Capitães-Mor* or *Donatários*. The captain-majors were granted leagues of coastline divided parallel to the Equator and extending inland from the coast to the line established by the Treaty of Tordesillas. They were then expected to oversee economic and military development of these lands. The system, however, proved problematic, and only two of the captaincies showed promise. In the northeastern *Capitania* of Pernambuco, Duarte Coelho Pereira subdued the Caeté Indians, expelled the French from the area, and set up the towns of Olinda and Igrassu. These successes were complemented by the introduction of sugarcane cultivation. In the south, the *Capitania* of São

---

[2] See the Connections Series book, *The First Horseman: Disease in Human History* (2007) by John Aberth.

Vicente, established in 1532 under Martim Afonso Souza at what had been the called the *porto dos escravos* (port of the slaves) near São Paulo, also prospered.

D. João III again placed Brazil under direct Crown control in 1548. The first governor-general, Thomé da Sousa (1549–1553), arrived with 1,000 troops in 1549 and established the new royal capital at Salvador (or *São Salvador da Bahia de Todos os Santos*). Da Sousa and his successors did much to entrench royal power and make the colony economically viable. The power of the coastal Indian tribes, including the Tamoio and Tupininquim, was broken. Tribal lands were cleared to facilitate large-scale sugarcane production on plantations that increasingly came to depend on imported African slaves purchased from native chieftains in West Africa and from the Crown colony of Angola in southwest Africa. In 1560, the governor-general Mem de Sá also led a royal fleet of 26 ships and 2,000 soldiers that attacked a nascent French colony called *France Antarctique* at what is now Rio de Janeiro. The French, however, had skillfully gained the support of the Tamoyo confederation of neighboring Indian *tribes* and were not definitively expelled until 1567.

As in India, missionaries arrived in Brazil to spread the Catholic faith, and in so doing, Jesuits, such as Manoel da Nóbrega, also helped expand Portuguese control. These Jesuits learned local dialects and established missions, churches, and schools. They also played a role in the founding of Rio de Janeiro, São Paulo, Receife, and Salvador. As in Spanish America, Jesuits like Nóbrega frequently clashed with colonists over the issue of the treatment of the indigenous population. These missionaries usually sought to prevent the enslavement of the Indians for the benefit of plantation owners. This stance exacerbated the need for African slave labor. Nóbrega became the first Provincial of the Society of Jesus in Brazil. He was instrumental in the establishment of religious and educational institutions, in the pacification of bellicose Amerindian tribes, and in the establishment of an episcopacy for the colony. D. Pero Fernandes Sardinha assumed office in the new bishopric of Salvador in June 1552. The city's impressive cathedral was completed in 1572, and a decade later there were more than 1,500 residents. In 1572, the huge distances of the expanding colony forced the creation of two adminstrative centers at Salvador and Rio de Janeiro.

By the end of the 16th century, the main outlines of Brazil's subsequent history were discernable. As in India, while nobles, adventure seekers, soldiers, priests, and *degredados*, or convict-exiles, had formed the initial core of the Portuguese colonial population, this equation was shifting by 1600 as merchants, bankers, craftsmen, and other tradesmen came to gradually recognize the potential of the vast natural resources found there. In the north especially, sugarcane from plantations (*fazendas*) and, as the century wore on, tobacco began to serve as reliable cash crops for the colonists and taxable products for the king's custom house in Lisbon. In turn, this created heightened demand for slaves from the African factories of the Crown. By 1585, black slaves probably represented about a quarter of the estimated settled population of 57,000 persons in Brazil. By the early 17th century total production of sugar in Brazil had already reached 14,000 tons. Tobacco had been cultivated by 1548, and a decade later it was common to find snuff in the markets of Lisbon. As we will see, while these intial successes for the colony were impressive, they would also

PHOTO 1.3 Sugar Plantation, Pernambuco. The slave-based sugar plantation economy of Brazil is reflected in this 1662 Dutch atlas. Sugarcane arrived in ox carts and was ground by the water driven power of the mill. Huge Portuguese profits had attracted the interest of the Dutch West India Company during the 17th century.

attract the attention of jealous European rivals as the 17th century unfolded.

DECLINE AND REBIRTH IN ASIA AND BRAZIL, 1600–1700

Not surprisingly, the opulent wealth reaped from the Asian spice trade, Brazil's growing sugar economy, and Portugal's mercurial rise combined to attract the jealousy of other European powers. The fact that the Spanish Habsburgs held the Portugese Crown from 1580 to 1640 only exacerbated these difficulties. A concerted attack by Spain's archenemies, the Protestant powers of England and particularly the United Provinces of the Netherlands, characterized the history of the 17th-century Portuguese overseas empire in Asia, Africa, and the New World. In Asia, by the mid-17th century, the earlier glories of the *Estado da India* were tarnished. In December 1662, Antonio de Mello de Castro, the newly arrived governor, reported that the *Estado* was nearly bankrupt: "The needs of this State are so many and so great . . . and there is not even a single penny to help meet pressing and necessary expenditures." Besides being financially distressed, the *Estado* also confronted a host of commercial, religious, and military enemies in Asia, including European rivals in the form of the Dutch (VOC) and English (EIC) East India Companies, as well as local indigenous powers, such as the Omani Arabs, the Marathas under Shivaji, the Muslim sultanates of Bijapur and Golconda, the powerful Mughal emperor Aurangzeb, and a series of petty rulers in littoral Africa.

The early 1660s marked the nadir of Portuguese power in Asia. Economically, problems had begun as early as the 1570s when the Levant trade revived. By 1600, the Crown managed to import "little more than 12,000 quintals, most of which was low-priced pepper" via the Cape of Good Hope. Moreover, while pepper prices generally rose in India, the price that the Crown could command for this commodity at sale in Lisbon fell from ca. 50 *cruzados* (gold coins) per quintal in the 1580s to 25 *cruzados* in the 1620s. These financial difficulties were exacerbated by the arrival of the English and Dutch Companies. The armed annexation of the Portuguese Crown by Philip II ushered in a protracted period of 60 years, the so-called Spanish Captivity (1580–1640), when Madrid bled Portugal and her empire dry in a doomed attempt to perpetuate Habsburg dominance in Europe. This annexation exposed Portuguese possessions in Brazil, Africa, and the

Indian Ocean to the onslaught of the Protestant powers, and a host of military setbacks for the *Estado* characterized the middle decades of the 17th century. Hormuz, the key to the Persian Gulf trade, was lost to a joint English–Persian attack in 1622. Melaka, the major entrepôt in the Indonesian trade fell to a prolonged VOC blockade in 1641. In 1650 Maskat fell to the sultan of Oman. By 1658, all of the Portuguese strongholds on Ceylon, locus of the lucrative cinnamon trade, had been captured by the Dutch. Finally, in early 1663 immediately following Mello de Castro's arrival, the *Estado* lost its remaining possessions on the pepper-rich Malabar Coast of India to the VOC. When the count of Obidos assumed the office of viceroy in 1652, the deed of transfer had still listed some 20 major coastal strongholds, but by the 1660s only half that number remained.

Diverse explanations have been given for this precipitous decline. Portuguese historians argued that this reversal of fortunes was occasioned by the Spanish Captivity. British historians of the 19th century argued that it was the corrupt nature of Portuguese administration that undermined the *Estado da India*. For C.R. Boxer, the most prolific historian of the past century in the field, the reasons for Portugal's imperial decline were more simple: "the superior economic resources, superior manpower, [and] superior firepower" of the Dutch. In the 1970s, the Danish historian, Niels Steensgaard, maintained that the entrance of the more advanced proto-capitalist entrepreneurial companies of the English and Dutch into the Asian trade doomed the monarchical monopolism of the Portuguese Crown to extinction. One constant in all this historiography was that the year 1663 marked an important watershed in the history of the *Estado da India*; for the loss in that year of Cochin is generally considered to have constituted the death knell for Portuguese power in Asia. As the Jesuit Manoel Godinho wrote in that fateful year on the *Estado*, "if it was a giant, it is now a pigmy; if it were great, it is now nothing."

Recent research has shown that during the last three decades of the 17th century, a significant rehabilitation campaign took place in Portuguese Asia. That the *Estado* was reduced in size is undeniable, equally so is that problems and setbacks continued. Nevertheless, there is definitive evidence to show that this campaign began with the reign of Prince Regent Pedro (1668–1702) and culminated with the viceroyalty of Luis de Mendonca Furtado (1671–1677). In theory, this reform campaign was grounded in the belief that the remaining

Asian holdings, if properly administered and exploited, in conjunction with the rich Rios de Cuama region of Mozambique, could serve as the basis for a profitable and viable *Estado da India*. In practice, this campaign reflects the fact that the harsh structural dichotomy advanced in the past between the monarchical monopolism of the Portuguese empire in Asia and those of the Dutch and English does not hold up. Rather a symbiotic relationship existed in the imperial competition in Asia among the European powers during the 17th century. The Portuguese learned lessons from their Protestant competitors and sought to implement them in their empire, while the Dutch and to a lesser degree the English, as we will see in Chapters 3 and 4, emulated some of the earlier practices of the Iberians.

Accordingly, the Portuguese undertook political, military, economic, and religious reforms during these decades. Perhaps the most crucial decision made by Pedro came in 1669, when he refused an attractive offer of an anti-VOC alliance in Asia made by Louis XIV's great minister Jean-Baptiste Colbert. Instead of recommencing open war with the much hated Dutch, Pedro instead began his reforms during the decade of the 1670s while his European rivals were warring with one another. Politically, the Crown effectively sought to re-establish control over the outlying fortresses of the *Estado,* including Mozambique, Macao, and Timor. Economically, by more efficiently mandating prompt departure dates, the Portuguese rejuvenated the *Carreira da India*. Regular sailings between Lisbon and Goa resulted, and pepper cargoes again reached the docks on the Tagus nearly every year. The Portuguese, using savvy business techniques, also bought pepper cargoes at the most advantageous prices possible. To once again enforce the *cartaz* system, fleets from Goa patrolled the Arabian Sea and Persian Gulf and many prizes were taken during these years. Militarily, a formidable *Terco* (regiment) was re-established in Goa, which successfully resisted the encroachments of the Marathas under Shivaji and his son Shambaji in the 1670s and 1680s. Portuguese war fleets also bested the fleets of the powerful sultan of Oman during this period as well.

Religiously, Pedro and Mendonca Furtado recognized the need to temper the zeal of the *religiosos* and the Inquisition. Various abuses were checked, most notably the lax interpretation of the 1559 law on Hindu orphans, in order to retain the commercial networks and capital of indigenous merchants living within the *Estado*. Great efforts were also made to develop the mineral and trade potential of the

Zambezi River Basin in Mozambique. As opposed to the dismal state of affairs described by Antonio de Mello de Castro in 1663, the *Estado* budget of 1680 showed a positive balance of some 271,000 *xerafins* for that year, perhaps the largest such balance in a century. Even though modern historians have been slow to appreciate these advances, they were certainly recognized by contemporaries in the Asian trade. As Gerald Aungier, the English Company President in Surat, notified his Company Directors in early 1674, "The Portuguese Follow their trade as well in India as Europe vigorously, they have sent this yeare fewer shipps full laden for Lisboa, two or three shipps for China, some to Mossambique, Monbass [Mombassa] & Patta & in October last they sent an Armada consisting of 5 shipps & about 10 small frigatts well manned to the Persian Gulph." All in all, it was a remarkable turn-around from the chaos and decline of the early 1660s and established the basis for the overseas empire in East Africa and Asia that would last until the late 20th century.

SEVENTEENTH-CENTURY BRAZIL: THE DUTCH CHALLENGE AND BEYOND

In Brazil, also, Portuguese fortunes suffered under the attacks of the rival Protestant powers and particularly the Dutch during the 17th century. By 1600, colonists from the Dutch province of Zeeland had established the Amazonas settlements on the Xingu River. In order to challenge more effectively the Portuguese position in Brazil and the African slaving posts that supported the colony, the Dutch estab-lished a West India Company (WIC) in June 1621 with many of the same powers earlier extended to the VOC (see Chapter 3). The direc-tors of the WIC had a simple strategy: Capture the capital city of the colony and the remainder would fall. Thus in May 1624, a Dutch fleet of 26 ships and 3,500 men attacked Salvador and compelled the Portuguese governor Diogo de Mendonca Furtado to surrender. This victory, however, was short-lived, as a Portuguese expedition of nearly 13,000 men recaptured the city in April 1625.

The WIC, however, was not deterred. In fact, from 1630 to 1645, the Dutch captured the northern half of Brazil. Pernambuco, Recife, and Olinda, the centers of the lucrative sugar economy, fell in February 1630. The Dutch also built a series of coastal forts to protect their new colony of *Nieuw Holland*. In January 1637, Johan

Maurits (John Maurice), count of Nassau-Siegen, arrived in Recife as colonial governor. Maurice of Nassau was a talented administrator who consolidated these gains and showed a strong interest in encouraging scientific and artistic endeavors in Brazil. Under his leadership, the town of Porto Calvao was retaken, the province of Ceará and the city of Fortaleza were captured, and Recife was rebuilt and expanded at great expense. In order to ensure a steady supply of slaves for the sugar plantations, Maurice sent an expedition in 1637 to attack the Portuguese lynchpin of the Guinea slave trade, the fort at São Jorge de Mina. In August, this Portuguese stronghold capitulated.

D. João IV's accession in December 1640, by severing ties with Habsburg Spain, could have ended these hostilities. But as in Asia, the burgher directors of WIC were much too intent on achieving economic dominance in the Atlantic economy to allow these political events to interfere. Instead, they exploited the many problems confronting the new Portuguese dynasty to escalate warfare in Brazil and West Africa. In 1641, the Dutch captured São Luis do Maranhão. That same year, an expedition of 21 ships and 3,000 men sailed to West Africa to attack Portuguese strongholds. Luanda, the capital of Angola, Benguela, São Tomé, and Annobon all surrendered by October 1641. D. João IV agonized as the keys to his Atlantic slave and sugar economy now rested in Dutch hands. The question was, Could they be recaptured?

From 1643 to 1654, the Portuguese, indeed, expelled the Dutch from most of these conquests. How? First, the formidable challenge embodied in Maurice of Nassau was prematurely removed. Maurice did his best to forge good relations with the Portuguese *moradores* (inhabitants) of northern Brazil. He gave them religious freedom, a limited voice in government, and improved the economic infrastructure of the colony. These very policies, however, alienated the dour Calvinist directors in Amsterdam, and he was recalled in 1643. Deprived of his leadership, the Dutch position quickly became untenable. Second, although Maurice had done his best to tie the Portuguese to the Dutch regime, there is clear evidence that this cultural fusion never took place. Numerically, the Dutch were at a distinct disadvantage with only 3,000 white *vriburghers* in 1644. This small community was surrounded by a much larger population of Portuguese and *mesticos* (persons of mixed ancestry), who were linguistically, culturally, and religiously tied to Portugal. The welcome news of D. João IV's revolution in Lisbon certainly helped motivate a revolt in the Dutch-controlled north, which began in 1645. Finally, D. João IV, in the global warfare against the Dutch, had been forced into a difficult imperial triage. He had to decide which of his overseas possessions to concentrate on defending with the limited resources at his disposal. The new king chose to concentrate on the Atlantic rim possessions. This decision was complemented by the very able commanders who implemented strategy, most notably Salvador de Sá e Benavides, who from 1647 to 1654 not only played a key role in expelling the Dutch from Angola but also assisted in the Brazilian campaign.

The second half of the 17th century, as in the *Estado India*, witnessed a rehabilitation of Portuguese power in Brazil. Problems, however, continued. The sugar and slave economy was re-established following the expulsion of the WIC. But the sugar boom in the Caribbean colonies of the Dutch, English, and French flooded European markets and prices declined sharply. These developments threatened the lifeblood of the colony. At the same time, the powerful racial and economic mix created by the plantation system could have exploded in the face of the Crown. Escaped slaves had already formed maroon settlements at odds with the dominant social and political structure of the colony. Cane farmers were also upset at the potential loss of their economic and social position. The plight of the Indians in Brazil was another divisive issue that the Crown and its subjects confronted during these years. The challenge of dealing with all these problems, as in Asia, largely fell to the councils and advisors of Prince Regent Pedro (Pedro II from 1683). Thanks to a mix of skill and luck, Portugal's Atlantic empire survived into the 19th century.

Economically, the relative decline of the sugar-slave plantation economy was offset by two factors. First, large-scale cattle and livestock ranching managed to offset some of these losses. These activities were familiar and socially acceptable to Portuguese nobles. Second, the longstanding quest to find precious metals finally yielded results in the last decade of the 17th century. Throughout the century, expeditions to the vast interior took place. The *bandeirantes*, organizers of private, free-booting expeditions, spearheaded this process from São Paulo, extending the western boundaries of Brazil in their quest for gold and Indians to enslave. In the 1690s, significant gold deposits were discovered in the southern Minas Gerais and Mato Grosso region. The resulting gold rush alleviated many of the economic tensions caused by the decline in sugar prices. The prospect of vast riches to the south also tempered the economic and social grievances among cane farmers and other Portuguese colonists who flooded the region from their homes in the northeast. Economic and social revolution was avoided thanks to the allure of gold and human greed.

The Crown also sought control over the maroon societies of escaped slaves in the colony. Palmares, or Quilombo dos Palmares, was formed in 1600 in the hills of northeastern Brazil. It constituted an independent "republic" with several towns and a population of over 10,000. The Palmarinos were skilled warriors who used a fighting style called *capoeira*, an aerobatic martial art. Their social and political structures were related to Angolan tribal structures, and the very word *quilombo*, which means "encampment," is Angolan in origin. The *quilombo* of Brazil can probably be traced to the Angolan *kilomb*, or male military society. Under leaders like Ganga-Zumba and Zumbi, the Pamarinos resisted more than twenty military expeditions sent against them by the Dutch and the Portuguese. According to a report sent to Lisbon, these successes could be traced to "military practice made warlike in the discipline of their captain and general, Zumbi, who made them very handy in the use of all arms, of which they have many and in great quantity—firearms, as well as swords, lances, and arrows." In the end, however, the developing absolutist regime in Lisbon and Rio de Janeiro could not tolerate this challenge. Ganga-Zumba accepted colonial control in 1677–1678. In the early 1690s, Domingos Jorge Velho led a fatal assault on the royal compound of Palmares at Macaco. Zumbi was wounded and betrayed. Jorge Velho beheaded him in November 1695 and then displayed his head at Recife to dispel any claims of immortality.

The plight of the Brazilian Indians also divided Portuguese society. The Jesuit Antonio Vieira (1608–1697), a great intellectual figure of this period, championed their cause. Vieira was a devoted missionary who translated the Catholic catechism into local Indian dialects and traveled widely winning converts for the faith. He was also a committed social reformer, who worked to free enslaved Indians and denounced the forced labor system. Predictably, the powerful plantation owners despised him, and in 1661 he was exiled back to Lisbon. There, the powerful count of Castelmelhor exiled him to Coimbra, where he wrote a book that postulated an ideal Portuguese empire. Of course, what was ideal for Vieira was not necessarily so for the power elite in Portugal and Brazil, and from 1665 to 1667, the Inquisition imprisoned him. Fortunately, the palace coup late in that year, which saw Afonso VI and Castelmelhor overthrown by D. Pedro, saved Vieira. He tutored Pedro as a youth, and the new Prince Regent allowed him to travel to Rome and eventually Brazil (1681), where he spent the last decades of his life ministering to the needs of the Indians.

By 1700, the Portuguese Empire had regained a vestige of its earlier glories. Breaking from the bonds of the Spanish Habsburgs was not an easy task, but by 1668 Madrid formally recognized the success of the 1640 revolution in Lisbon. The Braganza dynasty weathered a harsh trial by fire during its first decades. D. João IV, Afonso VI, and D. Pedro II all did their best to deal with the continental war with Spain and a tripartite global war against the powerful Dutch. D. João IV concentrated on saving the Atlantic Rim possessions, and by 1654 this task had been accomplished. The Crown colonies of Brazil and Angola survived and even prospered into the 18th and 19th centuries. Once this task had been accomplished, D. Pedro II turned his considerable talents to rehabilitating the *Estado da India,* which had been reeling in the early 1660s. Thanks to peace, reform, and skillful imperial appointments, such as Luis de Mendonça Furtado, the *Estado* had gained a degree of stability and economic feasibility that could hardly have been imagined in the dark days of the 1650s in Asia.

The significance for world history of the creation of the global empire of Portugal can hardly be overstated. Aboard Portuguese ships from 1500 to 1700, the very best and very worst of European society were exported to the rest of the globe; from the humanity of Francisco Xavier and Vieira to the inhumanity of the slave trade, the Inquisition, and the systematic extinction of indigenous cultures. In return, the symbiotic relationship that necessarily developed with the indigenous cultures of the empire ensured that European society was also exposed to a plethora of new intellectual, cultural, ethnic, racial, and medicinal forces, as well as a wide array of trading products. The hybrid cultures that resulted from this potent societal cauldron were then re-exported, for better or worse, around the globe. The wealth of the spice trade, as well as the slave trade, encouraged other world empires to develop. The dominance of the Portuguese on the Cape route to Asia logically forced their rivals to look for another gateway to the wealth of the spice trade. As we will see in Chapter 2, this quest would yield seminal albeit unforeseen results for the kingdoms of Castile and Aragon.

SOURCES

■ The First Portuguese Description of Calicut, 1498

Vasco da Gama (1469–1524) was born into a provincial noble family in the coastal town of Sines. He received a solid education, and following family tradition, he became a knight in the Order of Santiago, a confraternity that had its roots in the Iberian crusades against the Moors known as the *Reconquista*. After serving King D. João II in a variety of military and naval functions in the 1480s and 1490s, he commanded the first voyage to India for the Portuguese Crown between July 1497 and September 1499. Although a *Roteiro* (logbook or journal) was kept aboard da Gama's fleet, which survived, its authorship has never been definitively established. The two most likely candidates are Álvaro Velho, a solider who spent a good deal of time on the Guinea coast of Africa, and João de Sá, a trained notary who later worked at the India House in Lisbon.

As you read this section of the journal, what strikes you most about the description it provides of late-15th-century India? How was it possible for the Portuguese to believe that the inhabitants of Calicut were Christians? What paradigm does the author use to interpret events? Which sections do you think would be most interesting to King D. Manuel I? Do you think Vasco da Gama thought the rigors of the voyage were worth it as he met the Zamorin? Why? How would you try to negotiate trading privileges in da Gama's position? What do you think the Zamorin thought of the Europeans upon their arrival?

The city Calecut is inhabited by Christians. They are of a tawny complexion. Some of them have big beards and long hair, whilst others clip their hair short or shave the head, merely allowing a tuft to remain on the crown as a sign that they are Christians. They also wear moustaches. They pierce the ears and wear much gold in them. They go naked down to the waist, covering their lower extremities with very fine cotton stuffs. But it is only the most respectable who do this, for the others manage as best they are able. . . . The women of this country, as a rule,

---

Source: A Journal of the First Voyage of Vasco da Gama, 1497–1499, trans. and ed. E.G. Ravenstein (London: Hakluyt Soceity 1898; New Delhi, 1998), 49–50, 52–55

are ugly and of small stature. They wear many jewels of gold round the neck, numerous bracelets on their arms, and rings set with precious stones on their toes. All their people are well-disposed and apparently mild tempered. At first sight they seem covetous and ignorant.

[A Christian Church] When we arrived [at Calicut] they took us to a large church, and this is what we saw: The body of the church is as large as a monastery, all built of hewn stone and covered with tiles. At the main entrance rises a pillar of bronze as high as a mast, on the top of which was perched a bird, apparently a cock. In addition to this, there was another pillar as high as a man and very stout. In the center of the church rose a chapel, all built of hewn stone with a bronze door sufficiently wide for a man to pass, and stone steps leading up to it. Within this sanctuary stood a small image which they said represented Our Lady.[3] Along the walls, by the main entrance, hung seven small bells. In this church the captain-major [Vasco da Gama] said his prayers, and we with him.

We did not go within the chapel, for it is the custom that only certain servants of the church called *quafees*,[4] should enter. These *quafees* wore some threads passing over the left shoulder and under the right arm, in the same manner as our deacons wear the stole. They threw holy water over us, and gave us some white earth, which the Christians of this country are in the habit of putting on their foreheads, breasts, around the neck, and on the forearms.[5] They threw holy water upon the captain-major and gave him some of the earth, which he gave in charge of someone, giving them to understand that he would put it on later.

[A Royal Audience, 28 May] The king was in a small court, reclining upon a couch covered in cloth of green velvet, above which was a good mattress, and upon this again a sheet of cotton stuff, very white and fine, more so than linen. The cushions were after the same fashion. In his left hand the king held a very large golden cup [spittoon], having the capacity of half an *almude* [8 pints]. At his mouth this cup was two palmas [16 inches] wide, and apparently it was massive. Into this cup the king threw the husks of a certain herb which is chewed by the people of this country because of its soothing effects, and which they call *atambor*.[6] On the right side of the king stood a basin of gold, so large that a man might just encircle it with his arms: this contained the herbs. There were likewise many silver jugs. The canopy above the couch was all gilt.

---

[3] Probably the Hindu goddess Durga.

[4] Brahmin priests.

[5] Ashes that devotees of Shiva put on their bodies as a sign of devotion.

[6] Probably the betel leaf—a mild stimulant.

■ The First European Description of Brazil, April 1500

Péro Vaz de Caminha (ca. 1450–1500) was born in Porto, where he held a series of official positions, including serving on the city council. He was a knight of the king's household and had a solid education. Caminha also served with the troops from Porto in the Battle of Toro (1476). In 1499, he became the scribe for the second Portuguese India fleet under Pedro Alvares Cabral, which left Lisbon in March 1500. Cabral's fleet spent much of the following month exploring the coast of Brazil before resuming the voyage to India. To inform King D. Manuel I about his new discovery, Cabral sent one of his ships back to Lisbon on 1 May. Caminha compiled a long letter for the king describing this new discovery. Oddly, this letter, now sometimes called the "birth certificate" of Brazil, remained unpublished in the Portuguese archives until 1817. Caminha died in late 1500 fighting in Calicut.

As you read this portion of his letter, compare Caminha's description of the lands and people of Brazil with the description of Calicut provided in da Gama's journal. How do the possibilities for trade and conversion in Brazil compare with those in India? How do the possibilities for economic gain compare? Which passages in these selections most reveal Caminha as a man of early-16th-century Europe and how so?

[Affonso Lopez] captured two well-built natives who were in a canoe. . . . [I]n appearance they are dark, somewhat reddish, with good faces and good noses, well shaped. They go naked, without any covering; neither do they pay more attention to concealing or exposing their shame than they do to showing their faces, and in this respect they are very innocent. Both had their lower lips bored and in them were placed pieces of white bone, the length of a handbreadth, and the thickness of a cotton spindle and as sharp as an awl in the end. They put them through the inner part of the lip, and that part which remains between the lip and the teeth is shaped like a rook in chess. Any they carry in it there enclosed in such a manner that it

Source: Letter of Péro Vaz de Caminha to D. Manuel I from *The Voyage of Pedro Alvares Cabral to Brazil and India, from Contemporary Documents and Narratives,* trans. and ed. William Brooks Greenlee (London: Hakluyt Soceity, 1938), 5–33, passim.

does not hurt them, nor does it embarrass them in speaking, eating, or drinking. Their hair is smooth, and they were shorn, with the hair cut higher than above a comb of good size, and shaved to above the ears. And one of them was wearing below the opening, from temple to temple towards the back, a sort of wig of yellow "birds" feathers, which must have been the length of a *couto* [width of hand], very thick and very tight, and it covered the back of the head, and the ears. This was glued to the hair, feather by feather, with a material as soft as wax, but it was not wax. Thus the head-dress was very round and very close and very equal, so that it was not necessary to remove it when they washed. . . .

They seem to me people of such innocence that, if one could under-stand them and they us, they would soon be Christians, because they do not have or understand any belief, as it appears. And therefore, if the convicts[7] who are to remain here will learn their language well and understand them, I do not doubt that they will become Christians, in accordance with the pious intent of Your Highness, and that they will believe in our Holy Faith, to which it may please Our Lord to bring them. For it is certain this people is good and of pure simplicity, and there can easily be stamped upon them whatever belief we wish to give them; and furthermore, Our Lord gave them fine bodies and good faces as to good men; and He who brought us here, I believe did not do so without purpose. And consequently, Your Highness, since you so much desire to increase the Holy Catholic Faith, ought to look after their salvation, and it will please God that, with little effort, this will be accomplished. . . .

It seems to me, Senhor, that this land from the promontory we see farthest south to another promontory which is to the north, of which we caught sight from this harbor, is so great that I will have some twenty or twenty-five leagues of coastline. Along the shore in some places it has great banks, some of them red, some white, and the land above it is quite flat and covered with great forests. From point to point the entire shore is very flat and very beautiful. As for the interior, it appeared to us from the sea very large, for, as far as the eye could reach, we could still see only land and forests, a land which seemed very extensive to us. Up to now we are unable to learn that there is gold and silver in it, or anything of metal or iron; nor have we seen any, but the land itself has a very good climate . . . Its waters are quite endless.

---

[7] The Crown routinely used *Degregados*, or convict-exiles, on voyages of discovery. For the king, they were cheap and expendable; for the convicts such voyages held the promise of a better life.

■ The Second Capture of Goa, November 1510

Afonso de Albuquerque was born in 1453 at Alhandra near Lisbon and received a superior education at the court of Afonso V. After warring against Islam in North Africa periodically over the next 30 years, and serving as chief equerry for D. João II, he sailed for India for the first time in 1503–1504. His second and final voyage from 1506 to 1515 and term as governor of the *Estado da India* (1509–1515) witnessed the consolidation of Portugal's Asian empire. Albuquerque's *Commentaries* compiled from original letters and other documents by his son provides an exhaustive look at his notable career.

In the selection below, which factors are highlighted in the capture of Goa by the Portuguese? To what extent had the religious struggle known as the crusades been extended to India? What part of this description do you find the most surprising? Why? How do you think the Hindu inhabitants of Goa felt about this warfare between the Portuguese and the Muslims of Bijapur?

And now that the great Afonso Dalboquerque had made all arrangements to attack the city, as I have said, on the following day, before morning broke, which was the day of St. Catherine, the 25th day of the month of November of one thousand five hundred and ten.... The Turks, who were stationed therein, defended themselves for a long time, and prevented any entry of the enemy, and Afonso Dalboquerque, with the men he had in his company, on arriving at the palisades which Dinis Fernandez had already cut down, went up along the edge of ridge at the double. The Turks, because they did not fear any attack from that side, as soon as they felt themselves harassed by people at their back, after making a long resistance, began to retire from the stockades. The captains, when they perceived that the enemy were beginning to become embarrassed with the arrival of Afonso Dalboquerque, fell upon them so valiantly, carrying in their van the Apostle Santiago,[8] who was going with them as their guide, that in a short space of time they got into the

---

Source: The Commentaries of the Great Afonso de Alboquerque, Second Viceroy of India, by his son Afonso Braz de Alboquerque, translated from the Portuguese edition of 1774 and edited by Walter de Gray Birch (4 vols, London: Hakluyt Soceity, 1875–1883), 3: 9–10, 16–18.

[8] Saint James the Greater, an apostle whose putative relics at Compostela in northwest Spain had served as one of Western Christianity's most important pilgrimage shrines since the 9th century. Known as *Santiago Matamoros* (St. James the Moor-slayer), he served as the patron saint of the Christian *Reconquista* of Iberia. See the introduction to the first source.

stockades, and with the enemy in flight made their way pell-mell as far as the gates of the city, without looking behind them, killing and maiming many Turks.

In the city were captured a hundred large guns (*bombardas*) and a large quantity of smaller artillery, and two hundred horses, and many supplies and munitions of war. All these were ordered to be delivered to the factor for the king. And after the city had been pillaged, Afonso Dalboquerque told the captains to reconnoiter the whole of the island and to put to the sword all the Moors,[9] men, women, and children, that should be found, and to give no quarter to any one of them; for his determination was to leave no seed of this race throughout the whole of the island. And he did this, not only because it was necessary for the security of the land that there should be none but Hindoos within it. . . . And for four days continuously they poured out the blood of the Moors who were found therein; and it was ascertained that of the men, women, and children, the number exceeded six thousand. . . .

As soon as the despoiling of the land had been accomplished, Afonso Dalboquerque turned his attention without delay to the fortifications of the city, and ordered that a great quantity of cement should be prepared, and all the sepulchers of the Moors thrown down, in order to obtain plenty of stone. . . . And as he hoped to establish in Goa the principal seat of the Governors of India, he so arranged the plan that the palace of the Cabaio remained within the boundary. . . . At this time some men were progressing with the destruction of some old walls, in order to get stones for the works of defense, when they discovered in the foundations an image of the crucifix in copper. When the news of this ran through the city, Afonso Dalboquerque came down at once with all the people and clergy who were with him, and they carried the crucifix, with great devotion and many tears to the church. Great wonder was there that then seized upon the beholders; for within the memory of man there was no record of any Christians having been at that place, and they believed that our Lord had sent down that sign from Heaven, in order to show that it was his will that the kingdom should belong to the King of Portugal and not to the Hidalcao,[10] and that the mosques should become houses of prayer, wherein his name should be worshipped.

---

[9] Technically, a Berber or Arab-Berber Muslim of North Africa or Iberia.

[10] The Adil Shah dynasty (hence the Portuguese corruption) ruled over the powerful Muslim sultanate of Bijapur. This sultanate controlled Goa before the attack of the Portuguese in 1510.

■ Afonso de Albuquerque's Views on Asian Trade and Empire in a Letter to D. Manuel I, of 1 April 1512

Albuquerque is generally considered to be the great strategist of the Portuguese empire in Asia. Many of his long letters back to king Manuel I have survived the ravages of time. After reading this letter, do you think this reputation is deserved? What, according to Albuquerque, was the current state of affairs in the India trade? What did he see as the key to maintaining the status quo? How important were the factories of trading stations in the Indies for the well-being of Portugal? What was his advice on funding this growing empire without huge expenses for the Crown at home?

I have touched above on several matters for Your Highness concerning the India trade, this is because I see that Your Highness believes that this business is simple and safe. I note that your instructions and letters are full of blandishments and assurances for the Moslems from here, having certainty that in these parts that is how your interests will be best served, ordering me to avoid war as far as possible, and other words, that in your letters I see, tell me what to say to kings and lords of these parts where you wish to have trade and factories, buy and sell goods, keeping your people and your revenues secure. However, I then see that you command me to build very strong fortresses to secure your goods and your people, and I note that you want to take the spices and the other riches from India against the wishes of the Moslems and that you want to destroy the trade with Mecca, Jiddah, and Cairo. I see that the Moslems spend their money to defend it and, as far as they can, avoid accepting your trade and the establishment of your factories voluntarily. Those who have done so wait for the moment when they can take the noose from their necks and set to work against you.

I know for certain that this is the condition of the relations between Moslems and Christians, and the Moslems will do everything they can to ensure that it remains that way until the Final Judgment. I also see how Your Highness has taken from the Moslems the free trade and navigation that they formerly enjoyed and how their kings are deprived of the status, power and the authority they once had in India and are reviled and full of oppression, and you have taken from them

Source: Cartas de Affonso de Albuquerque seguidas de documentos que as elucidam, ed. R.A. de Bulhao Pato (7 vols, Lisbon, 1884–1935) I: 29–65.

all their domination of the ocean and coasts of their realms and lands, and some of them you have made your tributaries, and others out of fear seek to make peace with you.

Your Highness thinks you can keep these men under control with fair words and offers of peace and protection, and yet they are Moslems with many men and horses and much money. With strong fortresses, much cavalry, and good artillery and weaponry, I see Your Highness's position made secure in the lands of the Infidel; and yet you neglect India even though you stand in great need of all these things to secure it, it being the greatest enterprise that any Christian prince has ever undertaken, valuable both to the service of God and for your own renown and glory. . . .

And this problem, Sire, which I am here describing to you will last in India until they see their main strength in your power and strong fortresses or large bodies of troops to keep them quiet, and in this way you may trade merchandise without war and without so many conflicts in India. And three thousand men, at the salary which Your Highness now pays, cost around a hundred and twenty thousand cruzados a year, while the spices you have shipped each year from India, after deducting the salaries you pay here, losses at sea and the original outlay, are worth a million cruzados. Let Your Highness see if the tree which gives fruit every year should be well cultivated and well watered and treated with great favor. And again I repeat, if you want to avoid war in India and have peace with all its kings, you must send plenty of troops and good weapons, or else capture all the principal places on the coasts of their kingdoms. . . .

And also Sire you require that your men be paid wages, and I do not see any goods which can be used to pay these, the best capital that our factories have at present is whatever prizes and booty are captured from the Moslems, and from this source the expenses and costs of your fleet can be paid, and wages, and sometimes marriages, can be paid.

CHAPTER 2

The Spanish Empire in the New World, ca. 1480–1700

THE ENTERPRISE OF THE INDIES

As night fell on 13 August 1476, a drenched sailor washed up on the Algarve coast of Portugal. The man had been part of a trading voyage organized in Genoa that was sailing with a cargo to sell in Lisbon, England, and Flanders. Early that morning, the small Genoese fleet had been attacked by French corsairs. The bloody battle raged all day. Only two of the Genoese ships had escaped; the other three ships had burned and sunk. The aforementioned Genoese, using some of the wooden debris, had swum several miles to shore. One of the thoughts that sustained him was that he had a younger brother called Bartolomeu working as a chart maker in Lisbon. If he survived, why not head to that great city, the very epicenter of the nautical advances that were propelling the Age of Discovery to ever-distant lands? The man in the water that late afternoon was Christopher Columbus. His arrival in Lisbon several weeks later and his apprenticeship in Portugal during the next decade resulted in a project for discovery that would change the face of the globe as both his contemporaries and succeeding generations would know it.

Columbus was born into a lower-middle-class Genoese family in 1451. As with Vasco da Gama, not much is known of Columbus's early life. According to the later accounts of his son Ferdinand and Bartolomé de Las Casas, he supposedly attended the University of Pavia studying astronomy, geography, and cosmography. However, it seems more likely that the young Columbus, like his Portuguese contemporary, learned his nautical skills in the "school of hard knocks." He spent time in the family business and trading voyages. As he wrote to Ferdinand and Isabella in 1501, "I entered upon the sea sailing, and so I have continued to this day. That art inclines him who follows it to want to know the secrets of this world. Already forty years have passed that I have been in this employment." From 1461 to 1476, Columbus sailed along the Italian coast. He also may have voyaged to Tunis. Columbus learned valuable lessons on these voyages, but it was his subsequent apprenticeship in Portugal from 1476 to 1485 that perfected these skills and crystallized his grand project to reach Asia by sailing west.

To help finance his activities in Lisbon, Columbus embarked on a trading voyage to England, Ireland, and Iceland in 1477, where he heard stories about the Vinland of Leif Ericssoon, which, in turn, piqued his interest in a voyage west. Returning to Lisbon, he was taken into his brother Bartolomeu's mapmaking business. There was a large Genoese community established in the Portuguese capital and, thanks to these connections, the pair made a decent living. But once exposed to the possibilities that were opening up for Portugal, thanks to the Guinea trade, Columbus decided upon a self-improvement campaign, which yielded stunning results. First, he learned to read and write in Portuguese and Latin. The former was the *lingua franca* of the voyages of discovery; the latter was required for communicating with Europe's intellectual and cultural elites. Thanks in part to his varied commercial activities on behalf of powerful Genoese merchant families, Columbus also arranged a very favorable marriage. Sometime between 1478 and 1479 he married the noblewoman Dona Felipa Perestrello e Moniz. Her late father had been part of one of the early expeditions to Madeira and Porto Santo. He had been given the hereditary captaincy of Porto Santo and remained there until his death in the late 1450s. Columbus's mother-in-law gave him her husband's substantial collection of maps, charts, and books. Moreover, he and his bride lived on Madeira and Porto Santo in the early 1480s. During this time, he studied his father-in-law's maps, as well as the currents and winds of the Atlantic. Columbus also heard and read tales of islands and other lands farther west. By 1484, all of these influences had come together to form his grand plan for reaching Asia by sailing west.

Columbus's 'Enterprise of the Indies,' as he later called it, was therefore grounded on both his practical experiences as a mariner and his reading of scholarly works on geography. The theoretical underpinnings of the idea were not new. Both Aristotle and Strabo thought it possible to reach Asia by sailing west. Ptolemy's *Geography* postulated a Eurasian continent that dominated much of the Northern Hemisphere and might be reached by sailing west. Marco Polo's description of the riches of the islands including Cipangu (Japan), which extended perhaps 30 degrees of longitude out from the Asian mainland, also encouraged him. Finally, Columbus's heavily marked copy of Pierre d'Ailly's *Imago Mundi* contained the dictum that the Atlantic Ocean "is not so great that it can cover three quarters of the globe, as certain people figure it." The surprises that awaited him were due to his miscalculation of the earth's true circumference and thus the distance from Europe to Asia, and the formidable obstacle posed by the landmasses of North and South America. Columbus estimated that each degree of longitude was approximately 40 nautical miles at 28 degrees north latitude, the latitude of his proposed crossing. Since he believed that the distance from the Canaries to Japan was about 60 degrees of longitude, his estimate on the total distance was 2,400 miles, or 800 leagues. In reality, each degree of longitude is 60 nautical miles, and the actual distance between the Canaries and Japan is about 10,600 miles. Nevertheless, Columbus's plan received a lukewarm endorsement from the eminent Florentine scholar Toscanelli. The question was, would he find a patron for his voyage?

Given his connections in Lisbon, Columbus approached D. João II. The Portuguese monarch, however, was the genetic as well as philosophical heir to Prince Henry the Navigator. Nearly six decades of voyages, money, and energy had been expended by the Portuguese in the gradual push south along the African coast. The king was increasingly sure that there was indeed a cape at the bottom of Africa, and that India and China would soon be within his reach. After consulting with his experts, who were bothered by Columbus's overly optimistic mathematics and his admiration for Marco Polo, D. João politely refused. Columbus's rather hefty material demands and boasts did not help his cause. The king "observed that this Christovao Colum to be a big talker, and full of fancy and imagination." Nevertheless, D. João II was impressed enough to invite him back from Spain in 1488 for another interview. Ironically, soon after his arrival in December, Columbus witnessed the triumphant return of Bartolomeu Dias from his voyage around the Cape of Good Hope. The sea route to India by sailing south and east was now opened. D. João II had no further need of Columbus or his plan. A dejected Columbus left to sell his project elsewhere.

Ferdinand of Aragon and his cousin Isabella of Castile had married in 1469, portending a greater unity of the diverse kingdoms and provinces that make up modern Spain. Castile was the larger and more populous kingdom, while Aragon boasted a large Mediterranean empire. Unifying their separate kingdoms was never a goal. Rather, the pair sought to implement parallel policies in their realms. Together, the so-called 'Catholic Monarchs' established the power of the Crown at the expense of the traditional threats of the nobles and the Cortes, or representative assemblies, of their respective kingdoms. Ferdinand and Isabella also strove for religious conformity. Pope Sixtus IV issued a bull in 1478 that allowed them to establish the Inquisition in their domains, which they did in 1480. Although primarily intended to root out heresy against the teachings of the Roman Catholic Church, this institution also provided a weapon to cower all segments of Spanish society. Columbus had originally traveled to Spain in 1485 and had spent the next seven years trying to convince the Catholic Monarchs of the benefits of his project. But during these years, Ferdinand and Isabella had more important matters to deal with before seriously considering such risky overseas ventures.

The year 1492 was a seminal year in Spanish, European, and world history. In that year, Ferdinand and Isabella completed the Reconquest of Iberia. The process of expelling the Moors from Spain did much to unify the disparate ethnic groups that the Catholic kings ruled. Castilians, Aragonese, Galicians, Andalusians, Asturians, and many others joined the struggle against the remaining vestiges of Islam in the Spanish portion of the peninsula and gradually came to share a common language (Castilian) in the process. This much-needed cooperation later served Spain well both in its European wars and in the process of discovery and conquest of the New World. On 2 January 1492, Abu Abdullah Muhammad XI, the last Nasrid ruler of Granada, surrendered that city and its magnificent Alhambra to Ferdinand and Isabella. Muslim power in Iberia had ended. In March, in order to complete their policy of religious conformity, the Catholic

Monarchs ordered all the Jews in their domains to either convert to Christianity or to leave their kingdoms within four months.

Once these matters had been settled, Ferdinand and Isabella gave serious consideration to Columbus's plan. Portugal was the great rival. The Portuguese king D. Afonso V had even challenged Isabella's claim to the Castilian throne in the mid-1470s. No doubt harboring lingering antipathy toward the house of Aviz, the Catholic kings found much to like about the idea of challenging D. João II's emerging dominance in the Guinea trade. Columbus's plan provided such an opportunity. If he were successful in reaching Asia by sailing west, it would preempt nearly a century of painstaking Portuguese work along the African Coast. The Catholic Monarchs, moreover, in 1492 found themselves surrounded by restless hidalgos (nobles), who had just finished assisting with the *Reconquista* and who expected lands in return for their services. If Columbus were successful, these nobles might be appeased before they began fighting among themselves or against the Crown. Finally, Luis de Santangel, the keeper of the privy purse for Ferdinand, and a friend of Columbus, put together a creative funding package for the scheme which made it all the more attractive at court.

COLUMBUS'S FLEET OF 1492

After nearly seven years of demurring, the Catholic Monarchs gave their royal blessing for the project in August 1492. A formal contract was worked out. Ferdinand and Isabella agreed to outfit three ships with crews, provisions for a year, as well as trading products, such as the shiny beads and bells that the Portuguese had used to great effect on the west coast of Africa. After years of struggle, Columbus expected to be well compensated if he succeeded. He would be given the title 'Admiral of the Ocean Sea,' which in turn gave him administrative and judicial power over the lands he discovered; he would receive 10 percent of all the precious stones and metals that were found, and an eighth share of all the profits of the trade. Although these were bold claims, especially for a commoner to make, the Catholic Monarchs agreed. Why? They either did not expect much to come of the voyage, or they realized that such concessions could always be modified later.

Between May and July 1492, Columbus's fleet outfitted at the port of Palos de la Frontera. Why Palos and not Seville or Cadiz, the main ports of Andalusia? Well, in the summer of 1492, some 8,000 Jewish families were in the midst of embarking from Cadiz for other parts of Europe. Moreover, for a civic transgression, Palos had been fined the use of two caravels for a year. That was convenient. In all, about 2,000,000 *maravedis*, or about the monthly income of a Spanish marquis of the period, were spent on the 'Enterprise of the Indies.' Today, that amount would equal perhaps $175,000. The crafty Santangel provided a good portion of the 1,500,000 *maravedis* the Crown promised from the endowment of the *Santa Hermandad*, which provided the monarchs with a loyal royal militia. Columbus put up another 250,000 *maravedis*, which he borrowed from rich friends, and Santangel put up the rest. To pay for the salaries of the 90 men who sailed with Columbus, another 250,000 *maravedis* a month, a new tax was levied on the butchers of Seville. By early August, the *Niña*, *Pinta*, and *Santa Maria* were ready to depart. Columbus carried a passport in Latin: "By these presents we dispatch the noble man Christoforus Colon with three caravels over the Ocean Seas toward the regions of India for certain reasons and purposes."

After a shakedown voyage to the Canaries, the three ships departed for Asia in early September. Columbus believed that if he sailed due west, on a course of 270 degrees, he would hit the great island of Cipangu which lay on approximately the same latitude as the Canaries, or 28 degrees north latitude. Hold to that course and average about four knots an hour, and he would cover the 2,400 miles to Asia in three short weeks. By early October there was little doubt that the fleet had sailed nearly that far and no land had been sighted. Martin Alonso Pinzon, the commander of the *Pinta*, and others were growing tense. On 6 October, Pinzon called for a change in course. By 10 October, the fleet had been at sea for 34 days, with no end in sight to the voyage, and a mutiny brewing below decks. As his son Ferdinand later wrote, the crew was "saying that the Admiral in his mad fantasy proposed to make himself a lord at the cost of their lives or die in the attempt." The mutineers' plan was simple: they would "heave him overboard and report in Spain that he had fallen in accidentally while observing the stars; and none would question their story." But, in the end, the change of course was a fortuitous one. At about 2:00AM on the morning of 12 October 1492 a sailor aboard the *Pinta*, Juan Rodriquez Bermejo, sighted the moonlit shore of an island. Columbus's life was not only saved, but Asia, after 36 days and almost 4,000 miles, had apparently been found.

COLUMBUS'S LATER EXPEDITIONS AND DEATH

As we all know today, Columbus's fleet had not reached the outer islands of Asia, as he believed, but rather Watlings Island in the Bahamas, some 9,000 miles away from his destination. The new Admiral of the Ocean Sea, however, held on to the belief for the rest of his life that he had indeed reached the islands lying off the mainland of Asia. In all, following his epic voyage in 1492–1493, Columbus undertook three more voyages (1493–1496, 1498–1500, and 1502–1504) all in search of the Asian mainland. In the process, he discovered most of the main islands of the Caribbean: Hispaniola, Dominica, Cuba, Jamaica, the Leeward Islands, the Virgin Islands, Puerto Rico, Trinidad, the mouth of the Orinoco River in Venezuela, as well as Honduras, Costa Rica, and Panama. While this was an impressive geographical and nautical achievement, Columbus had a more checkered history in the attempt to establish a profitable Spanish presence in the New World. On his second voyage he discovered that his initial outpost on Hispaniola, called *Villa de Navidad*, was destroyed and its 39-sailor garrison wiped out in his absence by the angry Taino natives, who were repulsed by the avariciousness of the Spaniards in their never-ending quest for the source of the island's gold and probably also by their abuse of the islanders. He ordered a new settlement named in honor of his royal patron, Isabella, built on an inauspicious site on the island. On his third voyage, internecine fighting with Spanish colonists resulted in open rebellion against his authority. The outcry in Spain was such that even Ferdinand and Isabella lost faith in him. He was stripped of his title of Viceroy and Governor, and his successor, Francisco de Bobadilla, had Columbus arrested and sent back to Spain in irons. Although the Catholic Monarchs allowed him one more voyage, in search of a passage through the new lands he had discovered to the Asian mainland, his administrative and colonizing days were over. After his grueling fourth voyage, he returned to Europe to die in 1506 a broken man, far from the centers of power that he had worked so hard to cultivate and which his triumphant entries into Lisbon and Barcelona in 1493 had seemingly portended.

EARLY ATTEMPTS AT EMPIRE, 1493–1520

Nevertheless, between 1493 and 1520, the Spanish Crown began the arduous process of establishing an empire in the New World. In this process, there is much to recommend the argument that a unified Spain did not build this empire but rather that building this empire created a more unified Spain. On Hispaniola, the settlement known as Isabella was soon abandoned, and the construction of Santo Domingo began in 1496–1497. By then, the power of the local Taino chiefs, or *caciques*, had been broken. The Spaniards roamed the island at will, and the European population was estimated at 630 by Ferdinand Columbus. Some products of value had been sent back to Spain. Italian merchants present at Cadiz in March 1494, when the 12-ship fleet under Antonio de Torres arrived, sent a meticulous report back to their patrons. Thirty-thousand ducats worth of gold, "cinnamon enough, but white like bad ginger, pepper in shells like beans, very strong but not with the flavor of that of the Levant, wood said to be sandalwood but white," 60 parrots, and 26 Indian slaves "of different islands and languages . . . three of them *Canibali* who live on human flesh." While these goods were clearly exotic, they hardly justified the initial claims of Columbus to the Catholic Monarchs of the vast wealth of Asia that would soon be flowing into the royal coffers.

Before Columbus's arrival, the Arawak Taino Indians had lived on islands like Hispaniola and Puerto Rico in kingdoms based on a system of hierarchically arranged chiefs, or *caciques*. The Tainos were divided into three social classes: the *naborias* (workers); the *nitaínos* (nobles), which included the *bohiques*, or priests and medicine men; and the *caciques*, or chiefs. Each village, or *yucayeque*, was ruled by a chief. At the time Juan Ponce de León took possession of Puerto Rico in 1508, there were about 20 villages. Following the arrival of the Spaniards, the Tainos were forced to acknowledge the sovereignty of the king of Spain by payment of gold tribute, to work and supply provisions of food, and to observe Christian ways. As Columbus noted in his journal as early as 14 October 1492, the Tainos could be easily dominated: "These people are very unskilled in arms . . . with fifty men they could all be subjected and made to do all that one wished."

On the Caribbean islands, the Spaniards were largely frustrated in their search for precious metals, spices, and other valuable commodities. Most of the hidalgos who made the passage were quickly disillusioned and frustrated with the lack of ready gold and silver.

By the longstanding precepts of their class, they also shunned the idea of farming. To compensate for the disappointment of these aristocratic colonists, Columbus as early as 1499, had begun the exploitive *repartimento*, later in modified form called the *encomienda* system. This modified form of medieval feudalism was designed to provide the colonists with a stable and cheap supply of labor. The *encomienda* had been first used with the conquered Moors of Spain and the Guanches on the Canaries. In 1493, the Catholic Monarchs approved it for use in the New World. The Crown retained ultimate title to the land but a subject, called the *encomendero,* was given use of a parcel of land along with the inhabitants on it, who owed tribute and allegiance. In return, the *encomendero* promised to protect and, more importantly in the eyes of the pious Isabella, to instruct the Tainos in the liturgy of the Catholic faith. The right to use the land for their subsistence was also guaranteed. In essence, it entailed a practical *quid pro quo* between the Crown and Spanish colonists on one level and between the colonists and the Amerindians on another. The positive spin on the system was that it supposedly protected, educated, and civilized the peoples of the Caribbean and beyond. Predictably, Spanish colonists far removed from the effective power of the Crown rather brutally exploited their workers, who quickly died off. These abuses eventually led to a spirited moral and ethical debate in Spain and the empire led by the Dominican priest Bartolomé de Las Casas.

During these years, a profound cultural interchange took place between the Old and New Worlds. On a culinary level, Columbus believed that the key to remaining healthy in the new climate was to ingest primarily European dishes. As he wrote "under God, the preservation of their health depends on these people being provided with the provisions they are used to in Spain." As a result, wheat, barley, and grape vines were promptly planted. Horses, cattle, and pigs were also introduced to the Western Hemisphere. The Spanish first tasted new foods like maize, cassava, pineapples, and sweet potatoes. They were also exposed to the practice of smoking tobacco. Biologically, the distinct disease pools of the old and the New Worlds were also mixed with explosive, nearly apocalyptic results. European diseases like smallpox spread rapidly in the islands and within a few decades a good portion of the Taino population was wiped out. On Puerto Rico, when the Spaniards first arrived in 1508 there were probably close to 50,000 Tainos, but the combination of disease, flight, and the abuses of the *encomienda* system swiftly reduced this number to 4,000 in 1515, and by 1544 a local bishop could find only 60! On Hispaniola, the number of Tainos in 1492 may have been as high as 300,000. At least 100,000 died off between 1494 and 1496. In 1508, only 60,000 remained. In 1512, there were 20,000 left. In 1548, perhaps only 500 were alive.[1]

The immune systems of the Europeans fared better. Strengthened by centuries of encounter with these Old World diseases, the European colonists experienced far fewer losses. One medical legacy of the sexual relations between the two populations was the rapid spread of syphilis around the globe. There is a heated debate on whether the disease was first brought back by Columbus's crews to Europe or whether it already existed there. In all probability, the disease had been endemic in both hemispheres, and the sexual relations between the two groups ushered in with Columbus's arrival in 1492 propelled the disease into virulent epidemic proportions. When Columbus returned to Santo Domingo in August 1498 on his third voyage, for example, 160 of the Europeans, or about a quarter of the population, were then sick with the symptoms of syphilis. Of course, many of them had been living with three or four Taino women. The first documented outbreaks in Europe occurred in Barcelona in 1493 and Naples in 1494. Within four or five years, the disease had spread rapidly in Europe under a variety of names seeking to pass the blame for its existence: the 'Spanish disease' the 'Neapolitan disease,' the *mal francaise, mal anglaise,* or quite simply 'the pox.' By 1507, syphilis had spread as far as China.

THE VOYAGE OF MAGELLAN

Geographically, during the first two decades of the 16th century, the significance of Columbus's discoveries became clear to educated Europeans. It was evident that he had not reached Asia but instead discovered a vast continent that was a barrier to direct trade between Europe and Asia. In voyages between 1499 and 1502, Americo Vespucci explored 2,000 miles of this coastline, confirming the existence of a new continent. This achievement prompted Martin Waldseemüller to name

[1]See the Connections Series book by John Aberth, *The First Horseman: Disease in Human History* (2007), Chapter 2.

the new southern continent 'America' on his famous world map of 1507. Vasco Nunes de Balboa exploring the narrow Isthmus of Panama glimpsed the Pacific for the first time in 1513 and claimed this vast ocean and its adjacent lands and islands for Spain. Once it was clear that the New World was, indeed, a barrier to Asia, the logical question was, is there a passage through it? During the initial decades of the 16th century, various attempts were made to find such a passage, but only one expedition would succeed in this quest. The skilled mariner who accomplished this daunting task was named Fernão Magalhaes, or Ferdinand Magellan.

Magellan was born in Portugal in about 1480 into a minor noble family. He had served D. Manuel I from 1503 to 1513 in the *Estado da India*. Sailing to Asia in the fleet of D. Francisco de Almeida, Magellan fought in East Africa and India with the viceroy. Under Afonso de Albuquerque, Magellan took part in the capture of both Goa and Melaka. After returning to Lisbon, he fought in North Africa. Nevertheless, his subsequent petitions for rewards were rejected by D. Manuel. In 1517 he left Portugal for Spain. By 1518, Magellan had signed an agreement with Charles V. This pact promised considerable rewards in return for establishing the Spanish Crown in the spice-rich Molucca Islands, which Magellan said could be reached by sailing through a strait at the tip of South America. To bolster his case, he showed the emperor maps and charts that he said were based on secret documents stored at the India and Guinea Houses in Lisbon.

Magellan's fleet, of 5 ships and 270 men, departed in September 1519. After stops at the Canaries and the Cape Verde Islands, the fleet reached Brazil in December. Because Brazil belonged to the Portuguese Crown, Magellan stayed only a short time to resupply. The fleet next cruised south along the South American coast in early 1520 searching for the strait that would allow it passage to the Spice Islands. By March, inclement weather forced Magellan to winter in Patagonia. After putting down a mutiny, the voyage then resumed in September 1520. By October, the fleet entered the 373-mile strait that now bears Magellan's name. By 28 November, the three remaining ships entered the new ocean, which Balboa had sighted seven years earlier. Magellan called it the *mar pacifico*, or Pacific Ocean, because of its tranquil waters. Sailing northwest in an impressive achievement of seamanship, the ships covered over 13,000 miles of ocean in 98 sailing days. By March 1521, Magellan, now commanding about 150 men, reached the Philippine Islands, which he claimed for Charles V. Although relations were initially cordial with the local rulers, Magellan was killed in a battle on Mactan Island fighting against an indigenous force led by Lapu-Lapu on 27 April. Juan Sebastian del Cano assumed command of the *Victoria* with about 60 men, and after a difficult voyage across the Indian Ocean and around the Cape of Good Hope, he reached Spain in September 1522 with fewer than 20 men still alive. As the chronicler of the fleet, Antonio Pigafetta noted, "we had sailed 14,460 leagues, and completed the circuit of the world from east to west." The globe had at last been encompassed in a single voyage. Unfortunately, the rigors of passing through Magellan's Strait made it virtually useless for regular navigation. Nevertheless, the Spanish empire had expanded across the vast expanse of the Pacific Ocean.

In 1519, the year in which Magellan left Spain, the profits from this New World empire had been less than spectacular. By the time del Cano brought the *Victoria* back to Seville in 1522, all that had changed. Charles V was a dynastic fluke who inherited the Spanish kingdoms and empire of his maternal grandparents, Ferdinand and Isabella, as well as the Burgundian and Austrian possessions of his Habsburg paternal grandparents. But Charles was lucky not only at the dynastic game, as king of Spain he would hit the jackpot in the quest for overseas wealth. Ironically, this wealth would not result from new oceanic voyages like Magellan's, but rather from the exploits of hardened soldiers and fortune hunters seeking wealth, glory, and fame. The age of the explorers was ending, the age of the conquistadors was at hand. In the words of Bernal Dias del Castillo, the most plainspoken of these men, the conquistadors were driven by the desire to serve their king and God "and to grow rich as all men desire to do." Between 1519 and 1550, such men would win Spain a huge empire in the New World and obtain undreamed of riches for themselves and their monarchs.

CORTÉS AND THE CONQUEST OF MEXICO

The most famous of these men was Hernan Cortés. Cortés had been born into a minor noble family in 1485. At 14, he studied law at the University of Salamanca, but he soon became bored. In 1501, he decided to pursue a life of adventure. He sailed to Santo Domingo in 1504, and later accompanied Diego Velázquez to Cuba. In early 1517 Hernández de Córdoba, searching for a passage to Asia, had reached the Yucatán peninsula and through his contacts with the Mayans first heard stories of a rich civilization to the north. A fleet under Juan Grijalva had also reached the Mexican Coast and returned to Havana with even more stories of the great emperor Montezuma and his vast wealth. At this time, the Aztec civilization was at its height. Montezuma II ruled a vast Mesoamerican empire based in the great Valley of Mexico from his capital of Tenochtitlán. The Aztec Empire probably included some 20 million subjects. Velázquez initially chose Cortés to determine the veracity of these rumors. Yet, jealous of Cortés's skills, the governor soon regretted his choice and planned to relieve him of command. When Cortés learned of these plans, he quickly departed from Cuba in February 1519. He sailed with about 400 soldiers, 16 cavalry, and a few pieces of artillery. After landing on the Mexican Coast in early March, Cortés quickly captured the town of Tabasco, established a town at Vera Cruz, and had himself elected captain-general of the new colony. To demonstrate his resolve, he then ordered the ships burnt and headed inland.

In less than three years, Cortés reduced the vast Aztec Empire to vassalage to Charles V and Spain. Its vast riches in gold, silver, and precious stones were in part shipped across the Atlantic to Seville. How did Cortés accomplish this startling conquest? To begin with, an Aztec prophecy called for the return of the god Quetzalcoatl bringing good fortune with him. Cortés exploited this prophecy. Moreover, at the outset, his horses, armor, and weapons all reinforced this tendency of the Mesoamericans to look upon the Spaniards as gods. Of course, once the Spaniards had demonstrated human qualities, such as bleeding when wounded or beheaded, Cortés relied on more traditional, if ruthless, methods. He tricked Montezuma, placed him in irons, held him prisoner, and only ransomed him for a huge cache of gold and silver. Montezuma was later killed by his own people for his complicity with the Spaniards. Among other things, the emperor had yielded to Cortés's demand to end human sacrifices and to substitute Christian icons for Aztec gods in the city's main temple. After being expelled from Tenochtitlán during *La Noche Triste* (Night of Sorrow), in July 1520, Cortés built boats and brilliantly executed a siege of the capital that resulted in its capitulation on 13 August 1521. The Spaniards were assisted in this siege by the outbreak of smallpox in the city, which killed many and had a devastating effect on others' morale. Perhaps most important, Cortés, like the Portuguese in Asia, skillfully exploited the adage, 'the enemy of my enemy is my friend.' By the time he reached Tenochtitlán in early November 1519, he already had more than 4,000 Indian allies from the rival state of Tlaxcala supporting him.

Cortés's conquest of the Aztecs made him rich and famous beyond his wildest dreams. In return for his efforts in conquering the "New Spain of the Ocean Sea," he was made Marqués del Valle de Oaxaca (1529), a vast land grant that made him overlord of tens, maybe hundreds, of thousands of people. Thus established, Cortés began the cultivation of sugar in Mexico. To facilitate this process he was also one of the first Spaniards to import African slaves. Spanish

1. *Lienzo de Tlaxcala, Plate 45. Cortés on a causeway to Tenochtitlan passes a temple of the Golden Foci (Courtesy of the American Museum of Natural History).*

PHOTO 2.1   Dona Marina and Cortés attack the Aztecs. In this mid-16th-century Tlaxcalan depiction of the conquest of Tenochtitlán, Dona Marina, or La Malinche, plays a crucial role in assisting Cortés. She appears both in the battle along the central causeway of the city and in the boats crossing Lake Texoco. Known as the *Lienzo de Tlaxcala*, this series of pictures on fabric (lienzo) was probably crafted to celebrate the pivotal role played by Cortés's Indian allies. Note also the mixture of Mesoamerican and European artistic styles.

power quickly filled the vacuum left by the fall of the Aztec empire. Cortés ordered the construction of Mexico City on the ruins of Tenochtitlán, and by the mid-16th century this new city—Mexico City—was the center of the new colony. Cortés, however, like Columbus, did not die a happy man. His fame was such that it inspired jealousy and backbiting at the court of Charles V. Royal officials sent to investigate his activities soon arrived and undermined his influence in Mexico. Cortés made several trips to Spain to answer his critics and to solidify his relationship with the emperor. He even accompanied Charles V on his rather disastrous campaign of 1541 to Algiers, where his sound military advice was ignored. In the end, he was increasingly marginalized from court. According to one story, perhaps apocryphal, Cortés once forced his way through a crowd to the royal carriage and Charles had asked who he was. The conquerer of Mexico had supposedly replied, "I am a man who has given you more provinces than your ancestors left you cities." This was certainly not the way to win royal favor. In the end, Cortés had been undermined by his own fame; he died a rich but embittered man outside Seville in 1547.

PIZARRO AND THE INCAS

The next great New World civilization to fall to the Spaniards was the Incas in South America. The Inca Empire dated to ca. 1438, and conquests by the ruler Pachacuti. Geographically, it was the largest empire in the New World at the time of Columbus, spanning more than 3,000 miles from Peru through Ecuador, northern Chile, and even northwestern Argentina. In the Inca language of Quechua, the empire was known as *Tawantinsuyu*, or "land of the four quarters." The empire was divided into four parts meeting at the capital of Cuzco. In building it, the Incas had subjugated over a million people who had formerly lived in dozens of independent states with varying ethnic and linguistic backgrounds. The empire had been won thanks to an efficient military and the ability to integrate disparate elites and religious systems into their own. The Incas offered these conquered peoples a benevolent deal: cooperate and the elite would be well treated and allowed a degree of self-rule. The social system was more inflexible, with the royal family constituting a dominant force. Conquered peoples were required to render to the state a labor tax called the *mita*, similar to the *corvée* in France. Using this guaranteed source of free seasonal labor, the

Incas built a huge system of roads and terraced farmlands throughout the Andes. Maize (corn) and potatoes were extensively cultivated, and llamas and alpaca were raised as a source of meat, fleece, and for labor. The Incas were amazing engineers. Their ability to fit gigantic stones together, to execute huge earth-drawings, to build massive forts with stone slabs so precisely cut that they did not require mortar astounded the Spaniards. These achievements were especially impressive in light of the fact that the Incas probably had no formal writing system, but instead relied on *quipus*, or record-keeping devices based on a complicated system of knots. The wheel was also not used by them. Huge amounts of labor directed by the elite sufficed.

Rumors of this rich civilization to the south of Panama had reached the Spaniards by 1522. The conquistador who most desired to investigate these rumors was Francisco Pizzaro. Pizarro had been born in 1474, the illegitimate son of a low-ranking Spanish noble. Unlike Cortés, he was poorly educated. But he possessed the same burning desire to seek fame and fortune. Pizarro sailed to Hispaniola in 1502, and by 1519, was comfortably ensconced in Panama. Hearing news of this wealthy empire to the south, he formed a private partnership with a priest named Hernando de Luque and a soldier named Diego de Almagro to explore the west coast of South America and to find this rich civilization. Pizarro's first two expeditions yielded meager results. But after traveling to Spain and arranging a *capitulacione* from Charles V (July 1529) he was emboldened for a third attempt. The *capitulacione* made Pizarro governor and captain-general of the new province of New Castile, 200 leagues inland from the coast. In this province he was to enjoy all the rights and prerogatives of a viceroy. By January 1531, Pizarro and his brother Hernando had prepared their expedition of conquest. Sailing from Panama it numbered 180 men and 27 horses and a dozen or so guns, or harquebuses.

In conquering the Incas, Pizarro exploited many of the same techniques that had served Cortés so well. He also benefitted from the pyschological and biological advantages that had assisted his contemporary. First, Pizarro arrived in the lands of the Incas in the wake of the first epidemic of smallpox to ravage the region. This outbreak had probably killed the powerful Inca emperor, Huayna Capac. A civil war resulted between two of the emperor's sons, Huáscar and Atahualpa. This war had a devastating impact on the empire, and it was only resolved in early 1532, when Atahualpa had defeated and executed his half-brother. Soon after, Pizarro and his band of conquistadors appeared. The decisive moment of the campaign occurred at the town of Cajamarca on 15 November 1532 at the first meeting between Pizarro and the Inca emperor. Despite the fact that Atahualpa was in the middle of his empire and in command of an army of nearly 80,000 men, Pizarro ambushed and captured him in the main square of Cajamarca. In this encounter, the steel weapons and armor of the Spanish played a key role. Moreover, as in Mexico, the horses of the Spanish made a huge impression on the Inca troops. The hierarchical structure of the Inca Empire and the godlike status of Atahualpa provided Pizarro with a decisive edge in the ensuing events. He held the emperor captive for eight months. During that time, he sent out expeditions to explore the rest of the empire and arranged reinforcements from Panama under Diogo de Almagro. To save their sun-god emperor, the Incas paid a ransom of 13,000 pounds of gold and 26,000 pounds of silver, enough to fill a room 22-feet long and 17-feet wide. Yet, Pizarro, fearing Atahualpa's ability to rally his army, had him executed anyway in August 1533. Exploiting his military advantages and the resulting chaos within the empire, he captured the Inca capital of Cuzco in November. Almagro then headed south into Chile, while Pizarro in early 1535 founded a new capital called the 'City of Kings,' eventually known as Lima. The wealth of the Incas, like that of the Aztecs, was soon flowing into the royal coffers of Charles V.

THE AGE OF THE CONQUISTADORS

The exploits of Cortés and Pizarro were repeated during these decades by a host of other conquistadors, some famous, some more obscure. Pedro de Alvarado in the Yucatán (1522–1528) and Ecuador (1534), Gonzalo Jiménez de Quesada (1536–1538) and Sebastian Belalcazar (1533–1538) in Columbia and Venezuela, Francisco de Orellana (1541–1542) along the Amazon River, Almagro (1535–1537) and Valdivia (1540–1553) in Chile, Alvar Nuñez Cabeza de Vaca (1528–1536) along the Gulf Coast of America across Texas to the Rio Grande, Hernando de Soto (1539–1542) from the Gulf Coast of Florida to the Mississippi River, and Francisco Vasquez de Coronado (1540–1542) in the American Southwest in search of El Dorado—all claimed vast territories for Spain. By 1550, thanks to the exploits of these conquistadors, the Spanish Crown had won a huge New World Empire that stretched from Chile in the south to southern California and Florida to the north. All of these exploits were carried out by relatively small groups of private adventurers. Charles V never sent one of his own continental armies to the New World to facilitate these conquests. As Oviedo noted, "almost never do Their Majesties put their income and cash into these new discoveries." Pizarro's band of men at Cajamarca embodied a cross section of early modern Spanish and Spanish-American society—merchants, peasants, notaries, artisans, priests, and soldiers. Many of the men with Pizarro, as well as in the other expeditions of the years 1500 to 1540, were *encomenderos*. A vital part of this system, which gave the holder the right to tribute and labor from the Indians, was the military obligation to serve the Crown when necessary. This essentially feudal relationship was clearly spelled out in the formal contracts for the *encomendero*, which called for him to provide "arms and a horse" to serve the king. This system thereby relieved the Crown from sending large armies to the New World during the first decades of the 16th century. Of course, given the plethora of foreign policy and military demands on Charles V in Europe, it would have been nearly impossible for him to do so in any case. The problem of the decades after 1540 was to somehow reign in and control the conquistadors, who had largely been given a free hand in conquest during the preceding decades. This dilemma was solved by the gradual implementation of a formal Crown bureaucracy in the New World.

ADMINISTERING THE NEW WORLD

In predictable fashion for an early modern monarch, Charles V attempted to extract the maximum amount of profit from his new empire with a minimum amount of effort. This was the age of the 'New Monarchies,' when kings were striving for greater powers at the expense of the nobles, as well as more centralized control over their kingdoms. Charles V's first priority for the empire was to prevent the development of a recharged form of feudalism in the New World led by the conquistadors. That is why he was so sensitive to the fame of Cortés and Pizarro and rumors at court that they were seeking to create their own kingdoms from their conquests. Royal agents were swiftly dispatched to Mexico and Peru to prevent this, and to establish the basis of Crown rule. The emperor was determined to control his new empire, and between 1525 and 1600, the Spanish Habsburgs set up an administrative system that mirrored the one that existed in Europe for their far-flung possessions. Absolutism dictated that the king and royal power in Spain would dominate. At the top of this pyramid were the king and the Council of the Indies (1524) in Madrid and later the palace of Escorial. The Council of the Indies, made up of a half dozen legal experts, had complete control over legislation and policy regarding the empire. This body ultimately decided issues of law and order, the treatment of the Indians, economic policy, and even town planning. To implement the decisions of this council in the New World, two huge territorial viceroyalties were eventually set up. The viceroyalty of New Spain (1538) had jurisdiction over lands claimed from the American Southwest and Mexico to the southern border of Costa Rica; the viceroyalty of Peru (1542) administered most of South America. *Audiencias,* or royal courts, were set up for administrative and judicial functions. By 1661 there were 12 *audiencias* operating in the New World and another in Manila in the Philippines. Significantly, all of the judges, or *oídores,* of the *audiencias* were sent from Spain.

Although there was a confusing degree of overlapping authority, viceroyalties were subdivided into a combination of *audiencias* and captaincies-general depending on wealth, population, and military necessity. The latter were administered by captains-general, who had charge over political and military functions for the Crown. Some of the more notable captaincies-general included Santo Domingo (1540), Chile (1541), Guatemala (1560), and New Granada (1563). Serving below the captains-general, or *audiencias,* were provincial governors, *corregidores* (magistrates), and *alcaldes* (local judges). Ideally, one of the principal duties of the *corregidores* was to protect the natives from the abuses of the colonists, but many *corregidores* were notorious for their exploitation of the Indians. In the towns that were built largely using the *mita* labor of the Indians, town councils (*cabildos*) were established. Since Madrid and the emperor were thousands of miles away, a mind-numbing series of rules and regulations was drawn up for all these colonial administrators. Two of the most important were the 'New Laws' of 1542, which among other things prohibited the enslavement of the Indians, and the Ordinances on Discovery and Population of 1573, which mandated the consolidation and pacification of existing territories. This goal was to be accomplished in part by encouraging religious teaching through missionaries and the protection of the Indians. But as in Portuguese Asia, given the huge distances involved, it was easy to ignore many of these dictums from Madrid, and the temptation for corruption and abuses of the Indians proved overwhelming to many of the administrators and colonists.

THE PHILIPPINES, 1521–1700

Magellan had ended his personal voyage of circumnavigation cut down on the beach at Mactan in April 1521. Before this defeat, he had claimed the islands for Spain, calling them the *Islas de San Lazaro*. Magellan first landed on the island of Homonhon in March and cultivated good relations with Rajah Calambu of Limasawa and Rajah Humabon of Cebu. Impressed with Spanish weaponry, including 12 cannons and 50 cross-bows, these local rulers had suggested an attack on their rival, Lapu-Lapu, which ended badly for the Spaniards, and particularly Magellan. Thereafter, the Spanish Crown maintained an interest in colonizing the islands. The archipelago's proximity to the Spice Islands, as well as Malaysia and Japan, made it an attractive base from which to exploit the trade of the South China Sea and Indonesia. Although Spain renounced all claims to the Spice Islands to Portugal by the Treaty of Zaragosa (1529), this did not prevent colonization attempts from the viceroyalty of New Spain. The Portuguese after all, exploiting the subtleties of such treaties, had claimed and were developing Brazil in the midst of Spanish America, so it was only fair for Spain to have its own outpost in the midst of Portuguese Asia. In the 1520s expeditions had been sent out to explore these islands. Later, in 1541, the viceroy of New Spain, Antonio de Mendoza, selected Ruy López de Villalbos to lead an expedition. This four-ship fleet left Mexico in 1542. Villalbos explored Luzon, Samar, and Leyte Islands and renamed the group *Las Islas Felipinas*, in honor of the emperor Charles V's son, the Infante Philip. But Villalbos was forced to abandon any idea of permanent settlement due to hostile locals and a lack of supplies. The Philippines thus proved difficult to subdue.

In the 13th century, Malayan and Indian culture entered the southernmost portions of the archipelago, which formed part of the Majapahit Empire based in eastern Java, the last of Southeast Asia's great Hindu–Buddhist empires (ca. 1292–1478). In the late 14th century, Islam began to penetrate the southern Philippines, with the appearance of the scholar Makhdum Khan in 1380 being the the first recorded instance of Muslim missionary activity in the archipelago. Muslim traders quickly followed, settling in the south, where they formed powerful sultanates, including that of Sulu. In the north, Philippine tribes built city states, or *barangays*, in which a *datu* was the chieftan, or ruler. For a time, these states were vassals to the Ming dynasty in China. The Japanese even exerted influence over northern

Luzon. In short, the Spaniards had chosen to colonize an extremely rich and complex cultural cauldron that had a long history of absorbing foreign invaders and their influences. Clearly, more than the isolated expeditions of the first half of the 16th century were needed to accomplish this difficult task.

The conquest of the Philippines did not take place until the 1560s, when Miguel López de Legaspi arrived from Mexico with a large expedition. Legaspi attacked and defeated Tupas, the son of Humabon, and ruler of Cebu. Tupas was forced to place his domains under Spanish control. Legaspi then established the first Spanish settlement with the help of 5 Augustinian missionaries and 500 soldiers at San Miguel on Cebu. In 1571, Manila on the Pasig River was founded. As governor-general, Legaspi then transferred his capital from Cebu in the south to Manila in the north thanks to its fine natural harbor and rich agricultural hinterlands. In the decades that followed, Spanish authority increased, assisted in no small measure by the successful efforts of Catholic missionaries. Philip II decreed that the conversion of the Philippines to Christianity was not to be accomplished by force. The Augustinians, Dominicans, Franciscans, Recollects, and Jesuits followed these instructions for the most part and enjoyed notable success. At the same time, they were willing to incorporate some of the traditional customs and rituals of the islands into Philippine Catholicism. In 1593, Fr. Juan de Placencia completed a Spanish-to-Tagalog *Christian Doctrine* which transliterated Roman characters to Tagalog Baybayin characters, which a majority of the people on Luzon used. This linguistic triumph facilitated the conversion campaign, which succeeded on nearly all the islands of the archipelago with the exception of Muslim-dominated Mindanao in the far south.

Administratively and economically, the colony was intimately linked to the viceroyalty of New Spain. The viceroy and the royal *audiencia* in Mexico City exercised control through local governors-general. Economically, the *encomienda* system of New Spain was also introduced. This system supplanted traditional communal village structures and elevated the *datu* (village chief) class to rich landowners tied to the Spanish elite and Spain's colonial system. The peasants staged fairly regular uprisings against the exactions of this system. Tobacco, introduced from the Americas, also became an important cash crop for the colony. Ethnically, the community of Chinese merchants in Manila also increased dramatically between 1571 and 1700. On one hand, this group, using its capital and business networks in the South China Sea and Malaysia helped to make Manila a leading entrepôt in the region. At the same time, resentment against this group on the part of the Spaniards led to periodic crackdowns on the Chinese, as in 1603, when hundreds were killed.

By far the most important economic function of the Philippines for the Spanish imperial system was to act as an entrepôt between the New World and China. The Manila galleon system between Acapulco and Manila mirrored the Atlantic treasure-fleet system. In this lucrative trade, Chinese junks brought silk, porcelain, and other goods from Canton to Manila. These cargoes were then loaded with spices from the Moloccas and other Asian goods aboard the Spanish galleons bound for Acapulco, the Spanish colonies in America, and eventually to Spain. To pay for these Chinese goods, silver from the rich mines of Mexico and even Peru was used and entered the Indian Ocean trading system. Until 1593, three or more ships would depart annually from each terminus in the trade. But the exchange was so lucrative that in that year the merchants of Seville petitioned Philip II for a decree that limited the number of ships to two from each port. Of course, this led to the construction of huge 2,000 ton monsters usually built of hardwoods in the Philippines. The voyage across the Pacific usually took four months. It is estimated that during the 17th century at least one quarter of New World silver was going to China via this route. This vital link in Spain's global imperial system more than compensated for its periodic warfare with European and Asian rivals, as well as indigenous uprisings that the governor-general in Manila had to contend with during these centuries.

THE ECONOMIC STRUCTURES OF SPANISH AMERICA

Economically, hierarchical control was officially mandated by the Crown for its New World empire. Rather amazingly, all commerce with the empire was controlled by the *Casa de la Contratación* (House of Trade) in Seville, which was established in 1503. For both Columbus and the conquistadors, gold was the greatest attraction. In the Caribbean, gold was indeed found, panned primarily from streams. Between 1500 and 1520, perhaps 14 tons of gold were sent back to Spain from the Caribbean. In Peru, gold deposits were also discovered, which in the 1530s yielded great profits for the Crown. As Charles V wrote in 1536, "I am extremely pleased at the timely arrival of the gold from Peru and other parts; it amounts to nearly 800,000 ducats, a great help for our present needs." Beginning in the 1540s, however, silver began to dominate. Huge deposits were found in Mexico at Zacatecas and Guanajuato and particularly at Potosí in Peru. These deposits demanded more sophisticated mining techniques and huge amounts of labor. But as the cliché goes, 'necessity is the mother of invention' especially when precious metals were involved. The process of using mercury to help extract silver from waste was developed in 1555 and widely used in Mexico and Peru. By 1650, 181 tons of gold and 16,000 tons of silver had been mined from Spain's New World empire. As noted above, a sizable portion of this silver was also diverted to fund the Manila galleon trade.

In addition to mining, cattle grazing and ranching dominated the vast *encomiendas* that were granted in the decades after 1520. These activities were familiar to and socially acceptable for Spanish nobles.

PHOTO 2.2   Potosí, Bolivia. The famed silver mine at Potosí was the most lucrative one in the world during the late 16th and early 17th centuries, yielding millions to the Spanish treasury. This "mountain of silver" dwarfs the human elements in the painting, seemingly promising unlimited wealth.

Along the coastal plains, sugar plantations were also established, where African slaves were imported to replace the depleted Mesoamerican labor force. Tobacco, another crop requiring large-scale slave labor, became increasingly important in the 17th century. In true mercantilist style, most of the manufactured goods and luxury food-stuffs had to be imported from Spain. Hardware, weapons, cloth, books, wine, oil, and slaves were all in great demand in the colonies. Spain itself did not provide these goods in sufficient quantities, so a large parallel economy dominated by smugglers, pirates, and priva-teers developed to supply the rest. As for the legal trade, and this inter-change of products between Europe and America, a royal convoy system was set up by 1560. Two armed fleets were sent from Spain each year, one destined for Mexico, the other for Panama. After wintering in America, the ships would rendezvous in Havana the following spring for the return voyage to Europe. For the return trip, gold and silver from Peru would be shipped up the west coast of South America to Panama and be transported overland and then reembarked to Havana. The size of the fleets varied from 20 to 60 ships supported by five or six warships. Ideally, all shipping for the New World was restricted to these convoys. Because of the seasonal nature of these sailings, it was relatively easy for Dutch, English, and French pirates to attack the rich treasure fleets returning from the New World. Nevertheless, in over a century and a half of sailings, whole fleets were captured only three times. On the other hand, a late departure from Havana meant navigat-ing during the hurricane season, and this threat proved far more dan-gerous than pirates for many fleets. To infuse sufficient capital and products into the empire, the Spanish Crown was forced to temper its declared monopoly and to subcontract out various trading activities from 1550 to 1700. This was especially true of the slave trade, in which Portuguese, Italians, Germans, and other non-Spaniards dominated the *asiento,* or royal contract system, during these years.

SOCIAL AND CULTURAL LIFE IN COLONIAL SPANISH AMERICA

In Spanish America, the Crown attempted to control the interchange of human cargo between Spain and the New World. All emigrants were required to register at the House of Trade in Seville. This system allowed the Crown to prevent Jews and suspected heretics from embarking. In the century between 1500 and 1600, about 56,000 people officially departed from Spain for the New World. Illegal immigration also took place, but is difficult to gauge. One recent estimate is that from 1500 to 1650 as many as 437,000 Spaniards might have made the voyage. While this figure is probably an exaggeration, it is likely that at least a quarter of a million people emigrated during these two centuries. At the same time, given mortality rates and intermarriage with indigenous women, the pure Spanish population in the major urban areas of the empire remained relatively small. The children of such parents born in America were called *criollos*, or Creoles. *Mestizos* were the children of Indians and Europeans; *mulatos*, the children of Africans and Europeans; and *zambos*, the children of Africans and Indians. Increasingly, the *mestizo* population came to dominate numerically in the empire. This group became more numerous than both the pure Spanish and pure Indian populations, and it is this group that dominates in Latin America today.

Meanwhile, one of the major social issues confronting the Crown during the initial decades of the empire was how to treat the post-conquest indigenous Indian population. In this long and acrimonious debate, the key figure was the Dominican missionary Bartolomé de Las Casas, whose book *A Short Account of the Destruction of the Indies* (1542) was a harsh indictment of the abuses of the conquest. Las Casas argued that the Indians, like the Spaniards themselves, were the natural subjects of the Crown from the moment of conquest and, as such, should enjoy the same rights and privileges according to the laws of Castile. Moreover, he believed they were intellectually capable of living up to their duties. Las Casas wanted an imperial system in which the Indians would live under their traditional leaders but ultimately be subject to the power of Crown officials who would educate them in European practices. On the other hand, many colonists, championed by Juan Ginés de Sepúlveda, took a more dismal view of the potential of the Indians and instead demanded a paternalistic form of feudalism, in which their powers would be reconfirmed, especially in regard to the vital issue of forced labor.

By 1550, Charles V had resolved these issues, and the theory of empire that would continue down to the early 19th century emerged. The Indies were judged to be a distinct kingdom of the Crown of Castile ruled by its own royal council. Echoing Las Casas's views, the Indians were defined as subjects of the Crown; and free men who could not be enslaved unless they staged an armed rebellion.

Their rights to own property were recognized and they were subject to the Spanish courts. The Indians could sue and could be sued but their own laws were also to be respected, except where they were judged to be barbarous or clearly in defiance of Spanish law in the Indies. Their leaders, or headmen, moreover, were to be accepted as such and integrated into the royal bureaucracy. To appease the colonists, the *encomienda* system was formalized and forced labor under the *mita* system was allowed, provided the official wage-rate for such labor was met by the *encomendero*. It was a compromise system that erred on the side of the Indians, at least officially. One factor to keep in mind, however, is that the effective authority of the Crown in large expanses of the conquests was very limited throughout these centuries.

RELIGION AND THE MISSIONARY ORDERS

Religiously, the Crown by virtue of a series of papal bulls enjoyed a monopoly for spreading the Catholic faith in the New World, exclusive of Brazil. This royal monopoly, called the *Patronato Real*, gave the Crown vast powers. The monarch could appoint archbishops and bishops and controlled the emigration of both secular and regular clergy to America. The main missionary orders at the outset were the Franciscans, Dominicans, and the Augustinians. By the last half of the 16th century, they had been joined by the Jesuits. These orders established houses or missions for the spread of Catholicism throughout the vast Spanish possessions in the New World. By 1600, there were approximately 300 monasteries in New Spain alone, with perhaps 1,500 clergy in them. Although the effectiveness of the early missionary efforts was hindered by a lack of familiarity with indigenous languages, these efforts at conversion became increasingly impressive as time went on. Although the dreaded Inquisition was exported to Spanish America at the end of the 16th century, unconverted Indians were exempt from arrest and trial. As in Goa, the main victims of the Spanish Inquisition in the New World were New Christians.

Economically and socially, as in Portuguese Asia, the religious orders operating in the New World empire of Spain gained increased power during these decades as well. The religious orders came to control vast expanses of lands and wealth, which frequently put them

PHOTO 2.3   First Book Printed in the New World, 1543. This book of catechism by the Franciscan missionary Juan de Zumárraga was published in Mexico City. It was intentionally written in a plain and easy-to-comprehend style to facilitate the conversion of the native American population to Catholicism.

into conflict with the *encomienda* holders. The clergy, moreover, frequently criticized the actions of the colonists regarding the Indians and championed the causes of the indigenous population during these centuries. This tendency had begun as early as 1511 with the Dominican Antonio de Montesinos, who condemned the treatment of the Tainos on Hispaniola by the Spaniards. Although the *Patronato Real* ideally established Crown domination over the church in the New World, it also allowed for ecclesiastical interference into civil and political affairs as well. In fact, it was common for high-ranking churchmen like bishops to hold high political appointments. Despite such disputes, the campaign to entrench the Catholic faith continued. Even during the lean years of the 17th century, the Crown maintained its steadfast material and financial support for the activities of the *Patronato Real*. As Gil González Dávila noted, Philip IV in 1633, during the dark days of the Thirty Years' War and bankruptcy, made sure that 300,000 ducats was sent to the monasteries of New Spain and Peru to cover the cost of wine and oil. As a result of such support, the Catholic Church and its liturgy gradually and firmly became integrated into the new culture that the Spaniards created in the New World. Today, the church remains one of the strongest institutions in Latin America thanks to the efforts of the missionary clergy and the longstanding support of the Crown.

SURVIVAL OF EMPIRE IN THE 17TH CENTURY

During the 17th century, these fundamental institutions of Spanish America allowed it to survive the attacks of zealous rivals, such as the English, Dutch, and French. The New World Empire of Spain was even able to withstand a lack of large-scale support from Madrid. This dearth of support was tied to the plethora of problems that beset the reigns of both Philip III and Philip IV. Among these difficulties were the political and military dislocation caused by the Thirty Years' War (1618–1648) and a general economic crisis that was exacerbated by the huge influx of precious metals from America. In this survival of empire, four factors played a crucial role. First, the development of a large *mestizo* and *mestizaje* population, the progeny of the racial mixing and intermarriage in the empire, was crucial. This increasingly large and important segment of the colonial population had a strong interest in seeing the empire survive. Of course, in the 18th and 19th centuries, the so-called 'Creolization' of this group, a process in which identification with the hybrid society in the New World began to take primacy over traditional links with Spain would ultimately help destroy the empire. But down to 1700 this process was still probably in its infancy. Second, the huge amount of exploitable wealth in the New World gave this class and the Crown a strong vested interest in holding onto the empire. Despite the best efforts of the English, Dutch, and French during the 17th century, the military power of the Spaniards both at sea and on land was more than enough to hold onto these vast possessions (see Map 2.1). Third, the firm implantation of the Roman

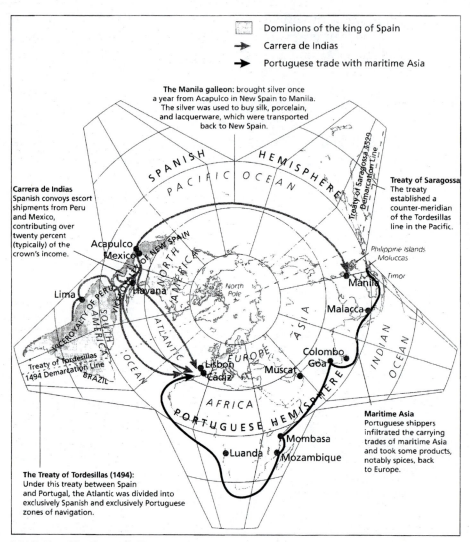

The Manila galleon: brought silver once
a year from Acapulco in New Spain to Manila.
The silver was used to buy silk, porcelain,
and lacquerware, which were transported
back to New Spain.

Dominions of the king of Spain

Carrera de Indias

Portuguese trade with maritime Asia

Carrera de Indias
Spanish convoys escort
shipments from Peru
and Mexico,
contributing over
twenty percent
(typically) of the
crown's income.

Treaty of Saragossa
The treaty
established a
counter-meridian
of the Tordesillas
line in the Pacific.

Maritime Asia
Portuguese shippers
infiltrated the carrying
trades of maritime Asia
and took some products,
notably spices, back
to Europe.

The Treaty of Tordesillas (1494):
Under this treaty between Spain
and Portugal, the Atlantic was divided into
exclusively Spanish and exclusively Portuguese
zones of navigation.

MAP 2.1   The Spanish Empire in 1600

Catholic religion also assisted the survival of empire. Millions of new
Christians were constantly assured by their spiritual leaders that the
Habsburgs and their minions were their rulers by the will of their 'new
god.' As good Christians, they were adverse to rejecting this part of
Spanish imperial Catholicism. Finally, as Gandhi once said, the only
way that 200,000 British could rule over 500 million Asian Indians in

the 19th and 20th centuries was through the cooperation and in some cases collaboration of the Indians themselves. Withdraw that tacit support and the empire would die. In the New World context of Spanish America, the same equation held true—200,000 Spaniards could maintain control over 150 million Indians only with the cooperation and collaboration of the Indians themselves. From the outset of the empire, the Spaniards had found it easy to recruit and exploit the *caciques* and other indigenous leaders to their advantage. This state of affairs would continue down to the 19th century. In the end, therefore, Columbus may have never found his route to Cipangu and the spices of Asia, but his voyages began a process that would finally define the limits of our globe and begin an interchange of ideas, products, and manpower that would define many of the structures of the modern world.

SOURCES

■ Christopher Columbus's Description of the New World, 15 February 1493

From the outset of his voyage, Columbus intended to keep a careful record. As he wrote 'I intended to set out and sail until I reached the Indies, there to deliver your Highnesses letters to their princes and to fulfill your other commands. I decided therefore to make this careful daily report on my voyage and of everything I should do, see or experience.' Columbus's original logbook, however, eventually disappeared, but not before the historian Bartolomé de las Casas made a digest of it, incorporating many of the admiral's original statements.

Columbus also wrote Ferdinand and Isabella an important letter on his voyage back to Spain aboard the *Niña* in February 1493. In the passages below from that letter, Columbus gives his initial description of the people and lands he encountered in the New World. As you read it, what strikes you most about the description Columbus gives? From this passage, do you get the impression that Columbus still believed he had reached Asia? Does the place have any economic value for the Crown? What other potential value can it have? Was Columbus a good salesman in this letter? What impression do you think his actions made on the inhabitants of these islands?

And as soon as I arrived in the Indies, in the first island which I found, I took by force some of them in order that they might learn [Castilian] and give me information of what they had in those parts; it soon worked out that they soon understood us, and we them, either by speech or signs, and they have been very serviceable. I still have them with me, and they are still of the opinion that I come from the sky, in spite of the intercourse which they have had with me. . . .

In all these islands, I saw no great diversity in the appearance of the people or in their manners and language, but they all understand one another, which is a very singular thing, on account of which I hope that Their Highnesses will determine upon their conversion to our holy faith, towards which they are much inclined. . . . In all these islands, it

---

Source: Journal and other Documents on the Life and Voyages of Christopher Columbus, trans. and ed. Samuel Eliot Morison (New York: The Heritage Press 1963) 184–186.

appears, all the men are content with one woman, but to their *Maioral* or king, they give up to twenty. It appears to me that the women work more than the men. I have been unable to learn whether they hold private property, but it appeared true to me that all took a share in anything that one had, especially in victuals.

In these islands I have so far found no human monstrosities, as many expected, on the contrary, among all these people good looks are esteemed; nor are they Negroes, as in Guinea, but with flowing hair, and they are not born where there is excessive force in the solar rays. . . . Thus I have neither found monsters nor had any reports of any, except in an island which is the second at the entrance to the Indies, which is inhabited by a people who are regarded in all the islands as very ferocious and who eat human flesh.[2] . . . In another island, which they assure me is larger than *Española*,[3] the people have no hair. In this there is countless gold, and from it and from the other islands I bring with me *Indios* as evidence.[4] . . . Their Highnesses can see that I shall give them as much gold as they want if Their Highnesses will render me a little help; besides spice and cotton, as much as Their Highnesses shall command; and gum mastic, as much as they shall order shipped. . . sell it for what it pleases; and aloe wood, as much as they shall ordered shipped, and slaves, as many as they shall order, who will be idolaters.[5] And I believe that I have found rhubarb and cinnamon, and I shall find a thousand other things of value.

■ Hernan Cortés Describes to Charles V What He Has Experienced and Seen in Mexico in his Second Letter to the Emperor (1520)

When Cortés departed from Cuba in February 1519 on his expedition to explore Mexico, he had done so technically in violation of orders from the royal governor Diego Velázquez. Although Velázquez initially appointed him to this command, he soon changed his mind. Before Cortés could be formally stripped of his powers, however, he

[2] The *Caribs*. This island was *Caire* (or *Charis* in Latin), the Carib name for Dominica.
[3] Hispaniola, which today includes the nations of Haiti and the Dominican Republic.
[4] This is the first time that the name that Columbus gave to the indigenous people of America appears.
[5] In other words, only natives who are not converts to Christianity will be enslaved.

Source: Oliver J. Thatcher, ed., *The Library of Original Sources* (Milwaukee: University Research Extension Co., 1907), vol. V: *9th to 16th Centuries*, 317–326.

hastily departed. By late 1520, when he dictated this letter, Cortés had already begun his preparations for conquering the Aztec capital of Tenochtitlán.

As you read this letter, try to imagine the foremost goals in Cortés's mind at this time. Why does he give so much detail on the city to Charles V? Why mention the religious practices? How would you rate his skills as a writer and politician?

In order, most potent Sire, to convey to your Majesty a just conception of the great extent of this noble city of Tenochtitlán, and of the many rare and wonderful objects it contains; of the government and dominions of Montezuma, the sovereign: of the religious rights and customs that prevail, and the order that exists in this as well as the other cities appertaining to his realm: it would require the labor of many accomplished writers . . . This great city of Tenochtitlán is situated in this salt lake, and from the main land to the denser parts of it, by whichever route one chooses to enter, the distance is two leagues. There are four avenues or entrances to the city, all of which are formed by artificial causeways, two spears' length in width. The city is as large as Seville or Cordova; its streets, I speak of the principal ones, are very wide and straight; some of these, and all the inferior ones, are half land and half water, and are navigated by canoes . . . This city has many public squares, in which are situated the markets and other places for buying and selling. There is one square twice as large as that of the city of Salamanca, surrounded by porticoes, where are daily assembled more than sixty thousand souls, engaged in buying and selling; and where are found all kinds of merchandise that the world affords, embracing the necessaries of life, as for instance articles of food, as well as jewels of gold and silver, lead, brass, copper, tin, precious stones, bones, shells, snails, and feathers . . . This great city contains a large number of temples, or houses, for their idols, very handsome edifices, which are situated in the different districts and the suburbs; in the principal ones religious persons of each particular sect are constantly residing, for whose use, besides the houses containing the idols, there are other convenient habitations. All these persons dress in black, and never cut or comb their hair from the time they enter the priesthood until they leave it; and all the sons of the principal inhabitants, both nobles and respectable citizens, are placed in the temples and wear the same dress from the age of seven or eight years until they are taken out to be married; which occurs more frequently with the first-born who inherit estates than with the others. The priests are debarred from female society, nor is any woman permitted to enter the religious houses. They also abstain from eating certain kinds of food, more at some seasons of the year than others . . . I said everything to them I could to divert them from their idolatries, and draw them to a knowledge of God our Lord. Montezuma replied, the others assenting to what he said, that they had already informed me they were not the aborigines of the country, but that their ancestors had emigrated to it many years ago; and they fully believed that after so long an absence from their native land, they might have fallen into some errors; that I having more recently arrived must know better than themselves what they ought to believe; and that if I would instruct them in these matters, and make them understand the true faith, they would follow my directions, as being for the best. Afterwards, Montezuma and many of the principal citizens remained with me until I had removed the idols, purified the chapels, and placed the images in them, manifesting apparent pleasure; and I forbade them sacrificing human beings to their idols as they had been accustomed to do; because, besides being abhorrent in the sight of God, your sacred Majesty had prohibited it by law, and commanded to put to death whoever should take the life of another. Thus, from that time, they refrained from the practice, and during the whole period of my abode in that city, they were never seen to kill or sacrifice a human being.

■ The Entrance of Cortés into Tenochtitlán, 8 November 1519

Bernal Dias del Castillo, also known as Bernal Díaz (1492–1584), was the last survivor of the conquerors of Mexico. He was born in 1492 and in 1514 first sailed to America as a soldier in the company of the new governor of Darién Pedrarias Dávila. In 1517, he sailed to the Yucatán Peninsula of Mexico, with Francisco de Córdoba's expedition. He returned to Mexico in 1518 with Grijalva, and in 1519, with Hernan Cortés. On the expedition of Cortés, Dias took part in scores of battles and was present for the conquest of Tenochtitlán. As a reward for these services, Dias was appointed governor of Santiago

Source: The Conquest of New Spain by Bernal Díaz, trans. J.M. Cohen (London: Penguin Classics 1963, Reprint) 216–217.

de los Caballeros in Guatemala and was also given vast estates. It was not until he was 76 years old (1568) that he completed his *True History of the Conquest of New Spain*.

As you read this selection, which aspects of Aztec society strike you most? What impression does Dias give the reader on the motives and qualities of his compatriots? What is his view of the Aztec elite and Montezuma? How objective a reporter does Dias appear to be? On what do you base this judgment? How do you think the Aztecs viewed the Spanish at this point?

Early next day we left Iztapalapa with a large escort of these great Caciques, and followed the causeway, which is eight yards wide and goes so straight to the city of Mexico [Tenochtitlán] that I do not think it curves at all. Wide though it was, it was so crowded with people that there was hardly room for them all. Some were going to Mexico and others coming away, besides those who had come out to see us, and we could hardly get through the crowds that were there. For the towers and the *cues*[6] were full, and they came in canoes from all parts of the lake. No wonder, since they had never seen horses or men like us before!

With such wonderful sights to gaze on we did not know what to say, or if this was real that we saw before our eyes. On the lake side there were great cities, and on the lake many more. The lake was crowded with canoes. At intervals along the causeway there were many bridges, and before us was the great city of Mexico. As for us, we were scarcely four hundred strong, and we well remembered the words and warnings of the people of Huexotzinco and Tlascala and Tlamanalco, and the many other warnings we had received to beware of entering the city of Mexico, since they would kill us as soon as they had us inside. Let the interested reader consider whether there is not much to ponder in this narrative of mine. What men in all the world have shown such daring? But let us go on. . . .

When we came near to Mexico, at a place where there were some other small towers, the great Montezuma descended from his litter, and these other great Caciques supported him beneath a marvelously rich canopy of green feathers, decorated with gold work, silver, pearls, and chalchihuites,[7] which hung from a sort of border. It was a marvelous sight. The great Montezuma was magnificently clad, in their

---

[6]Temples.
[7]Semi-precious green stones of malachite and turquoise.

fashion, and wore sandals of a kind for which their name is cotaras, the soles of which are gold and the upper parts ornamented with precious stones. . . .

When Cortés saw, heard, and was told that the great Montezuma was approaching, he dismounted from his horse, and when he came near to Montezuma each bowed deeply to the other. Montezuma welcomed our Captain, and Cortés, speaking through Dona Marina,[8] answered by wishing him very good health. Cortés, I think, offered Montezuma his right hand, but Montezuma refused it and extended his own. Then Cortés brought out a necklace which he had been holding. It was made of those elaborately worked and colored glass beads called margaritas, of which I have spoken, and was strung on a gold cord and dipped in musk to give it a good odor. This he hung round the great Montezuma's neck.

■ Las Casas's Report on Spanish Atrocities in the New World

Las Casas was born into a merchant family in Seville in 1484 and received a solid education. Between 1502 and 1513 he sailed several times to the New World and received an *encomienda* and indentured labor of Indians for his efforts. But his presence at the brutal conquest of Cuba in 1513 prompted him to break definitively with the *encomendero* elite. He became a priest in the Dominican order and for the rest of his life struggled in both Europe and the New World crusading for the rights of the indigenous peoples within the empire. In 1542, he wrote his *Short Account of the Destruction of the Indies*. This work was dedicated to Prince Philip of Spain, later Philip II. Las Casas claimed it was written to inform the Crown of what was really happening in the New World, and as a warning that if such atrocities continued, God might inflict punishment on Spain for these sins.

---

[8]A Nahuatl-speaking woman whom Cortés received as a slave. He baptized her a Christian and gave her the name Marina. She served as Cortés' interpreter, counselor, and mistress, bearing him a son, the first Latin American. Many conclude that Cortés could not have succeeded without her aid. See Photo 2.1, page 73.

Source: A Short Account of the Destruction of the Indies by Bartolomé de Las Casas, written in 1542, ed. and trans. Nigel Griffin (London: Penguin Classics 1992) 22–23.

As you read the selection, ask yourself if you can determine the level of Las Casas's sincerity in making these claims? What do you think was the reaction of Charles V and Philip to such descriptions? How would the Spanish colonists respond to these charges? Do you think all the Spaniards were as evil as he presents, and the Indians as pure?

The fifth kingdom [of Hispaniola] was known as Higuey and its queen, a lady already advanced in years, went by the name of Higuanama. They strung her up and I saw with my own eyes how the Spaniards burned countless local inhabitants alive or hacked them to pieces, or devised novel ways of torturing them to death, enslaving those they took alive. . . All I can say is that I know it to be an incontrovertible fact and do here so swear before Almighty God, that the local peoples never gave the Spanish any cause whatever for the injury and injustice that was done to them in these campaigns. On the contrary, they behaved as honorably as might the inmates of a well-run monastery, and for this they were robbed and massacred, and even those who escaped death on this occasion found themselves condemned to a lifetime of captivity and slavery. I would go further. It is my firm belief that not a single native of the island committed a capital offence, as defined in law, against the Spanish while all this time the natives themselves were being savaged and murdered. Despite the enormous provocation, very few of the natives, I hazard, were guilty of even those sins which do not lie within the ambit of human law but are properly the province of God, such as hatred and anger, or the thirst for revenge against those who committed such enormities on them. It is my own experience of these peoples, gained over many years, that they are no more given to impetuous actions or to harboring thoughts of retribution than are boys of ten or twelve years of age. I know beyond any shadow of a doubt that they had, from the very beginning, every right to wage war on the Europeans, while the Europeans never had just cause for waging war on the local peoples. The actions of the Europeans, throughout the New World, were without exception wicked and unjust: worse, in fact, than the blackest kind of tyranny.

CHAPTER

3

The Dutch Empire in Asia and the Atlantic World, ca. 1600–1700

THE CHALLENGE FOR THE ASIAN TRADE

In September 1583, the Dutchman Jan Huyghen van Linschoten arrived in Goa aboard a Portuguese fleet carrying the new Archbishop Vicente de Fonseca. He had begun his travels at the age of 16, when he left the Netherlands for Seville. After the conquest of the Portuguese Crown by Philip II, he continued on to Lisbon. There, he arranged employment in the entourage of Fonseca. There was nothing new in Dutchmen with nautical or other skills obtaining employment in the Portuguese *Estado da India*. What distinguished Linschoten was that he spent the next nine years living in Goa, learning the intricacies of the Portuguese imperial system. Upon his return to Europe in the 1590s, Linschoten, to the delight of many Protestants, published a treatise on the strengths and weaknesses of the entire Portuguese system. His book was quickly translated into French, Latin, and English and enjoyed a very wide audience among the European elite. The following were among Linschoten's principal points: Contrary to the traditional impression, the Portuguese empire was vulnerable; this vulnerability was tied to the crushing military expenses the Portuguese had made in defense of their over-extended possessions; and finally, the *Estado* was weakest in the Indonesian Archipelago.

These were chaotic years in the history of the Netherlands. The Low Countries, increasingly wealthy thanks to a rich soil and an expanding share of the profitable European carrying trade, had been a part of the huge dynastic inheritance of Charles V. Holy Roman Emperor, ruler of the European domains of Austria and Burgundy, as well as heir to Spain and the vast possessions of Castile and Aragon in America, Charles V juggled the geopolitical, economic, and religious problems of his empire for 40 years. In 1556, he divided this empire between his son Philip II and his brother Ferdinand, and retired to a monastery. Who could blame him? The problems inherent in ruling such a vast empire, especially in the age of Luther, Calvin, Henry VIII, and Francis I, had proven too much for any man to sustain. For Philip II, the good news was that his part of the inheritance included the rich lands of the Netherlands. The bad news was that his inheritance included the rebellious provinces of the Netherlands.

The Dutch revolt against Habsburg Spain began in the 1560s, fueled by resentment against largely absent rulers like Charles and Philip, the appointment of foreign friends of the emperors to high office, and the rapid spread of Calvinism. In 1566, Calvinist revolts broke out in Flanders. Although these riots were repressed, the greatest landowner in the Netherlands, William of Orange (the Silent), refused an oath of allegiance. Moreover, he was soon recognized as titular leader by the rebellious Sea Beggars, who had begun their naval campaign against Spanish fleets. From 1572 to 1576, open warfare raged in the northern Netherlands. Most notably, the provinces of Holland and Zeeland revolted against Philip II and recognized William of Orange. The Prince of Orange, meanwhile, openly embraced Calvinism. In 1579, the formal battle lines for the revolt were drawn when the largely Catholic, French-speaking southern provinces agreed to the pro-Habsburg Union of Arras, while the northern Dutch-speaking provinces embraced the Union of Utrecht, rejecting Habsburg (and, therefore, Spanish) claims. For the next 68 years, the struggle continued with a much-needed truce from 1609 to 1621. For most of this period, the Dutch United Provinces of the Netherlands operated as a de facto independent state, recognized and supported by Elizabeth I and Protestant England and periodically by a French state also embroiled in bloody civil and religious warfare.

THE VOYAGE OF HOUTMAN, 1595–1597

Before the forced union between Portugal and Spain in 1580, Dutch merchants had been the principal carriers of pepper and other Asian goods shipped from Lisbon to Amsterdam and the rest of northern Europe, making a tidy profit in the process. Somewhat ironically, the combination of Philip II's successful claim of the Crown of Portugal and the Dutch revolt against him had effectively shut these Dutch merchants out of this lucrative role as middlemen in the European leg of the spice trade from Asia. This shift furnished a strong incentive to obtain these spices directly. Several expeditions searched in vain to find either a Northwest or Northeast Passage during the final decades of the 16th century. If found, such a passage would have allowed Dutch merchants to reach the wealth of Asia without directly challenging the entrenched position of the Portuguese in that trade. Once it became clear that sailing north to the Arctic would yield little more than frostbite, the Dutch turned to the only other proven option: the Cape of Good Hope route. In this quest they were emboldened by the pronouncements of Linschoten. Taking his advice on Indonesia to heart, the first Dutch expedition for the Indian Ocean commanded by Cornelius Houtman sailed in April 1595. Houtman was well prepared for this challenge; he was an experienced merchant who had lived in Lisbon and knew the intricacies of the spice trade. Houtman had also read Linschoten's book and had the benefit of maps and sailing instructions drawn up by him as well.

Houtman's voyage, however, was a difficult one. The fleet was outfitted by the *Compagnie van Verre* (Long Distance Company) at a cost of ca. 290,000 guilders. This Company was dominated by nine affluent Amsterdam merchants, who a few years earlier had funded a fact-finding trip to Lisbon for Houtman and his brother Frederik. Nevertheless, while Houtman was well versed in the trade, to put it mildly he lacked people skills. His overbearing personality managed to alienate just about everyone he came into contact with during the voyage. The first stage to the Cape of Good Hope was routine, but scurvy broke out due to a lack of fresh fruit and vitamin C. To save his crews, Houtman landed on the inhospitable island of Madagascar. In a hellish six-month stay, so many men died that one of the bays came to be called *Hollantsche Kerckhoff* (Dutch cemetery).

PHOTO 3.1   The Great Market at Bantam, 1598.   This illustration from the *Historie van Indien* by William Lodewijckszoon demonstrates the thriving trade on islands like Java during the 16th century. A key for the various stalls was incorporated into the illustration. Such works were designed to whet the Dutch appetite for increased trade in the Spice Islands.

After the crews recovered, the journey continued. In June 1596, nearly 15 months after leaving the Netherlands, Houtman's four ships finally reached the kingdom of Bantam on Java, where the local Muslim sultan promptly agreed to a trading agreement. Yet, this promising beginning was short-lived. Why? First, although Linschoten had informed Houtman that Portuguese power in the archipelago was minimal, the reality was that the Iberians still had a sufficient presence on Java to lobby against the Dutchmen, particularly with monetary inducements to the local sultans. This opposition in conjunction with Houtman's overbearing behavior and the unruly actions of his crews soon turned the favorable reception sour. Several armed attacks by the Javanese killed a dozen of Houtman's crew and forced him to abandon the island. In August 1597 the remnants of Houtman's fleet reached Texel. The 28-month voyage had taken a harsh toll. Only 89 of the original 249 men had survived. Despite the difficulties of the voyage, however, the three ships held a cargo of 245 bags of pepper, 45 tons of nutmeg, and 30 bales of mace. What counted most to the burghers of Amsterdam who had founded the Company was that the windfall from these prized commodities not only covered the cost of the fleet but provided a profit as well. Moreover, Houtman, for all of his flaws, had demonstrated the pivotal reality of the Asian trade: namely that it was possible for the

Dutch and others to send ships around the Cape of Good Hope and return with the wealth of the East Indies in their holds. Not only could the pretensions of the Iberians be challenged, but it was clear that local rulers in Asia would generally welcome competitors to the entrenched power of the Portuguese. These realizations helped fuel the mercurial rise of the Dutch Republic to a global maritime power in the following six decades.

COMPETING DUTCH COMPANIES, 1597–1602

Spurred on by the profits from Houtman's voyage, five new companies were formed in different Dutch towns in the next year. These companies outfitted 22 ships. During the next five years, 70 ships departed for Asia, most for the spice-producing islands of Indonesia. The most successful was the 1598–1600 expedition of Jacob Corneliszoon van Neck. His eight-ship fleet departed in May 1598. Van Neck reached Bantam with three ships by November 1598. There, he quickly exploited his favorable reception and loaded a sizable cargo. On New Year's Eve, his other five ships appeared and were "joyously received." Van Neck then began the voyage home with four of his ships, while ordering the other four to the Moluccas to procure more nutmeg, cloves, and mace. His return to Amsterdam in July 1599 with these richly loaded vessels set off days of civic celebration in the city since "so long as Holland has been Holland . . . such richly laden ships have never been seen." Van Neck's vessels brought back some 300 tons of pepper and another 125 tons of cloves. The sale of these spices yielded capital that paid off the cost of the entire venture as well as a profit of 100 percent. When the remaining four ships returned in 1600 loaded with the spices of Ternate, Banda, and Amboina, the profit margin increased to a staggering 400 percent!

Not surprisingly, the allure of such huge profits created fierce competition among the various Dutch companies. Frequent disputes broke out among the captains and crews of competing companies. Local sultans in Indonesia also exploited the heightened competition between the Portuguese and Dutch, and among the Dutch themselves. They raised spice prices, tolls, tariffs, and harbor fees. Moreover, as time went on, the prices that could be commanded in the Netherlands for spices fell due to the large and uncontrolled cargoes that competing companies imported. By 1601, it was clear that something would have to be done. The eight competing companies had already sent out some 14 fleets and nearly 70 ships. Dutch factors had been set up in Bantam and at least five other islands in the Moloccas, as well as on the Malaysian peninsula. Moreover, the ship *Liefde* had gone ashore on Kyushu in Japan, and the captain and crew had begun trading negotiations there. These disparate activities had to be streamlined and consolidated for the Dutch to challenge Portugal effectively.

THE FOUNDATION OF THE UNITED DUTCH EAST INDIA COMPANY, 1602

The man largely responsible for accomplishing this difficult task was Johan van Oldenbarneveldt, chief minister of the province of Holland and one of the most powerful politicians in the Netherlands. In 1600, van Oldenbarneveldt convinced the States of Holland to appoint a commission to study this problem. This commission had recommended the merging of all the competing companies into a single national monopoly company. While this made a good deal of sense, the major investors in the existing companies were far from thrilled.

Nevertheless, in March 1602, van Oldenbarneveldt with the support of Maurice of Nassau, prince of Orange, finally convinced the States-General of the United Provinces of the Netherlands to amalgamate the disparate companies into one "United East India Company," or *Verenigde Oost Indische Compagnie* (VOC). The charter of the VOC well reflected the political, economic, and social structures of the Dutch Republic. Merchant capitalism, the power of the burgher oligarchy, and the regionalism of the provinces were merged with the geopolitical necessities inherent in European and overseas war with the Iberians. The VOC, the States-General, and the Dutch Republic were united in this struggle and would rise or fall together. This national crusade dominated the history of the Netherlands and the Asian trade for the next century, and the United Company was well prepared for the struggle. The VOC was given a monopoly for the trade east of the Cape of Good Hope and west of the Straits of Magellan. The Company could wage war, negotiate peace and alliances in the name of the *stadtholder* (governor) of the Dutch Republic, and build fortresses wherever and whenever it was judged advantageous. It could establish colonies, coin money, and seize foreign ships. The VOC paid no import duties and paid only 3 percent on exports. In short, the Company had full administrative, judicial, military, and legislative authority over its area of operations in the Indian Ocean Basin, the South China Sea, and the Pacific.

The VOC embodied one of the first early capitalist joint-stock companies. The initial capital pool was set at 6,500,000 guilders, to be raised in subscriptions of 3,000 guilders. The federated union of the United Provinces was mirrored in the Company's union of six chambers, or *kamers*, the most important in Amsterdam. To oversee the Company's general activities, a directorate of 60 members was chosen by local boards. Real governing power rested in the Board of 17 members, the *Heeren XVII* (Seventeen Men), whose representatives were based on the share each chamber contributed to the joint stock. Money equaled power. Since Amsterdam subscribed half of the capital pool, it received eight representatives on the Board. Among other things, the Seventeen nominated the governor-general (after 1608) for Dutch possessions in Asia. Reflecting the extremely close ties of the VOC to the States-General, another committee of 10 members was established at the Hague to transact business and liaison with the States-General.

THE DUTCH STRATEGY

The history of the VOC during the 17th century can be divided into three periods. The first witnessed the consolidation of the Company's activities from 1602 to 1636. This was followed by a period of conquest and rapid expansion, which took place from ca. 1636 to 1672. The final period from ca. 1673 to 1700 was characterized by a degree of stagnation occasioned by the attacks of European and indigenous rivals in Asia, as well as complications exacerbated by problems at home. Perhaps the easiest way to summarize these periods is to say that the Dutch first strove to establish a foothold from which to challenge the Portuguese; they then took the offensive against the core of the *Estado da India*, and in the end, became the new Portuguese in the trade with all that implied. In this campaign, the Dutch had advantages, some real, some more fanciful than fact. Local rulers around the Indian Ocean Basin initially welcomed them as a much-needed counterbalance to the long entrenched power of the Portuguese. The VOC, therefore, found it easy to arrange favorable trading agreements. Even the sultan of Achin (Acheh), who had been insulted by Houtman, underwent a marked change of heart. Of course, the fact that his legal action in the Amsterdam courts on behalf of some of his wronged merchants yielded a judgment of 50,000 guilders certainly helped this transformation. Thereafter, the sultan not only welcomed VOC merchants but he also provided letters on behalf of other Dutchmen leaving for the Indian entrepôt of Surat addressed to the Mughal emperor Akbar.

Another supposed advantage for the Dutch was that the harsh social distinctions in the *Estado da India* between warriors and merchants that were part of the traditional monarchies of Europe did not develop within the ranks of the VOC. For the Portuguese, it was common for fleet commanders to be nobles with little or no experience at sea. Such men were also theoretically prevented from engaging in common trade, since it would imperil their noble status. For the Dutch, high-ranking officials were frequently both traders and warriors. Additionally, the Dutch had very little interest in spreading their brand of the Christian faith. While the Portuguese had increasingly labored under the financial and cultural drag of the *Padroado Real* and the Goa Inquisition, the Dutch were free to pursue trade alone. By concentrating their activities in the East Indies, the VOC also avoided an armed showdown with the huge land armies that had checked the inland expansion of the Portuguese on the Indian subcontinent and in Persia and China. Exploiting such advantages, the VOC sent out huge fleets during its first five years. These fleets carried large quantities of munitions, as well as specie to pay for the much-coveted spices. Following Linschoten's advice, the Company centered these early activities in Indonesia, especially on the island of Java. The Dutch were welcomed by the local sultans of the archipelago as long-awaited saviors from the bane of the Portuguese, and they exploited this fact to sign commercial treaties with these rulers. As time went on, Dutch power increased and subsequent treaties became decidedly more one-sided, with the VOC enjoying the status of protectors in return for a cheap and regular flow of spices.

Down to 1609, as the war with Habsburg Spain continued in Europe, the Dutch permitted the London (or English) East India Company (EIC) to trade in the archipelago as well. After all, the Protestant English had been one of the Republic's most loyal allies in this struggle. This reality allowed the EIC to send out 26 ships to Asia from 1601 to 1612. But James I adopted a more measured tone than

Elizabeth I regarding Habsburg Spain, signing a separate peace in 1604. This diplomatic rebuff, coupled with the Twelve Year Truce that the Dutch signed with the Spaniards in 1609, allowed the VOC to take a more aggressive stance in the trade. Over the next 15 years, the Dutch would ruthlessly expel their Protestant brothers from the trade in Southeast Asia. For the burghers of Amsterdam, money was more important than religion.

EMPIRE BUILDING IN INDONESIA, CA. 1609–1629

During this initial stage of empire building, the most important individual was Jan Pieterszoon Coen. Coen had been born in 1587, and had worked in the counting house of a Flemish merchant in Rome. This apprenticeship lasted six years and served Coen well in his later activities for the VOC. In Italy, he learned the intricacies of double-entry bookkeeping, as well as obtaining a degree of fluency in Latin, Portuguese, Spanish, and French. Coen first sailed to Asia in 1607 as a junior merchant. In 1612, he returned to Indonesia as a senior merchant. His formative experiences in the trade were well reflected in a report he submitted to the *Heeren XVII* in 1614, titled *Discourse Touching the Dutch Indian State*. The directors realizing the brilliance of this work appointed Coen director-general of commerce. Coen's basic strategy for dominating the spice trade was straightforward and ruthless. First, the Dutch had to expand their so-called country trade in the Indian Ocean Basin in order to increase profits. As the Portuguese before them had discovered, European products, with the sole exception of weapons, had found few markets in Asia. So, in order to avoid the export of vast quantities of bullion from home to fund the purchase of spices, an intra-Asian trade had to be developed. For example, textiles from India had to be obtained as cheaply as possible to resell in Indonesia at a hefty profit, which could then fund the purchase of spices for shipment to the Netherlands. Establishing bases around the rim of the Indian Ocean Basin was therefore a priority for the Company's trade to flourish. Second, Coen wanted the Dutch to establish a monopoly over cloves, nutmeg, and mace. Since the sources of these spices were restricted to a relatively few islands in the archipelago, setting up such a monopoly would be far easier than attempting to control a product like pepper, which was grown over a huge geographic region. Finally, Coen wanted the Dutch to establish their own independent Asian capital to direct all these activities. Colonists sent out from the Netherlands would implant Dutch culture and make the prospect of extended residence in Asia more palatable (see Map 3.1).

Of course, not everyone in the VOC hierarchy agreed with Coen's plans, which portended a trading monopoly based on a thinly disguised extortion racket of sham treaties with local rulers enforced by military might. In opposition to this view, rivals such as Laurens Reael and Steven Van der Hagen argued that "the merchant's profit lies not so much in selling his wares at a high price as in the extent of his sales and retailing." They believed that the VOC had no right to enforce a monopoly in Indonesia unless it could provide the archipelago with rice and Indian textiles at fair and freely negotiated prices. In this, they were espousing embryonic proto-capitalism. Yet, Coen countered that the indigenous producers should be compelled to sell their spices at prices fixed by the VOC. Moreover, this monopoly should be maintained at all costs against Asian merchants, the Catholic Iberians, as well as those "false friends," the English. These views largely coincided with the tenets of late mercantilism, which the Portuguese had long embraced. The size of the economic pie was fixed, and to gain the greatest part of it

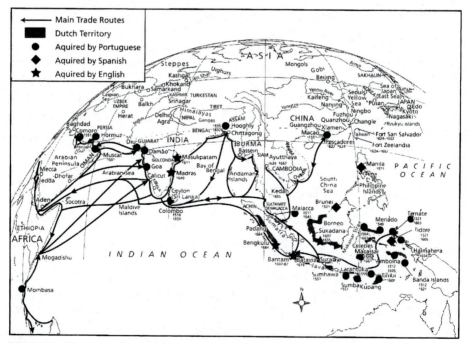

MAP 3.1   European Imperialism in the Indian Ocean, 1500–1700

meant taking it from one's competitors or enemies through military force. By April 1618, Coen won this power struggle when he was named governor-general. He would hold this post until 1623 and then again from 1627 to 1629. During these years, Coen swiftly and ruthlessly sought to implement his strategy. His successors as governor-general would continue these same policies. As a result, the history of the VOC for the remainder of the 17th century was one of frequent warfare in Indonesia and the rest of the Indian Ocean Basin.

It was the English Company that suffered the initial attacks in this Dutch quest for a spice monopoly. In Coen's view, the weakness of his predecessors had allowed the English to establish a credible presence in the trade. They had set up trading factories in Makassar and at Bantam on Java, as well as bases on two of the Banda islands, Run and Nailaka. As early as 1612, the Dutch began a campaign to undermine the English. Dutch agents sought to discredit the English as mere "pirates" with the local rulers and advised them not to trade with them. English ships were frequently harassed, their cargoes seized on bogus technicalities, and their crews imprisoned. Rising Dutch pretensions and the haughty character of Coen had prompted Matthew Duke to inform the London Directors: "Theis buterboxes are groane soe insolent . . . that yf they be suffred but a whit longer, they will make claims to the whole Indies, so that no man shall trade but themselves or by thear leave: but I hoope to see ther pride take a falle." Based on such reports, the EIC sent out a powerful fleet of six ships in 1618 under Sir Thomas Dale to protect English interests in the archipelago. But Dale's fleet was no match for the naval forces that Coen could muster. By 1620, the governor-general had established the VOC at a strong fortified base at Jakarta on Java, which he renamed Batavia, "as Holland used to be called in the days of old." John Jourdain, the English chief of the Bantam factory, was killed in action, and Dale died from disease. Only news from Europe that an Accord (1619) had been reached between the two Protestant companies saved the remaining English from the wrath of Coen, and this was only a respite not a full pardon.

This Accord, agreed to by the Seventeen in preparation for the end of the Twelve Year Truce with Spain (1621), promised the English one-third of the spice trade from the Moluccas, Bandas, and Amboina and one-half of the pepper trade of Java. In return, the English agreed to provide 10 ships for a common defense fleet against the Portuguese. Coen was incensed at this ill-advised agreement, which undermined his earlier efforts. As he wrote to the *Heeren*, "The English owe Your

Excellencies a great debt of gratitude, for they had assisted themselves straight out of the Indies, and You have put them right back in the middle again." From 1620 to 1624, Coen did all he could to undermine this agreement, harassing the English factory on Java, which had shifted from Bantam to Batavia. He also continued with his aggressive plans for monopoly. Although repulsed from Macao by the Portuguese in 1622, two years later the VOC managed to establish a factory on Formosa (Taiwan). In 1621, Coen conquered the Banda islands, expelling the English from Run and allowing them to remain only on Nailaka. The Bandanese were harshly treated by the governor-general, whose zeal for his cause rationalized all atrocities. The lands on these islands were taken over by the Dutch, who worked them with slave labor. On the island of Lontor, nearly 50 tribal chiefs were tortured and then executed, and 800 islanders were enslaved and shipped to Java. On the island of Run, on the clove-producing island of Ceram, and elsewhere the grim story was essentially the same.

PHOTO 3.2 Jacob Mathieusen and Wife, ca. 1650. Mathieusen was a senior VOC merchant in Batavia. Although the Dutch were making huge profits there, both Mathieusen and his wife dress in the somber clothing common to Calvinists. Their one extravagance was a slave who shades them with a parasol or *pajong,* a status symbol in Asia. Behind them, VOC ships prepare to sail for Europe.

Coen also strove to entrench operations in India and Persia. In 1620, Pieter van den Broecke reached the rich Gujarati entrepôt of Surat as "director of Arabia, Persia, and India." Broecke quickly founded factories in northwest India to assist with the lucrative textile trade. Settlements were also set up in Persia by Hubert Visnich at Gombroon (Bandar Abbas) and Ispahan in the early 1620s. There, the Dutch were soon doing a brisk exchange of Indonesian spices for Persian silks. During the 1620s, Dutch shipwrights also began to construct vessels in India for the Asian country trade. By 1623–1624, the Surat factory was well established despite the opposition of the Portuguese. In January 1623, the English members of the joint "Council of Defense" also asked the Dutch to provide ships to bring their remaining factors from Banda, Amboina, and the Moluccas to Java since no ships or funds had appeared since the Accord. Coen was happy to grant this request, provided a fair price was paid. He then departed for Amsterdam in February to lobby for an increase in Dutch colonists to populate and work the growing list of islands under VOC control. Although there was some opposition in the Netherlands to his harsh methods, Coen was reappointed governor-general in September 1624 and prepared to return to Batavia.

On the eve of his departure, however, news reached Europe of one of the most explosive episodes in the history of the Asian trade, the "massacre of Amboina." In March 1623, Gabriel Towerson, the chief factor of the English Company on Amboina, along with 9 of his countrymen, 10 Japanese mercenaries, and a Portuguese employee were all beheaded on the orders of the Dutch governor of the island, Herman Van Speult. The charge: that they had conspired to attack Fort Victoria and kill Van Speult in order to seize the rich trade of the island. While the truth regarding these charges will never be known, at the very least it seems that Van Speult, embracing the harsh line toward monopoly initiated by Coen, erred on the side of rashness and not prudence. In Europe, the case created a firestorm of protest and ill feelings between the erstwhile allies. Van Speult died in 1626 before he could formally respond to the English complaints. A judicial panel eventually acquitted the Dutch officials in the matter, while criticizing their legal procedures and haste. Nevertheless, the stench from the massacre lingered. The Treaty of Westminster, which ended the First Anglo-Dutch War (1652–1654), included a clause of compensation for the victims' families in the amount of £3,615. Moreover, Charles II cited the massacre as one of the reasons for renewed warfare in the mid-1660s. But in Indonesia, the executions had the desired effect: the English Company soon abandoned its efforts on Japan and mainland Southeast Asia. Their overawed factory at Batavia was also of little use. In 1628, the English managed to return to Bantam and this factory survived until 1682. But it was clear that the Dutch had won the European struggle for the spice-producing islands of Indonesia. The English, as we will see in Chapter 4, would have to concentrate their trading activities elsewhere.

After Coen's return to Batavia in 1627, the consolidation of the VOC monopoly continued. There were, however, difficulties. Internal political rivalries on Java between rival Muslim sultans embroiled the Dutch in frequent warfare. Of these powers, the interior kingdom of Mataram was the most dangerous threat to Dutch pretensions. It had expanded under sultan Agung (r. 1613–1645). Agung expected Dutch support against his rival sultans in Madura and Surubaya, but Coen refused. Agung first besieged Batavia in late 1627 to little effect. In 1629, Batavia was again besieged by Agung's forces. Once again, the combination of Dutch military might, their fortifications, the ability to reinforce by sea, and their superior artillery again decided the issue. Although Agung periodically waged war with Batavia throughout the 1630s, Dutch power was secure on the island, and Coen's plans to plant a true colony took hold. Agung's only consolation was that the Dutch governor-general died from dysentery during the second siege in September 1629. Coen, however had done much to establish the VOC on a solid footing. A flourishing country trade had been set up from the ports of the Red Sea to those of China. They had also gained effective control over the production areas of the spices, an economic reality that certainly facilitated their trade. By choosing Batavia on the northern coast of Java, the Dutch also avoided dependence on the alternating monsoon winds for passage around the Cape of Good Hope. Instead, the VOC could exploit the Sundra straits and the trade winds of the thirties and forties of south latitude, a safer and more reliable course.

CONSOLIDATION AND EXPANSION UNDER VAN DIEMEN

The second period in the history of the VOC from ca. 1636 to 1672 witnessed a sustained attack on the most important possessions of the rival Portuguese *Estado da India*. Initially, this campaign of open warfare was orchestrated by Anthony Van Diemen (1593–1645). Van Diemen had been born in 1593 to middle class parents. Like Coen, he trained in a counting house. In 1616, he became a merchant and settled in Amsterdam. He was soon bankrupt. To escape his creditors, Van Diemen took the assumed name of Theunis Meeuwisz, joined the VOC, and sailed to Batavia as a soldier in 1618. After all, 15,000 miles would put a lot of distance between him and his debts. Coen heard his story and was impressed by his intellect, his force of character, and his resourcefulness. The governor-general was so impressed that he gave him a job as his private secretary, a position of great trust. Van Diemen, for the next three and a half years, kept the account books. When the Seventeen ordered Van Diemen sent back to the Netherlands to address his problems, the governor-general refused to comply. When Coen returned himself to Amsterdam in 1623, he promoted Van Diemen to senior merchant to give him more leverage in the colony. Coen's return for his second term as governor-general ensured Van Diemen's rise. In 1627 he became director-general, the second highest position in Asia. Van Diemen was traveling in late 1629 when Coen died and this afforded the Seventeen an opportunity to bypass him for the post of governor-general. It was only in January 1636 that Van Diemen finally obtained this much-coveted office. For the next nine years, he oversaw a rapid expansion of the Company's operations and sustained warfare with the Portuguese from India to Melaka.

In Indonesia, Van Diemen tightened the spice monopoly. Emboldened by their newfound wealth, the *Heeren XVII* ordered not only that the monopoly be strictly enforced, but that production be controlled to ensure maximum profits. Although nutmeg production was already effectively managed in the Bandas, the Seventeen wanted this system extended to clove production in Amboina and the Moloccas. Production would be restricted and redistributed primarily by cutting down and destroying the clove trees. The local population would be forced to grow other crops, such as rice. In turn, a sharecropping system would be installed which would reduce them to perpetual debt and servitude to the VOC. Van Diemen did his best to implement this system despite personal reservations on the destruction of the spice trees. But given his far-reaching commitments, complete control over cloves was not achieved before his death in 1645. Islam, moreover, was attracting many converts in the archipelago, reinforcing the self-confidence of the sultans in their opposition to the Dutch. His successors, however, continued these policies. Following a bloody five-year war, the sultan of Ternate was reduced to vassalage, and the Dutch achieved their goal at last. In fact, they may have succeeded too well. In 1656, the production of cloves was so low that it could not meet the demand in Europe and Asia.

During the first years of the VOC there had been no intention of attempting to monopolize the Malabar Coast pepper trade or the rich trade in cinnamon based on the island of Ceylon. By the mid-1630s, however, the VOC was so strong in the East Indies that Van Diemen decided to extend the Company's monopoly to these additional spices and concurrently to take the offensive to the very heart of the Portuguese empire. His years as governor-general witnessed almost continual warfare with the *Estado da India*. Van Diemen's strategy was simple: use the superior fleet of the VOC and the large numbers of Dutch troops and Asian retainers at his disposal to attack the Portuguese whenever possible. One facet of this campaign was to erect a blockade of Goa during the traditional sailing season from September through June. Van Diemen believed that depriving Lisbon of the flow of spices carried by the ships of the *Carreira da India* and interdicting the arrival of fresh troops and money from Portugal would cripple the *Estado*. In 1635, a large VOC fleet departed from Batavia for Persia with orders to begin the blockade of Goa. For the next eight years, the blockade of Goa continued with periodic battles at the mouth of the Mandovi. While this strategy was effective, the VOC never captured Goa. The Portuguese, during these lean years, shifted their trade to other possessions on the west coast of India, such as Cochin, and a tenuous link was maintained with Lisbon. The last of Van Diemen's blockading fleets departed from Batavia in late 1643. The following year, orders arrived with Johan Maetsuycker mandating a truce with the Portuguese.

WARFARE WITH THE PORTUGUESE ON CEYLON, 1638–1658

Warfare raged on Ceylon as well. Western legends of the wealth of this lush island dated back to the descriptions of Ptolemy and Marco Polo. Cinnamon grew in plenty along the coastal rim while, in the interior, emeralds, elephants, timber, and areca nuts could be found. Finally, there were rich pearl fisheries in the Gulf of Manar between the island and India. By the mid-1630s, the stage could hardly have been better set for Dutch designs. As the VOC had methodically expelled the Portuguese from much of their trade in the Indonesian Archipelago and elsewhere, the Portuguese had sought to solidify their holdings on Ceylon. The Portuguese controlled much of the coastal belt of the island based at powerful fortresses at Colombo and Galle. In the 1620s, they had added forts at Batticaloa and Trincomalee. But they were not content with these coastal possessions. In 1630, the captain-general Constantine de Sá attacked the inland kingdom of Kandy ruled by the Sinhalese king Senerat. De Sá knew the difficulties, but proceeded all the same. He paid a heavy price. In August 1630, his army was badly mauled and the captain-general slain. His head was then paraded on a spike before Senerat.

Things would get worse. In 1634, Prince Maha Asthana ascended the throne with the title Raja Sinha II to honor an ancestor who had heroically resisted the Portuguese in the late 16th century. This bit of foreshadowing came to fruition in 1636 when the young king was insulted by the new captain-general of the island, Diogo de Mello de Castro. The king sent an urgent appeal for assistance to Van Diemen, who was overjoyed at the formal invitation to help expel the Portuguese. Van Diemen had already ordered his admiral of the 1637–1638 fleet for Goa to stop at Ceylon and offer the king 50 percent more than the Portuguese for his cinnamon. The governor-general promptly changed these orders and instructed him merely to "direct affairs in such a way that we may obtain from the king . . . a good, profitable, and binding contract for a great quantity of cinnamon." Mello de Castro, meanwhile, marched on Kandy to settle scores with Raja Sinha II. He sacked the city in revenge for Constantine de Sá's debacle, but did not have a force sufficient to garrison the place. On his retreat to the coast, the Portuguese suffered heavy losses, and yet another captain-general was slain.

Formal warfare between the Europeans began in May 1638 when a Dutch fleet helped the Sinhalese expel the Portuguese from their fortress at Batticaloa. That same year the VOC sent cinnamon bought for 53,000 guilders home to Amsterdam, where it sold for double that amount. Life, for the moment, was good for the VOC. For the next 20 years, warfare raged periodically on the island. The Portuguese were well entrenched in their coastal fortresses and proved difficult to displace. Generations of Portuguese had lived from the rich trade of the island. Many of the *casados* (married settlers) in India, Ceylon, and elsewhere had no intention of returning to Portugal and were determined to fight to the end. As Van Diemen wrote, "Most of the Portuguese in Asia look upon this region as their fatherland, and think no more about Portugal."

Perhaps recognizing this fact, the governor-general, just before his death in April 1645, agreed to a short-lived pact with the Portuguese that called for a division of the cinnamon-producing lands along the coast and a joint attack on the Sinhalese.

MALACCA AND JAPAN

In Malaysia and Japan, Van Diemen also carried on a sustained campaign against Portuguese power. One of the cornerstone fortresses of the *Estado da India* was Melaka, or Malacca, a strategically located entrepôt near the tip of the Malay peninsula, which had been taken by Afonso de Albuquerque in 1511. This multicultural enclave bristled with products and merchants from throughout Asia. For Van Diemen, its prosperity was a thorn in the side of the emerging Dutch empire. Dutch attacks on Melaka began as early as the Third Fleet of the VOC in 1606. By the mid-1630s, Van Diemen was determined to reduce Melaka once and for all. Goa, blockaded for most of the year, could offer little support. In late 1639, Van Diemen sent a fleet of 12 ships supported by 25 Achinese galleys to besiege Melaka. In May 1640, Adriaan Antonoiszoon sailed from Batavia with a fleet of 18 ships and 1,000 men to again surround the Portuguese fortress. He was soon supported by another 40 small ships and perhaps 1,500 soldiers provided by the sultan of Johore. This siege lasted from August 1640 until January 1641. Both the Portuguese garrison and the besiegers suffered greatly from disease and other privations. Finally in mid-January, the Portuguese garrison, reduced to fewer than 200 men, agreed to surrender. Van Diemen was overjoyed. For Johore, however, this victory proved to be a mixed blessing. Although the sultan's powers grew to include Achinese territories on the peninsula, the Riau archipelago, and parts of east Sumatra, the VOC promptly insisted on a monopoly of trade within his dominions. Foreign ships, including those from Gujarat, were also forced to purchase Dutch passes.

In Japan, the Dutch managed to replace the Portuguese as the principal European traders on the island during Van Diemen's administration. In this power shift, however, the VOC did not have to expend any of its own firepower. The Tokugawa shoguns took care of this purge of the Iberians for them. The Dutch had been welcomed to Japan as a counter-balance to the power of the Portuguese initially. In 1600, the shogun Ieyasu (r. 1600–1605) protected the Dutch crew of the *Liefde* and allowed it to remain in Tokyo harbor. In 1609, a VOC factory was established at Hirado. In the 1620s, the Dutch experienced problems with the shogun for a time after Pieter Nuyts, the new governor of the Dutch fort on Formosa, demanded the recognition of VOC "sovereignty" over the island. In 1628, Nuyts had also foolishly attempted to seize two ships outfitted by the magistrate of Nagasaki. Instead, he himself was taken and forced to bargain for his own release. Fortunately, in the wake of this debacle, the Dutchman who would consolidate the position of the VOC appeared. His name was François Caron. Born in Brussels in 1600 to Huguenot parents who eventually settled in the United Provinces, Caron sailed as a cook's mate to Hirado in the service of the VOC in 1619. There, he quickly learned the Japanese language and the customs of the country, skills that served him well. He quickly rose in the Company hierarchy: merchant, senior merchant, second in command at Hirado (1633–1638), and chief of the factory in February 1639.

By that year, the Tokugawa shogun Iemitsu (r. 1623–1651) decided that he had seen enough Christianity in his domains. Portuguese Jesuits had been active in Japan from the late second half of the 16th century and had some success in conversions. For the increasingly xenophobic shoguns, this was too much. In 1609, the huge Portuguese carrack *Madre de Deus* had been burnt in a Japanese attack. In 1636, the Iberians, to prevent the spread of their religion, had been restricted to the island of Deshima in Nagasaki harbor. All Portuguese descendants had also been expelled and prohibitions were put into effect on foreign travel. In 1638, a stronger edict had been issued in light of continuing missionary activities to burn all Portuguese ships arriving in Japanese harbors. In 1640, the leading citizens of Macao sent a 60-man delegation to seek the repeal of this ban, which threatened their longstanding trade with the islands. On the shogun's orders they were all beheaded. Even Van Diemen was taken aback. As he wrote, "when it rains on the Portuguese we likewise get wet from the drops." Fortunately, Caron was astute enough to avoid a trap set for him in early November 1640 by the commission charged with suppressing Christianity in the shogun's domains. For his efforts, the VOC in July 1641 was allowed to transfer its activities on Deshima in place of the Portuguese. Profits of nearly a million guilders a year soon resulted from this tiny area of less than three acres in the middle of Nagasaki harbor. Caron returned to Batavia in early 1641. He would subsequently achieve notable results against the Portuguese on Ceylon and rise to director-general, only to be expelled from the VOC in 1650 for private trading. After a forced retirement in the Hague, he was, as we will see in Chapter 4, lured to the service of Colbert's East India Company, charged with undermining the activities of the Dutch Company, which he had done much to entrench.

Anthony Van Diemen died in April 1645. His nine years as governor-general witnessed the consolidation and expansion of VOC activities throughout Asia. The country trade was flourishing. Dutch factories from the Persian Gulf to Japan maintained a regular correspondence with Batavia and dispatched products there for eventual shipment to Amsterdam. Batavia had also been transformed by Van Diemen. Coen's modest settlement had expanded into a rich and prosperous city, its canals lined with townhouses reminiscent of the homeland. The strong fort had been complemented by the construction of reformed churches, a Latin school, and an orphanage. A multicultural mix of merchants from throughout Asia sought profit in its markets. Millions of pounds of pepper, cloves, nutmeg, mace, and cinnamon entered Europe through the efforts of the VOC, and huge profits were made. The Dutch Company was quickly becoming the most powerful commercial entity in the world. In recognition of his services, Van Diemen's wife was granted a hefty pension by the Seventeen. The question confronting the VOC in 1645 was, Could a worthy successor to Van Diemen be found to continue this phenomenal period of growth? Moreover, what would the long-term impact be of the decades of ruthless monopoly in the Asian trade? Initially greeted as liberators from the Portuguese, the Dutch were on the verge of becoming the new Portuguese in the trade. While they did not have the baggage of religious zealotry that had fairly or unfairly attached itself to the *Estado da India*, their single-minded worship of profit, perhaps exacerbated by the predestination doctrine of their Calvinist faith, made them much less suave colonizers than the Portuguese. The Iberians, after all, had intermarried with local populations wherever possible, and produced generations of Euro-Asian offspring. Their language, moreover, continued as the *lingua franca* of the Asian trade. Even in Batavia it was heard almost as commonly as Dutch.

THE DUTCH WEST INDIA COMPANY, 1621–1700

The formidable success of the VOC encouraged the Dutch to challenge for a sizable share of the Atlantic trade during the 17th century, as well. Dutch privateers had successfully attacked Spanish galleons throughout most of the 16th century, and private Dutch merchants had invested legally and otherwise in the overseas empire of Spain and Portugal. By the early 1620s, the States-General decided to begin a more systematic campaign. In June 1621, this desire resulted in the granting of a formal charter establishing the Dutch West India Company. In structure, the WIC largely mirrored that of the VOC with the sole exception that it could not conduct military campaigns without the approval of the States General. It had five *kamers*, or chambers, and nineteen members of the board of Directors, the *Heeren XIX*. The Company received a trading monopoly from the west coast of Africa to the eastern edge of New Guinea, including the Pacific Ocean. Nevertheless, from the outset the WIC was expected to concentrate on establishing bases between the west coast of Africa (slaves), Brazil (sugar), the Caribbean Islands (sugar and rum), and North America (furs, naval stores). The timing of the founding of the new Company was no accident. The Twelve Year Truce with Spain ran out in 1621. Philip III, moreover, had died in March of that year and his 16 year-old son inherited a kingdom that was reeling from the combination of previous imperial commitments and the prospect of even more difficulties thanks to the escalating campaigns of the Thirty Years' War. Portugal was still ruled by the Spanish Habsburgs and thus Brazil, Angola, and other Portuguese possessions on the west coast of Africa were fair game for the WIC.

The period from ca. 1621 to 1642 witnessed rapid expansion and generally favorable results for the Company. In North America, the Dutch had claimed territory since 1609 and the voyages of Henry Hudson. The colony of New Netherland, centered on the Hudson River valley and adminstered from New Amsterdam, included parts of present-day New York, New Jersey, Connecticut, and Delaware. In the 1620s, to protect these interests, forts were built at Fort Amsterdam (Manhattan Island), Fort Orange (Albany), Fort Nassau on the Delaware River, and Fort Good Hope at Hartford. Beginning in 1628, the Company used the *patroon*, or patron, system to develop this colony. Members of the WIC received huge land grants with powers of local government and a share of the fur trade in return for settling 50 colonists. While the arrangement looked good on paper, only one of the five patroonships showed signs of progress. Kiliaen Van Rennselaer, a diamond merchant from Amsterdam, set up his patroonship called Rensselaerswyck, near Albany. By the 1660s, Rensselaerswyck had more than 40 houses and 200 inhabitants over one million acres in upstate New York. In North America, the main rivals of the Dutch were the English, who were in the midst of establishing themselves in Virginia and New England.

In the Caribbean, the WIC found itself in competition with the declining power of the Spaniards and the rising pretensions of the English and the French. By the 1640s the WIC, building in some cases on earlier expeditions, founded colonies on the Leeward Islands of Saba (1640), St. Eustatius (1636), St. Maarten (1631), and off the coast of Venezuela on Aruba (1636) and Curaçao (1600). Curaçao became the administrative center for the WIC. The island also built up a sizable share of the slave trade to the Caribbean as the century unfolded. It has been estimated that during its history, the WIC transported more than 500,000 slaves from West Africa to the New World on the dreaded "Middle Passage." From these bases in the Caribbean, the WIC also carried out another of its main functions: privateering against the shipping of the Spanish empire. Perhaps the most notable success in this campaign came in 1628. In September of that year, Piet Heyn, the first vice-admiral of the WIC, commanding a fleet of 31 ships, cornered the annual Spanish treasure fleet in the bay of Matanzas near Havana and forced it to surrender without a fight. The silver captured aboard these galleons yielded the WIC some 12 million guilders.

As noted in Chapter 1, the WIC also enjoyed great success in depriving the Portuguese of their imperial possessions in Brazil and on the West African coast during the 1620s, 1630s, and 1640s. In this struggle, the WIC was assisted by the cordial reception it received from indigenous peoples in those areas, such as the Tupis and the Ndongo, who detested the Portuguese and wanted to use the Dutch as a counterweight. During the 1620s, Dutch fleets attacked Salvador da Bahia in Brazil and even captured this northern capital for a time. In 1630, a large fleet under Hendrick Corneliszoon Loncq captured Pernambuco, Recife, and Olinda in the sugarcane plantation region of the northeast. To complement these victories, the WIC then turned its attention to West Africa and the slaving stations of the Portuguese. These strongholds had also been under attack by the WIC since the mid-1620s. In August 1637, a Dutch fleet of 9 ships and 800 men, supported by more than 1,000 Africans, attacked and captured Sao Jorge da Mina. In 1641, a WIC fleet of 21 ships and 3,000 men sailed to West Africa with orders to attack the remaining Portuguese strongholds there, including, São Tomé, Angola, and Benguela. Luanda, the capital of Angola, Benguela, São Tomé, and Annobon all surrendered. From 1621 to 1647, some 30,000 slaves from these new slaving posts in Africa reached Dutch Brazil through the efforts of the WIC. The fortunes of the Company seemed assured.

Unfortunately from the Dutch perspective, the next three decades witnessed the rapid decline of these impressive gains. This decline can be traced to several key factors. In Brazil and Angola, the Portuguese under D. João IV had marshaled as many military forces as possible and launched a spirited counterattack in the late 1640s and early 1650s that at least in Brazil played on the traditional cultural and religious ties of the colonists to the Portuguese Crown. The WIC certainly facilitated this turn of events by recalling the astute and talented Maurice of Nassau in the midst of this offensive in northeastern Brazil. From 1647 to 1654, the WIC was expelled from nearly all of its conquests in Brazil, Angola, and West Africa. The Peace of Westphalia of 1648, which formally recognized Dutch independence and ended the long struggle with Spain, also helped to undermine the Company. This treaty deprived the Company of its longstanding and lucrative privateering opportunities against the Spaniards in the New World. In North America, rejuvenated colonial schemes first under Cromwell and then under Charles II had also resulted in decisive military action against the Dutch colony. In the midst of his anti-Dutch campaign of the mid-1660s, Charles annexed New Netherland and granted it to his brother James, Duke of York. James, who had a strong interest in colonial affairs, especially regarding the African trade, sent a fleet under Sir Richard Nicolls to seize this possession of the WIC. In September 1664, confronted by this fleet, the Dutch director-general, Pieter Stuyvesant, surrendered Fort Amsterdam, and the rest of the colony soon followed. These losses in Brazil, Angola, and North America dealt a fatal blow to the WIC. By 1674, the dire financial situation of the Company forced its dissolution. A year later a new, albeit scaled down, WIC was founded exclusively for trade. This entity managed to survive on the slave trade passing through Curaçao and sugar produced in Suriname, but the glory days of the Dutch Atlantic Empire were over.

THE MAETSUYCKER YEARS IN ASIA, 1653–1678

In the Indian Ocean Basin, meanwhile, Van Diemen's immediate successors were less than impressive. The Cape of Good Hope colony was founded in 1652 at the direction of the Seventeen. The true successor to Van Diemen and Coen was Johan Maetsuycker. Maetsuycker was a Roman Catholic who had studied law. In 1635, as the Seventeen were searching for a qualified lawyer to assist the expanding activities of the court of justice at Batavia, Maetsuycker offered his services. To receive the appointment he promised to profess Dutch Reformed Protestantism. Arriving in Java in 1636, Maetsuycker spent the next six years compiling the Statutes of Batavia, the legal code that served as the basis for Dutch colonial possession in Asia for the next 200 years. He returned to Batavia in 1644 with orders from the Seventeen to belatedly put the Ten Year Truce between the United Provinces and a newly liberated Portugal into effect. Although some hard-liners, including Van Diemen, sought to only periodically adhere to its provisions, Maetsuycker worked diligently to follow his orders on the matter until the truce expired in early 1652. From 1646 to 1650, he served as governor of Dutch Ceylon. He became governor-general in 1653 and held this post for the next 25 years, the longest term in the Company's history.

Maetsuycker's tenure began on a high note. In 1655, he sent a fleet of 14 ships and 1,200 men under Gerald Hulft to Ceylon. The time was right to finally end the longstanding war there with the Portuguese. In December 1640, the Duke of Braganza, had claimed the Portuguese throne, a bold act that began 28 years of periodic warfare in Europe against Spain, as well as continuing overseas warfare in Brazil, Africa, and the Indian Ocean against the Dutch. In the triage of resources that followed for D. João IV, the *Estado da India* received far less support than both Brazil and the African possessions throughout the new king's reign, which ended in 1656. Reenergized with these reinforcements, the Dutch captured Colombo in May 1656, and by July 1658, the Portuguese had been expelled from the island. Yet, this long awaited victory on Ceylon was somewhat deceiving. Maetsuycker and the VOC soon faced a series of daunting challenges that began to undermine the preeminent position in the trade that they had attained by the late 1650s. On Ceylon, once the Portuguese had been defeated, Rijkloff Van Goens, the VOC governor, became the foremost proponent of inland territorial expansion as part of a strategy to obtain an effective monopoly over the lucrative cinnamon trade. He actively pursued such a policy in the face of mounting deficits during the 1660s and 1670s.

Maetsuycker initially favored a cautious policy on Ceylon. But, during the mid-1660s, the increasing threat from European competitors forced the governor-general to reverse his views on the advisability of Van Goens' designs. In 1660, the English ship *Anne* appeared on the Sinhalese coast. This event signaled renascent EIC activities on the island, and fueled apprehension in Batavia and Amsterdam alike. As Maetsuycker wrote, the English were determined "to induce Rajah Sinha to make common cause against us and secure for themselves free trading in Ceylon. This is a serious matter." The Rajah, still seeking to play the Europeans off against one another to his advantage, asked for formal Dutch protection over the bays of Batticaloa and Trincomalee. Vans Goens proposed taking them outright "so that we could exclude any other nation from the island." News that a palace coup in Kandy had temporarily rendered Rajah Sinha militarily impotent decided the issue. As the governor-general and Council informed the Seventeen: "We have after due consideration given orders for the execution of [Van Goens's] plan." Van Goens exploited the situation with ease. Batticaloa and Trincomalee were quickly taken and fortified and the Dutch began to expand to inland. Batavia was delighted with these initial reports, and the Council was soon convinced that it would be advisable perhaps to conquer the entire island and make Dutch power on Ceylon comparable to what it was in Indonesia.

MOUNTING PROBLEMS FOR THE VOC, 1660–1700

The financial and military strain of this expansionist policy, however, soon became painfully evident in Batavia and Colombo. Van Goens's troops may have occupied new inland territories, but underlying this façade of early success was the fact that the governor had committed the Company to a policy that its resources could not sustain. Maetsuycker registered his "great uneasiness" with the military situation on Ceylon as early as October 1668, when he informed the Seventeen that "our posts are now extended so far in the interior and spread so far apart that by any sinister design of Rajah Sinha they are entirely at his mercy." This able king had promptly restored order in Kandy and in 1670 launched the type of counteroffensive that the Batavia Council feared: Van Goens's men suffered heavy losses and had soon retreated to their pre-1665 positions. This warfare continued for the next two years. For Maetsuycker, the cost could not be denied: in the late 1660s the Company's annual deficit on Ceylon was already averaging 250,000 guilders, the figure would soon reach 730,000 guilders. Van Goens's expansionist desires also facilitated Colbert's wish that France share in the rich cinnamon trade of the island. Faced with a continuing campaign against the Dutch, Rajah Sinha was exceedingly receptive to the French director-general François Caron's diplomatic feelers that called for the establishment of trading operations on the island and the granting of either Batticaloa or Trincomalee to Colbert's *Compagnie*.

Much the same situation existed for the Dutch on the Malabar Coast and particularly in the pepper-producing region surrounding Calicut. Open warfare had begun between the VOC and the Zamorin in the mid-1660s, following that potentate's decision to raise the price of pepper. At times, the fighting had been particularly vicious. John Petit, the English factor in Calicut, described one incident when Dutch Company troops launched a surprise attack on the Zamorin's camp. After overcoming the guards "whome they killed with little trouble . . . they came upon where the king's wife and other women of quality were lodged," and shot and killed several of them including "the king's daughter into the thigh & his wife into the eye." Although the Dutch were eventually able to field over 1,000 men, mostly native retainers, in this struggle, this necessitated leaving Cochin and the remaining Dutch possessions on India's west coast virtually undefended. The Zamorin badly needed assistance to prosecute this war and exact revenge for the outrages of Van Goens's troops. Caron began negotiations toward procuring trading privileges and land to erect factories. The local ruler, in the midst of this campaign against the Dutch, had proven receptive. As a sign of goodwill, he granted the *Compagnie* the small coastal village of Alicot, located at the southern limits of his domains. Commenting on the gravity of the problems then confronting him, Maetsuycker lamented, "What a fearfull charge doth Ceylon and Malabar draw after it, and how many years hath this continued in hopes of a profitable issue . . . God in mercy put an end to these bad times and cause them to issue for the best."

One reason for the increasing problems for the United Provinces in general and the VOC in particular related to shifting alliances and the military revolution of the late 17th century in Europe. Before 1667, the Protestant Dutch had managed to remain France's ally in their joint struggle against Habsburg Spain. The wars of Louis XIV beginning in 1667, however, fundamentally altered this alliance. The Dutch at the behest of Johan de Witt, grand pensionary of the Dutch Republic, shifted to an alliance with the English to blunt the expansionist plans of Louis in the Spanish Netherlands. Down to the Peace of Utrecht in 1713, ending the bloody wars of Louis XIV, the United Provinces were periodically at war with France. The ascension of William of Orange to the throne of England in the Glorious Revolution of 1688–1689 additionally solidified this *volte-face.* In the periods 1667–1668, 1672–1679, 1686–1697, and 1701–1713, wars raged, all fueled by France's quest for dominance over western and central Europe. This warfare not only upset the regular trade of the VOC, but it also undermined the ability of the States-General to provide assistance and aid to the Dutch Company. The military revolution of this period, in which the average size of European armies rose from ca. 30,000 in 1648 to over 100,000 by the end of the century, also put the Dutch, with a population of perhaps 2 million, at a distinct disadvantage against a power like France, whose population was about 20 million.

Despite these problems at home, the VOC managed to ship a record cargo to Amsterdam in 1670 of 9.2 million pounds of black pepper and 134,000 pounds of white pepper, the largest of the century. Moreover, Maetsuycker commanded a fleet of some 65 Dutch ships, the most powerful European fleet in Asian waters. Thirty to forty of these ships were actively involved in the country trade. But territorially, economically, and geopolitically, the 1670s probably constituted the peak of Dutch power. Thereafter, continually defending this position against European and Asian rivals, as was the case for the Portuguese earlier, took a higher and higher toll. Warfare expenses ate into Company profits and loans from Asian bankers at increasing rates of interest became more common. In Batavia and elsewhere, administrative or household expenses continued to rise. Private trading at Company expense and outright corruption also mounted. Prices on the products that the VOC monopolized, such as black pepper and cloves, also declined marginally in Europe during these years. The VOC was also slow to exploit the changes in the

Asian trade with Europe. The Dutch had constructed a good part of their monopoly around the goods that had dominated European markets in the 16th and early 17th centuries, principally spices. But as the 17th century wore on, the profit margin on other products gradually challenged these goods. Indian cotton textiles, traditionally confined to the country trade, became the fashion in Europe and a huge demand for them ensued. Moreover, it was the English Company, well positioned in India at Bombay on the west coast, Madras on the east coast, and in Bengal in the north, that reaped the greatest advantage. Similarly, after the Manchu emperor Kangxi opened up the ports of China to Western trade in 1685, the VOC failed to appreciate the true potential of tea in European markets. The Dutch, adhering to their traditional monopoly model, attempted to ship the relatively small quantities of tea they purchased in China through Batavia, instead of opening up a direct trade to Amsterdam. As a result, the flavor and quality of the transshipped tea could not compete and this increasingly lucrative trade was also lost to the English Company in the last decades of the 17th century. Nevertheless, the VOC remained a powerful force in the Asian trade down to the mid-18th century. Thirty to forty ships a year sailed from Amsterdam each year and dividends of 20 percent were maintained throughout the 17th century. Yet, if the Seventeen and men like Coen, Van Diemen, and Van Goens had followed the advice of Linschoten more closely, instead of emulating many features of the Portuguese empire, perhaps these profits and dividends would have been even higher. We will never know. What we do know is that in six thrilling decades, the United Provinces, thanks in large measure to the efforts of the VOC in Asia, became the predominant mercantile power in the world and Amsterdam the richest and most prosperous city Europe had witnessed to that time.

SOURCES

◼ Jan Huyghen van Linschoten Reveals the Secrets of Portuguese Asia

For a century, the Portuguese Crown had been obsessive about maintaining secrecy regarding the sailing routes and other details regarding the sea route to India and its Asian empire. During his years in Goa, however, Linschoten's position as a trusted confidant to Archbishop Vicente de Fonseca gave him access to maps, log-books, and other "secret" documents on the trade. Linschoten even made copies of some of these treasured maps. When Fonseca died in 1587 on a trip to Lisbon, Linschoten decided to return to Europe and make money from selling these secrets. He left Goa in January 1589, but when his ship was attacked by English pirates near the Azores, Linschoten spent nearly two years there before reaching Lisbon in 1592. He soon returned to his home town of Enkhuizen in the Low Countries and began publishing his much-valued knowledge of what had hiterhto been the "secret" inner workings of Portuguese Asia.

As you read this selection, what strikes you most about late 16th century Goa? Do you get the impression that Linschoten is an objective observer? Would this passage encourage or discourage Portugal's European rivals in their quest to challenge for a share of the trade? How much power does Linschoten bestow upon indigenous merchants?

The Citie of Goa, is the Metropolitan or chiefe Cittie of all the Orientall Indies, where the Portingales have their traffique, where also the Viceroye, the Archbishop, the Kings Councel, and Chauncerie have their residence, and from thence are all [places in] the Orientall Indies, governed [and ruled]. There is likewise the staple for all Indian commodities, whether all sorts of Marchants doe resort, coming thether both to buy and sell, out of Arabia, Armenia, Persia, Cambaia, Bengala, Pegu, Sian,[1] Malacca, Iava, Molucca, China, etc. . . . in Goa there come as well Gentlemen, as marchants

---

Source: The Voyage of John Huyghen van Linschoten to the East Indies, trans. and ed. A.C. Burnell and P.A. Tiele (2 vols, London: Hakluyt Soceity 1885) I: 177, 184–185.

---

[1]Siam, or Thailand.

[and others], and there are all kindes of Indian commodities to sell, so that in a manner it is like a Faire. This meeting is onely before Noone, everie day in the yeare, except Sondayes and holie dayes: it beginneth in ye morning at 7 [of the clocke] and continnueth till 9 [of the clocke], but not in the heate of the day, nor after Noone, in the principal streete of [the] Citie named the straight streete, and is called the Leylon, which is as much to say, as an outroop:[2] there are certain criers appointed by the Citie for ye purpose, which have of al things to be cryed and sold: these goe all the time of the Leylon or outroop, all behanged about with all sorts of gold chaines, all kindes of costly Iewels, pearles, rings, and precious stones: likewise they have running about them, many sorts of [captives and] slaves, both men and women, young and old, which are dayle sould there, as beasts are sold with us, where everie one may chuse which liketh him best, everie one at a certaine price. There are also Arabian horses, all kinde of spices and dryed drugges, sweet gummes, and such like things, fine and costly coverlets, and many curious things, out of Cambaia, Sinde,[3] Bengala, China etc. and it is wonderful to see in what sort many of them get their livings, which every day come to buy [wares], and at an other time sel them again. . . . There are some married Portingales, that get their livings by their slaves, both men and women, whereof some have 12, some 20, and some 30, for it costeth them but little to keepe them. These slaves for money doe labour for such as have neede of their helpe, some fetch water, and sell [it for money] about the streetes: the women slaves make all sorts of confectures and conserves of Indian fruites, much fine needle worke, both cut and wrought workes, and then [their maister] send the fairest and youngest of them well drest up with their wares about the streetes to sell the same, that by the neatnes and bewtie of the said women slaves, men might be moved to buy, which happeneth more for the affection they have to the slaves and to fulfill their pleasure with them, then for any desire to the conserves or needle workes: for these slaves doe never refuse them, but make their daylie living thereby, and with the gaines that they by that meanes bring home, their maisters may well keepe and maintaine them."

---

[2]"Leylon" means "auction," from the Portuguese *leilão*
[3]Sind. The Indus region of modern Pakistan.

■ A VOC Treaty with the King of Cochin

Rijkloff Van Goens was one of the leading figures of the VOC during the second half of the 17th century. Born in 1619, Van Goens had sailed to Batavia with his father in 1628. Orphaned soon thereafter, he had been placed in the household of the Dutch governor at Pulicat in India, where he learned much about the company's trade in India and demonstrated considerable business acumen and a ruthless efficiency in diplomacy. Between 1654 and 1663, Van Goens established his reputation as one of the most formidable military commanders in the Indian Ocean. His capture of five well-armed Portuguese carracks in 1654 earned him the title "Commissioner, Superintendent, Admiral, and General by land and by sea on the coasts of India, Coromandel, Surat, Ceylon, Bengal, and Melaka" in 1657. Named governor of Ceylon in 1662, Van Goens directed the final stages of the onslaught against the *Estado da India* on the Malabar Coast in late 1662 and early 1663, when his fleet captured Cannanore, Cranganor, and finally Cochin from the Portuguese.

As you read the treaty ending this campaign, what does it reveal about the overall strategy of the Dutch in the Asian trade. Why would indigenous powers agree to such pacts? Do you think this treaty was designed to facilitate primarily economic or geopolitical priorities for the VOC? What is the most important clause? Why do you conclude that? If you had to rank these articles from most important to least, from the perspective of the VOC, what would your list look like? Defend your rankings. What about the king of Cochin's perspective? How might he have viewed this contract in its entirety? Why does the VOC require that the contract be written on a golden scroll?

Article I: That there will always be a good, firm, & durable peace, union, and confidence among the parties which both assure.

Source: Treaty and Perpetual Alliance made between the VOC, by the Admiral Ryclof van Goens in the name of the Governor-general and Council of the Indies on the one part and Moetadavile, King of Cochin, and his princes on the other, 20 March 1663. Published in Jean Dumont, ed., *Nouveau recueil de traitez d'alliance etc. entre les rois, princes et etaits souverains de l'Europe, depuis la paix de Munster jusques MDCCIX* (2 vols, Amsterdam: F.L. Honoré 1710) I: 125–129, passim.

Article II: The king of Cochin cedes the right of this town & all the countryside & all the islands . . . in the same manner as the Portuguese possessed them, which rights he grants, cedes, and transfers to the Company, so that they may be eternally possessed by the Company.

Article III: The king of Cochin recognizes having been reestablished by the Company in his kingdom, & thus he accepts the Company as his Protector.

Article IV: The king of Cochin assures the Company that all the pepper and all the cinnamon that is found in his country . . . will be delivered to the Company alone, & and all the said pepper will be embarked from Cochin in the Company's ships, without any other nation having a share.

Article VI: The king of Cochin promises to give all the aide and assistance, in everything within his powers, for the execution of the fourth article & the others proceeding it, & require that he favor the Company with building three forts, one for the security of the Porca River, at the most convenient place of Gerea, and the third on Baypin, opposite the town, for the greatest security of Cochin, & in several other places, if they are needed.

Article VII: The Admiral promises in the name of the Company, to place a garrison for the security of the King & this Contract, in the town of Cochin, in the castle of Suna, at Palepot, Baypin & Porca, if it is judged necessary.

Article IX: All the Christians, who have traditionally have been in the jurisdiction of the town of Cochin & who dwell along the coastline, will be subjects to the Justice of the Judges, that the Company will establish at Cochin, under the authority of the governor of Ceylon.

Article XII: The king promises that he will prohibit pepper and cinnamon from being transported by land.

Article XIII: The plain, where at present all the coconut trees have been cut down surrounding the town, will not be replanted without the consent of the Company.

Article XVI: The merchants of this country, who carry on their commerce with the Company, will not be charged extraordinary impositions above the customary ones, unless on the consent of the Company, which protects them.

This Contract will be written in its entirety on a golden scroll and two paper copies, in the Malabar language and in Dutch which are the languages of the two parties. Thus agreed and concluded, as it is also signed in the Palace of the king of Cochin at Suna and in the town of Cochin, the 20th of March 1663.

■ The Purchase of Manhattan Island by the Dutch, 5 November 1626

Peter Minuit, born in Wesel in 1580, was a Walloon, or French-speaking, Protestant whose family fled from the southern Netherlands to the Protestant north during the Dutch Revolt. In the employ of the Dutch West India Company, Minuit reached the mouth of the Hudson River in May 1626 as the third director of the WIC in the colony of New Netherland, which had been established on the southern end of Manhattan in 1624. To bolster the colony, Minuit purchased the island of Manhattan from the Lenapes Indians for 60 guilders or the equivalent of $24.00 at the time. This new possession was called New Amsterdam, and the 270 Dutch settlers traded European goods for furs to be sold back in the Netherlands. Minuit served as director of New Netherland until 1633. The document below was presented to the States-General by Peter Schaghen, the government's representative on the Board of the *Heeren XIX* in the summer of 1626.

As you read this document, what evidence is given for the future prosperity of this new Dutch colony? What were the primary goals of the new settlers? Which American products were deemed appropriate for the European market? What would they be used for?

"High and Mighty Lords,

Yesterday the ship the *Arms of Amsterdam* arrived here. It sailed from New Netherland out of the River Mauritius on the 23d of September. They report that our people are in good spirit and live in peace. The women also have borne some children there. They have purchased the Island Manhattes from the Indians for the value of 60 guilders. It is 11,000 morgens in size [about 22,000 acres]. They had all their grain sowed by the middle of May, and reaped by the middle of August. They sent samples of these summer grains: wheat, rye, barley, oats, buckwheat, canary seed, beans and flax. The cargo of the aforesaid ship is:

7246 Beaver skins
178 1/2; Otter skins
675 Otter skins
48 Mink skins

Source: The letter of Peter Schaghen. From *The New Netherland Project: Documents* found at http://www.nnp.org/documents/schagen_main.html. The original document is in the Rijksarchief, The Hague.

36 Lynx skins

33 Minks

34 Muskrat skins

Many oak timbers and nut wood. Herewith, High and Mighty Lords, be commended to the mercy of the Almighty,

Your High and Mightinesses' obedient, P. Schaghen

Herewith, high and mighty Lords, be commended to the mercy of the Almighty. In Amsterdam, the 5th November, A. D. 1626.

Your High Mightinesses' obedient, P. Schaghen.

Received, 7th November, 1626."

■ An Early Description of Jakarta (Batavia) by Joris Van Speilbergen, 1616

Joris Van Speilbergen (1568–1620) was the second Dutchman to circumnavigate the globe between 1614 and 1617. He had previously sailed to West Africa (1596) and the Indian Ocean (1604–1607) in the service of various Dutch trading companies. In 1614, Van Speilbergen departed from the Netherlands with a six-ship fleet in the employ of the VOC. His goal was the spice-producing Molucca islands. Van Speilbergen's fleet sailed west through the Straits of Magellan, across the Pacific to the Philippines, where he engaged a Spanish fleet, before reaching the island of Java in 1616.

As you read the selection below, what is your impression of the status of the VOC on Java at this time? What challenges did the Dutch face in their attempt to break into the Indonesian trade? What methods and techniques did they employ in their campaign for Asian trade? What is the most interesting fact that Van Speilbergen presents in his description?

"On the 15th of September [1616] we arrived at Jacatra, and there our ships were caulked and coppered before loading; whilst we were doing this we were still constantly mindful of Don Jan de Silva's armada, for we were well aware and had been circumstantially informed that he was to come from Malacca to Bantam and Jacatra for the purpose of conquering us. On the 30th of the said month we received reliable

---

Source: The East and West Indian Mirror, being an account of Joris Van Speilbergen's Voyage Round the World (1614–1617) trans. and ed. by J.A. J. de Villiers (London: Hakluyt Soceity 1906), 149–152.

tidings of Don Jan de Silva's death at Malacca, which we opined to have been occasioned by poison, and that his fleet, being much weakened and diminished both in men and in stores, had started to return to the Manilles [Manila] . . . During the time that we lay at anchor at Jacatra several ships arrived from the Molucques, Banda, and other parts, laden with all kinds of spices for the account of the General Company [VOC]. Meanwhile vessels also arrived at various times from home, among them four ships of extraordinary size, well equipped with soldiers, sailors, stores, and large quantities of Spanish reals,[4] another that came from Japon, similarly laden with reals, and uncoined silver, besides copper, iron, and all kinds of good provisions, nearly all of which had been captured and taken by the conquest of a Portuguese ship proceeding to Macoro [Macao].

Among the aforesaid Dutch vessels was the ship *West Vriesen,* from Hoorn, on board of which some mutiny had been got up by 28 men who had intended to overpower the said vessel and make themselves masters of it; by the treachery having come to light, the ringleader of the aforesaid traitors was quartered at Bantam, some of them hanged, after their fingers had been cut off, and the rest, who were least guilty, condemned to the galleys and other forms of slavery. [October] On the 20th there arrived at Jacatra the ship named *Eendracht,* of Hoorn, under the command of Jacques le Maire, having set out from the Netherlands on the 15th July 1615, and come south of [the Straits of] Magellanes,[5] and whereas it was found that the said vessel was not associated with the General Company and that she had set out on this voyage without their orders, the President, Jan Pieterssen Coenen [Coen], confiscated the said ship on behalf of the General Company and transferred her crew to our vessels."

---

[4] A royal (*real*) silver coin, or dollar (*peso*), used in Spain and her overseas empire, sometimes called "pieces of eight," since eight *reales*=one *peso*.
[5] Le Maire's ship was the first European vessel to round Cape Horn on this voyage.

CHAPTER

4

The English and French Empires in the New World and Asia, ca. 1600–1700

PRIVATEERS AND THE PERIPHERY OF WORLD EMPIRE

In late 1522 Alonso de Avila y Benevides and Antonio Quinones, two of the Spaniards present for the conquest of Tenochtitlán, received a commission from Hernan Cortés. They were ordered to sail back to Seville with three caravels loaded with Charles V's share of Montezuma's treasure and other booty, including jaguars, macaws, parrots, and slaves. Avila and Quinones expected a royal welcome. Even though their cargo was only a part of the vast Aztec treasure, it was nonetheless impressive. As Cortés wrote to Charles V, it included "things so marvelous that they cannot be described in writing nor can they be understood without seeing them." The return voyage, however, was anything but profitable. As the heavily loaded ships made slow progress across the Atlantic, a fierce storm freed one of the jaguars, which managed to rip the arm off one man and the leg off another before jumping overboard. It took three months to reach the

Azores, where Quinones was killed in a bar fight over a local woman. Finally off Cape St. Vincent, in June 1523, the three ships were attacked by a fleet of French corsairs under the command of 'Jean Florin.' Two of the Spanish vessels, including the flagship with Charles V's share of the loot, were captured. Much to the glee of the Frenchmen, the Spanish ships held 680 pounds of pearls, 500 pounds of gold dust, cases of gold and silver ingots, and boxes of amazing jewelry. Not bad for a half day's work.

Seventy years later in August 1592, an English fleet organized by Sir Walter Raleigh and commanded by Sir John Burrough was cruising off the Azores also hoping to intercept a Spanish treasure fleet. Instead, a huge 1600-ton ship appeared. At 165 feet in length, it was the largest ship that any of the Englishmen had ever seen. The ship was the Portuguese carrack *Madre de Deus* returning to Lisbon from Goa. The ship's holds and decks were overflowing: 400 tons of pepper, 45 tons of cloves, 35 tons of cinnamon, 3 tons of nutmeg, diamonds, emeralds and other jewels, amber, and rich textiles. This lumbering monster was no match for more maneuverable English vessels. The captain-general of the *Madre de Deus* soon surrendered. The cargo taken was estimated to be worth nearly £500,000, or half of all the monies then in the royal treasury. It was a windfall for the fragile finances of Elizabeth I (r. 1558–1603), who was the 'chiefe' investor of the voyage.

These two episodes encapsulate the overseas fortunes of the English and French during the 16th century. Both internal and external factors served to marginalize and largely exclude these powers from the mainstream sources of the wealth of overseas expansion. Externally, this process began in 1494 at Tordesillas when D. João II of Portugal and Ferdinand and Isabella of Spain agreed to divide the rapidly expanding world of the Age of Discovery between them. This division was not only sanctioned by the papacy, it was also enforced by the military might of the Iberians. Internally, the 16th century had witnessed political and dynastic chaos in both England and France. Henry VIII had boldly broken with Rome over his divorce from Catherine of Aragon. But this act had led to dynastic and religious uncertainty, which sapped England's resources and energies. In France, much of the 16th century had been dominated by a bloody civil war, which also merged dynastic and religious elements. These developments ensured that the two kingdoms were condemned to operate on the periphery of the overseas world and its wealth. The English and French were reduced largely to the role of privateers living off the crumbs of the bountiful table enjoyed by Spain and Portugal. Only in the 17th century would these powers actively seek to undermine the power of the Iberians.

THE ENGLISH EMPIRE IN THE NEW WORLD
AND ASIA, 1500–1700

The initial steps in English expansion were designed to find, like Columbus, an alternate sea route to Asia by sailing west. This quest for a Northwest Passage would avoid the power of the Portuguese on the African coast, as well as the conquests of the Spaniards in the Americas. The Iberians had shown little interest in the North Atlantic, despite the fact that it was a huge fishery teeming with cod, a valuable source of protein for the early modern diet. The man who first staked England's claim to North America was John Cabot, or 'Giovanni Caboto.' Cabot, who had been born in 1451 in Genoa, believed, albeit incorrectly, that most of the spices from Asia came from the *northern* part of that continent. His project called for finding a shorter route to the Indies than Columbus by sailing in more northern latitudes. Henry VII (r. 1485–1509) of England proved to be a willing customer. The English king had rejected Columbus's plan and regretted it. Cabot also agreed to sail on "his own proper charges," meaning that the parsimonious Henry would not have to fund the expedition. In March 1496, Cabot received Letters-Patent that granted him "full and free authoritie, leave, and power, to sayle to all partes, countreys, and seas, of the East, of the West, and of the North, under our banners and ensign."

Cabot departed from Bristol in May 1497 with a small ship called the *Matthew* and fewer than 20 men. By late June, he reached the coast of North America, probably near Belle Isle, Newfoundland. Cabot claimed the land for Henry VII and explored the region for several weeks before returning to Bristol. For his pains, Henry granted him a pension of £20 a year. In 1498, John Cabot made another voyage. This time, Henry allowed him to impress, or conscript, English ships and sailors. His fleet of five ships departed in May. One ship returned to Bristol soon afterwards. As for Cabot, he "found his new lands only in the ocean's bottom, to which he and his ship are thought to have sunk, since, after that voyage, he was never heard of more." For England, however, the fundamental point was that Cabot had staked her claim to North America before his watery demise.

THE NORTHWEST PASSAGE

Sir Humphrey Gilbert thereafter became the champion of the search for a Northwest Passage. From 1576 to 1578, he backed the three voyages of Martin Frobisher to the Canadian Arctic. In November 1578, Gilbert himself outfitted and commanded a fleet of seven ships, which sailed from Plymouth for America. His fleet, however, was quickly scattered by storms. In 1583, he finally took a five-ship fleet to Newfoundland, which he claimed for Elizabeth I. Gilbert's work was continued in the decades that followed by explorers like Henry Hudson, who not only sailed up the river that now bears his name but also discovered the vast fur-producing region around the Hudson Strait and Bay.

PRIVATEERING AND PERMANENT COLONIES

While these efforts were underway, the English Crown and enterprising seamen employed more direct methods to share in the wealth of the New World. As everyone in Europe knew, the real money generated in the Atlantic World was tied to the slave trade and plantation economies of Spanish America and Brazil. Of course, the huge amounts of precious metals being shipped from Peru and Mexico through Havana on treasure fleets bound for Seville constituted an alluring jackpot. As early as the reign of Queen Mary (r. 1553–1558), English ships were visiting Guinea in search of slaves to sell in the New World. Under Elizabeth I the escalating war with Philip II facilitated bolder measures in the Atlantic. John Hawkins and his cousin Sir Francis Drake began slaving voyages in the early 1560s. Despite the Spanish monopoly (*asiento*), the pair easily bartered slaves on Santo Domingo. This trade came to an abrupt end when the pair and their small fleet were caught at anchor by a much larger Spanish force at San Juan de Ulua in 1568. The English suffered heavy losses, and only the ships of Drake and Hawkins managed to escape the carnage. This incident heightened Drake's hatred for Philip II and the Spaniards. In 1573 he exacted revenge by raiding the waters around Darien (Panama). With the assistance of French privateers and *cimaroons* (African slaves who had escaped from the Spaniards), Drake even captured the silver train from Peru as it neared Nombre de Dios. This act not only stunned the Spaniards, it also made Drake and his crew rich for life. On this voyage, Drake also climbed a tree on the Isthmus of Panama and became the first Englishman to glimpse the Pacific Ocean. From 1577 to 1580, Drake continued his exploits by completing the first circumnavigation of the globe by an Englishman. This voyage exposed the weaknesses of Iberian imperial pretensions, something the defeat of Philip II's armada of 1588 reconfirmed. In the following decades Elizabethan England undertook a much more aggressive colonization campaign in both the New World and Asia.

In the New World, these schemes were centered in more temperate regions than the early voyages of exploration near Newfoundland. The man who was instrumental in establishing the initial English outposts in the New World was Humphrey Gilbert's half brother, Sir Walter Raleigh, one of Queen Elizabeth's favorites. In 1584, Raleigh received a 10-year royal patent on exploration in the New World, which gave him proprietary rights over all territory he occupied in the New World upon payment of one-fifth of the precious metals mined in those lands. In seeking a base for operations, both Elizabeth and Raleigh wanted a site that could provide New World wealth, as well as afford a strategic location from which to attack the annual Spanish treasure fleets. In April 1584, Raleigh sent out an exploratory voyage, which cruised along the coast of North America from Florida to North Carolina. These lands were given the name Virginia, and in 1585, Raleigh underwrote the first colonization scheme under Sir Richard Grenville on Roanoke Island. The colonists, however, who had embarked mainly in search of gold, abandoned the place when Drake appeared in 1586. In 1587, 117 colonists were sent out to Roanoke under John White. Problems with the local Indians forced White to return to England looking for assistance. After several delays, he returned to Roanoke in August 1591, only to find that the whole colony had disappeared without a trace.

It was not until the reigns of the Stuart kings James I (r. 1603–1625) and Charles I (r. 1625–1649) that successful permanent settlements were established, facilitated by James I's more cordial relations with Spain. A theory of settlement and empire had also emerged by this time based on economic, religious, political, and social principles. Economically, the New World colonies could enrich the Crown (through customs duties) and private citizens (by investments) alike by providing commodities that were in demand. In an age when a country's wealth was judged by the amount of gold and silver it possessed, the most important of these products was precious metals. Fish was also coveted especially since the English had traditionally imported large quantities from Dutch middlemen. Wine and other luxury goods usually imported from Portugal and southern Europe might also be obtained. Finally, the vast virgin forests of North America could provide timber and other naval stores for the emerging English navy. Traditionally these goods had been imported from the Baltic also through Dutch middlemen. Religiously, the desire to spread the Gospel certainly existed among English Protestants. As John Smith noted in Virginia, "The gaining of provinces addeth to the King's Crown; but the reducing heathen people to civility and true religion bringeth honour to the King of Heaven." Politically, anti-Spanish sentiments and the need for New World strongholds from which to attack Spanish America also formed part of the theory of settlement. Socially, widespread unemployment and the rapid growth of cities like London had led to the belief that England was overpopulated and that the New World was a necessary destination for this surfeit of subjects.

Nevertheless, one chronic problem for the English Crown in the quest for overseas empire had been the shortage of sufficient money for these projects. English monarchs were still dependent on essentially medieval forms of taxation, which were far less lucrative than the taxes paid to many other European rulers of the age. Elizabeth had overcome this difficulty by skillfully accepting the profits of privateers like Drake. By the initial decade of the 17th century, both Elizabeth and especially James I would also embrace the nascent joint-stock company model to underwrite the financial commitments of colonization.

VIRGINIA AND MASSACHUSETTS

In 1606 a Virginia Company was incorporated. Initially it contained the twin Virginia Company of London and the Virginia Company of Plymouth. Although these joint-stock companies possessed identical charters they were designed to colonize different areas of the Atlantic seaboard of North America. The London Company had permission to establish a colony from the 34th parallel to the 41st parallel (roughly Cape Fear to Long Island Sound). The Plymouth Company had a similar grant between the 38th and 45th parallels (from around Chesapeake Bay and the contemporary border between Maine and Canada). In the overlapping territory, the Companies were prohibited from setting up colonies within one hundred miles of each other. The London Company was largely the work of Sir Thomas Smythe, a prominent merchant who had earlier helped to organize the East India Company. He served as treasurer of the London Company until 1619 and was instrumental in sending out the colonists who entrenched the young colony.

The first Company fleet sailed in December 1606, with 144 men aboard. In May 1607, these settlers landed on Jamestown Island and established their settlement on the banks of the James River. They were soon able to "beare and plant palisadoes" for a small wooden fort. But there were many difficulties. These included the antipathy of the Algonquins and the need to either find or grow sufficient quantities of food. In fact, only 60 of the original 214 colonists were able to survive the "starving time" winter of 1609–1610. Nevertheless, thanks to the efforts of Captain John Smith and others, the colony managed to survive. Following the marriage of Pocahontas, the daughter of the Algonquin chief Powhatan, to John Rolfe in April 1614, a period of relative peace and prosperity followed.

Rolfe also came upon the crop that would ensure the survival not only of Jamestown but of the English colony in Virginia: tobacco. The local tobacco was judged to be too harsh for European tastes, but as early as 1612, Rolfe began to experiment with sweeter and more aromatic West Indian varieties. By 1617, the colonists were growing enough of this crop to send a shipment to England. Thanks in part to the public relations campaign of Walter Raleigh and the English tour of Rolfe and Pocahontas in 1616–1617, it soon became a fashionable habit. With relatively low prices, this consumer boom lasted throughout the 17th century, despite the diatribe of James I against the "manifold abuses of this vile custom of tobacco taking." To facilitate the expansion of tobacco production on plantations, African labor, first as indentured servants and then as slaves, was imported into the colony from Angola by 1620. In 1624, the Virginia Company was dissolved, and Virginia became a royal colony.

In 'northern Virginia,' the Plymouth Company had less success. The Company attempted to establish a colony along the Kennebec River (Maine) in 1607. But by 1608, this settlement was a complete failure. The rocky soil and harsh climate in 'northern Virginia' prevented any serious attempts at settlement until the 1620s, when James I chartered the Plymouth Council for New England. This grant included lands from present-day New Jersey in the south to Nova Scotia in the north. Sir Edwin Sandys, Treasurer of the Company and a man with

PHOTO 4.1   View of Tobacco, 17th Century.   A New World crop encountered by Columbus, tobacco was believed to have medicinal applications especially for digestion. This belief and its narcotic properties ensured its rapid exportation around the globe. In this Dutch illustration, Cupid carries the pipe and pouch since its pleasures, like lovemaking, were fleeting.

Purtian sympathies, allowed the Pilgrims to settle in the northern sector of the Company's holdings. The *Mayflower* and its Pilgrim passengers reached Cape Cod in November 1620 and founded Plymouth Colony. The 1620s and 1630s witnessed the relatively rapid settlement of the New England region by the English. The Massachusetts Bay Colony in the area around Boston was the most important. In 1629, a powerful group of Englishmen, mostly Puritans, had formed the Massachusetts Bay Company to settle this region.

This was, however, a chaotic period in English history. Charles I, striving for Absolutism, ruled without Parliament for eleven years (1629–1640). Archbishop Laud also enforced a hard line toward religious 'dissenters.' As a result, the kingdom lurched toward Civil War and Revolution. Laud's religious persecution of dissenters also led to an increasing flow of Puritan settlers to Massachusetts. Led by stern religious ideologues, such as John Winthrop, these colonists established a community with a special covenant with God—"a city upon a hill" to quote Winthrop's famous phrase. The colonists celebrated their first Thanksgiving in July 1630. As in Jamestown, however, there were great difficulties. Lack of food, disease, and harsh weather claimed over 200 colonists during the first winter. Warfare with the surrounding native American tribes continued throughout the century, most bloodily in the Pequot War of 1637 and King Philip's War with Metacom and the Wampanoag in the 1670s. Nevertheless, held together by the harsh discipline of Winthrop and his successors, the colony grew. As early as 1631, there were over 2,000 people living in the Massachusetts Bay Colony. The political problems in England of the 1630s led to a huge influx of settlers during that decade, and the population of New England was around 20,000 in 1640. By 1700 the number of colonists in what had began as 'northern Virginia' had probably reached 100,000.

THE CARIBBEAN, SOUTH AMERICA, AND THE "TRIANGULAR TRADE"

While John Winthrop and his successors were creating their own version of God's plan on earth, Oliver Cromwell and his Puritan supporters strove for similar ends at home in England. The Civil War culminated in January 1649 with the execution of Charles I. The English Republic, or Commonwealth (1649–1653), and Cromwell's rather dictatorial rule as Lord Protector (1653–1658) followed. Cromwell believed that he had been chosen by God to purify a decadent England. Just as important, the gentry and merchants of London who supported him expected a rigorous extension of the English empire overseas. In this quest, breaking the power of the Dutch was pivotal. The 1651 Navigation Act, which decreed that all goods flowing into and out of England had to be carried in English ships, was a first salvo. The First Dutch War of 1652–54 escalated the struggle, which brought the English into the Caribbean and South America in a more substantial way.

Earlier, the English had settled on the more peripheral islands of the Caribbean and had attempted several settlements on the South

American mainland. In 1623, Thomas Warner began to colonize St Christopher (St. Kitts). Warner was granted a Royal Commission from Charles I in 1625 for the islands of St. Christopher, Nevis, Barbados, and Montserrat. Nevis was settled in 1628 and Antigua and Montserrat in 1632. On Barbados, Captain Henry Powell landed in February 1627 with 80 settlers and 10 slaves to settle the island. By the end of the 1630s, sugarcane also had been introduced. Not surprisingly, the demand for slaves and indentured servants rapidly increased. In 1655 Cromwell sent an expedition to the Caribbean which took Jamaica from the Spaniards. The English also established South American bases at Guyana and Surinam. All of these colonization efforts in the Caribbean and South America pitted the English against the Dutch West India Company as well as the entrenched power of the Spanish empire.

By the mid-17th century, the English position in the New World was relatively secure. Nevertheless, while the power of the Spanish Crown was weakening in both Europe and America, that of the Dutch was still strong. As noted in Chapter 3, the Dutch West India Company had effectively challenged the power of Spain in the Caribbean and Portuguese holdings in Brazil. The Second (1664–1667) and Third (1672–1674) Dutch Wars were fought as a result of the commercial and imperial competition between the two Protestant powers. The optimism following the Restoration of Charles II in 1660 had led to a much more aggressive commercial policy vis-à-vis the Dutch. English privateers attacked Dutch ships at will. In January 1664, Robert Holmes captured several slaving outposts of the WIC along the West African Coast. In August 1664, Colonel Richard Nicolls compelled the surrender of New Amsterdam, dealing a death blow to the Dutch colony of New Netherland. The settlement on Manhattan island was quickly renamed New York in honor of Charles II's brother, James, duke of York. In 1672, a reconstituted monopoly company for the African trade called the Royal African Company was formed. Between 1680 and 1688 this company sent an average of 5,000 slaves a year to the New World. By 1698, the clamor to allow all merchants, especially those from West Country ports such as Bristol, to also engage in this lucrative trade convinced Parliament to open up the trade, and in a brief period of time, the average number of slaves transported per year rose to 20,000.

By 1700, the English had thus established the basis for a New World Empire that would flourish down to the American Revolution

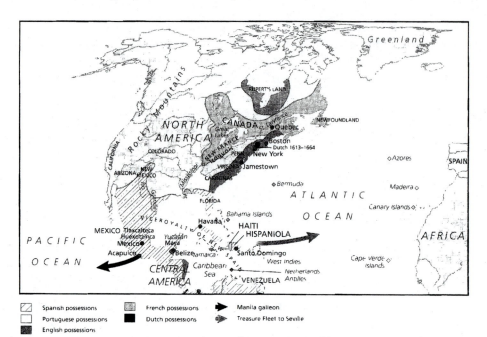

MAP 4.1   Land Empires in North America, ca. 1700

(see Map 4.1). A lucrative trading system, usually known as the 'tri-angular trade,' had also developed. This trade exploited resources and products found throughout the empire. These included the vast fisheries and forests of New England, the tobacco and cotton of the southern colonies, the sugar, molasses, and rum of the Caribbean islands, the slaves of West Africa, and the manufactured goods of England. These products were bought and sold in various combinations by English merchants. Several 'triangular' or 'quadrangular' routes were possible. London and Bristol merchants could send ships loaded with firearms, tools, other manufactured goods, and liquor (especially rum) to West Africa and trade for slaves. After the grueling 'Middle Passage' of up to 10 weeks between Africa and the New World, the slaves who survived (perhaps 75 percent) were sold to the plantations in the Caribbean and Brazil for sugar, molasses, and rum, which commanded huge profits in Europe. Of course, slaves were also sold in the North American colonies as well, in return for fish, lumber, and other naval stores, which were also in demand at home. Alternatively, merchants in Boston or Newport might send their ships loaded with New England products like fish and lumber and sail directly to the Caribbean, where these good were in demand and obtain sugar, molasses, and rum. These goods could then be taken either to West Africa and exchanged for slaves or to England and exchanged for manufactured goods that were in demand in the colonies. The most notable feature of this complex trading network was that it usually yielded profits for the merchants involved and in doing so did much to entrench the English empire in the New World.

THE ENGLISH EAST INDIA COMPANY

In the aftermath of Drake's successful circumnavigation of the globe and the defeat of the Spanish Armada, English merchants, such as Sir Thomas Smythe, were also emboldened to challenge for share of the rich Asian spice trade. On 31 December 1600, Elizabeth I granted a monopoly charter of 15 years to the "Governor and Company of Merchants of London Trading into the East Indies." The Company initially had 125 shareholders, a capital of £72,000, and was run by a governor and 24 directors. Smythe had been instrumental in organizing the Company and arranging the charter from the queen. He also served as its governor for most of the next 20 years.

As with the Dutch, the initial problem for the English was developing a strategy for taking on the imperial edifice of the Portuguese. While the Dutch received their answer from Jan Huyghen van Linschoten, the English received much-needed intelligence from Ralph Fitch. In January 1583, Fitch departed with a group of merchants for Asia via the traditional route through the Levant. After sailing across the Mediterranean and stopping in Aleppo in Syria, the English embassy crossed southern Mesopotamia to Baghdad and continued down the Tigris river to Basra by July 1583. Fitch then sailed down the Persian Gulf to the great Portuguese fortress of Hormuz.

In Hormuz, Fitch and his companions were arrested as spies in October 1583 and sent in chains to Goa. The viceroy D. Francisco de Mascarenhas had them interrogated and held in prison until late December. As Fitch wrote, they "were charged as spies, but they could prove nothing by us." Finally, thanks to a 2,000 ducat bond put up by the English Jesuit Thomas Stevens, Fitch was liberated with the stipulation that he remain in Goa. By April 1584, however, he had seen enough of Portuguese hospitality and fled. Fitch traveled around much of north India and eventually reached the court of the Mughal emperor Akbar at Fatehpur Sikri. He then spent the years 1585–1588 sailing down the Ganges and visiting Bengal, Pegu, Burma, and Malaysia, before reaching the Portuguese stronghold of Melaka (Malacca). He finally returned to London in April 1591. Once home, he wrote on his vast experiences and consulted with Smythe and others on the details of the Asian trade and the power of the Portuguese.

RIVALRY WITH THE DUTCH IN INDONESIA, ca. 1600–1623

Initially, the English, like the Dutch, decided to concentrate their activities where the power of the Portuguese was judged to be weakest: Indonesia. In 1591, even before the East India Company (EIC) was formed, some merchants sent out a three-ship fleet of exploration and privateering under James Lancaster. Lancaster departed from Plymouth and reached the Malaysian Peninsula in June 1592. He spent the next four months seeking to intercept and capture every ship he could but with limited success. After a voyage to Ceylon, his crew forced him to sail home. Lancaster reached England in May 1594 with only one ship and 25 men remaining. Fortunately, he was able to redeem himself in 1594–1595, when he sacked Pernambuco in Brazil and returned with a huge cargo of booty. As a result, Smythe and the EIC Directors selected Lancaster to command the first fleet of the Company in 1601. This five-ship fleet cost the Company £40,000 to outfit. Another £6,860 was spent on purchasing English goods to sell or trade. Lancaster was also given £21,700 to buy spices and other goods in Indonesia.

The fleet enjoyed great success. Lancaster reached Indonesia by June 1602. Like the Dutch, he discovered that many of the local sultans had tired of the Portuguese. As a result, he negotiated a commercial treaty with the sultan of Acheh in northwestern Sumatra. Lancaster also established the first English factory in Indonesia at Bantam on Java, sent an envoy to the Moluccas, and returned with a rich cargo of spices in September 1603. As a reward, he was knighted by Elizabeth I. The second voyage of the Company (1604–1606) under Henry Middleton followed a similar route to Acheh, Bantam, and the Moluccas and enjoyed a similar degree of financial success. Nevertheless, this

promising beginning was tempered by both internal and external problems. First, the EIC down to 1614 was not a true joint-stock company.
Each voyage was subscribed separately and the profits divided at the
end. This meant that it was difficult for the English to compete against
the much better subscribed VOC, which had a huge permanent joint
stock capital pool for operations. From 1614 to 1657, the EIC used short-
term joint stocks. It was not until Cromwell's 1657 Charter that the EIC
finally embraced a permanent joint stock pool. Thus, organizationally
and materially, the EIC paled in comparison with the VOC during these
early decades. From 1602 to 1625, while the Dutch were sending hundreds of ships to Indonesia, the English were sending dozens.

During these decades, the English slowly expanded their activities in Indonesia in the face of growing Dutch opposition. In addition
to the Bantam factory, settlements were set up on Makassar, the Banda
islands of Run and Nailaka, as well as on Amboina in the Moluccas.
The Dutch did their best to undermine the English diplomatically by
deriding them as pirates to the local sultans. Using its superior naval
power, the VOC also harassed EIC shipping in the archipelago. As
noted in Chapter 3, this campaign culminated under governor-general
Jan Pieterszoon Coen. The most controversial act in this campaign of
aggression was the Amboina massacre of March 1623, when Gabriel
Towerson and 20 others were beheaded on the orders of the Dutch
governor of the island, Herman Van Speult. The backlash against this
act lingered throughout the remainder of the century. Van Speult's
actions, however vicious, were effective in undermining the EIC in
Indonesia. The Java factory, shifted to Batavia in 1619 as part of an
accord with the Dutch, returned to Bantam in 1628 and continued to
function until 1682. But it was clear that huge profits for the London
Company would not result from the Indonesian trade.

THE SHIFT TO PERSIA AND INDIA, ca. 1620–1700

The English Directors had already decided that the Company would
have to diversify its trading activities. This realization was occasioned by the traditional difficulties the Europeans had in selling
their goods, such as woolens, in tropical Asia to purchase spices and
other commodities. Consequently, all of the European powers
needed to develop an intra-Asian trade network to avoid sending
out huge quantities of bullion. Indian cotton textiles could easily be

exchanged in Indonesia and elsewhere for spices and other products. India, therefore, became one of the foci of the English from the early years of the Company. Smythe also decided that it was preferable to set up trading activities in areas where strong local powers could protect them from Dutch attacks. The period from ca. 1606 to 1639, therefore, witnessed attempts to gain formal trading privileges from strong indigenous powers, such as the Shah of Persia, the Mughal emperor, the Zamorin of Calicut, and the king of the Muslim sultanate of Golconda.

In India, the position of the EIC was consolidated thanks to two factors: (1) a succession of embassies to the Mughal court of the emperor Jahangir (r. 1605–1625); and (2) a string of naval victories off Surat over the Portuguese. The embassies began with the Third Fleet (1606–1607) under Captain Keeling, which anchored off Surat in August 1608. William Hawkins, who had worked for the Levant Company and knew Turkish, then disembarked as James I's ambassador to the Mughal court. Hawkins spent two years at Agra, and Jahangir was favorably impressed. He even took him into his service and promised "that he, the Emperor, would allow him £3200 a year with increase till he came to 1,000 horse. So my first should be 400 Horse. For the nobility of India have their titles by the number of their Horses from 40 to 12,000, which pay belongeth to Princes." But the intrigues of Portuguese Jesuits and the Dutch at court ultimately forced Hawkins to leave empty handed. By the Voyage of 1610 under Henry Middleton, the directors had decided to make India and Surat the EIC's "main and principal scope." Middleton reached the Gulf of Cambay in late 1611. Rebuked by Mughal officials under pressure from the Portuguese, he then spent most of early 1612 harassing shipping in the area and fighting skirmishes with the Portuguese that impressed Jahangir's officials. In September 1612, Thomas Best also added to the maritime reputation of the English by forcing a superior Portuguese fleet to withdraw from the Gulf of Cambay. The English received permission to set up a factory at Surat in 1613. This important trading concession was solidified first by Nicholas Downtown's naval victory in January 1615 over a large Portuguese fleet of 11 ships and some 3,000 men under the command of the viceroy D. Jerónimo de Azevedo. Finally, the embassy of Sir Thomas Roe to Agra from 1615 to 1619 reconfirmed the royal *farman* for Surat and helped extend it to other parts of the Great Mughal's domains. Factories were soon set up in Agra, as well as in the textile centers of Ahmadabad and

Broach. One ship a year was sent back to London from Surat in the years 1615–1620, two in 1621 and 1626, three in 1622, 1625, and 1629, and seven in 1628.

Once established in Surat, principal entry port for the Mughal empire and embarkation point for the hajj traffic to Mecca, it was logical for the EIC to expand its operations to the Red Sea and Persian Gulf. Once again, the main problem was the power of the Portuguese, and especially their fortress at Hormuz. Relations with the Safavid ruler Shah Abbas (r. 1588–1629) were improving, and the Company directors were anxious to import Persian silks. The Portuguese were keenly aware of these plans. In 1619, a fleet under Ruy Freire de Andrade arrived in the Gulf region to destroy foreign competitors and to enforce the long-standing pass system. In late 1620, four English ships under Andrew Shilling held their own against Andrade's fleet. In 1621, nine English ships arrived near the Portuguese forts at Hormuz and Qeshm. The Persians and Portuguese were warring openly, and the Persians asked the EIC for assistance in attacking these strongholds. Although there were risks involved, the English decided to take a chance. The ensuing sea and land siege resulted in the capture of Qeshm in February 1622, with the loss of only three Englishmen, including the Artic explorer William Baffin. In late April, Hormuz fell after a bloody siege, in which 20 English and more than a thousand Persians were killed. Shah Abbas was overjoyed with the expulsion of the Portuguese from his domains. The EIC received half the spoils from these fortresses and the right to half the custom duties at Hormuz, later transferred to Gombroon (Bandar Abbas).

The trading activities of the EIC, however, remained relatively modest in comparison with those of the Portuguese and Dutch. In India, additional factories were set up at Calicut, thanks to an agreement with the Zamorin, and in the powerful sultanate of the Golconda on the Coromandel, or southeast, Coast at Masulipatnam (1611, 1632) and in 1639 at Madras, where Fort St. George was built a few years later. Farther north, the EIC also set up factories at Balasore in Orissa (1633) and in Bengal at Hugli (1651). In Southeast Asia, a grant from Sontagam, king of Siam, permitted an English trading post at Ayutthaya (1611). The Company's administrative structure owed much to Keeling, the first "Factor-general and Supervisor" in Asia. Keeling placed the factories "to the Northwards," meaning those in the Persian Gulf region, Gujarat, and Malabar under the control of the Surat factory; and those "to the Southwards," meaning the Coromandel Coast of India to the east under the supervision of Bantam. By 1618, the chief factors in Surat and Bantam had taken the title of President. But during the period from ca. 1625 to 1661 the EIC did its best merely to survive. Complications engendered by the Thirty Years' War (1618–1648), the uncertainties of Charles I's reign, the Civil War, the Commonwealth, and Cromwell's Protectorate all took a toll. During the First Dutch War of 1652–1654, the servants of the EIC did their best to exploit the protection provided by their indigenous hosts, well aware of the military superiority of the VOC.

Economically, returns on investments never equaled those made with the First Joint Stock (1613–1621), whose capital of £418,691 had yielded a profit of nearly 88 percent. The Second Joint Stock (1617–1632), which yielded a 12 1/2 percent profit, and the Third (1631–1642), which yielded 35 percent, were still respectable. But the impact of the Civil War was reflected in the Fourth (1642–1649) and United (1650–1655) Joint Stocks which were lucky to break even. The Company's monopoly was not even secure. In 1635 and 1637, Charles I granted charters to Sir William Courteen to enter the Asian trade. As the king declared, "[The East India Company has] neither planted nor settled a trade in these parts, nor made such fortifications and places of surety as might encourage any hereafter . . . neither have we received any annual benefit from thence." The Courteen Associates did much to undermine the Company's activities over the next 15 years.

Matters improved marginally in October 1657 when Cromwell granted the Company a new charter. This document sanctioned a permanent joint-stock capital pool. It was only after the Restoration of 1660, however, that several key events facilitated the recovery and expansion of the Company's activities. First, in April 1661, Charles II granted a charter that reconfirmed the points in the 1657 document. A permanent joint-stock pool was reconfirmed: the Company could detain and repatriate any interlopers; it could make war and peace with non-Christian rulers; and it could exercise civil and criminal jurisdiction in its settlements. Second, as part of his dowry for the marriage alliance with Portugal in that same year, Charles II received the island of Bombay, along with Catherine of Braganza. The new Portuguese governor of the *Estado da India*, Antonio de Mello de Castro, refused to turn over the place until 1665. By 1668, Charles II had tired of the expenses related to the settlement and leased it to the EIC for £10 a year in gold. Blessed with a fine harbor and a strategic location on the west-central coast of India, Bombay finally provided the EIC with the independent base for operations that it had lacked. During the next 30 years, and especially thanks to the policies of Gerald Aungier, head of the Western Presidency from 1668 to 1677, Bombay prospered. Aungier expanded the town, fortified it, and assured its economic position by offering religious freedom in the enclave. Rich Hindu, Jain, and Parsi merchants in the neighboring Portuguese Province of the North, who had long suffered under a series of anti-Hindu laws, flocked to Bombay with their families and capital. One sign of this rapid economic expansion was that income from the tobacco tax increased threefold in less than a decade. By 1690, the seat of the Presidency was shifted from Surat to Bombay in recognition of this newfound wealth and power. Meanwhile, at Fort St. George in Madras on the east coast, the wise policies of William Langhorn produced similar results. Langhorn also offered religious freedom to attract Hindu, Jewish, Armenian, and Catholic merchants to the settlement. He even encouraged the construction of a large Catholic church in Madras some 20 years before the first Anglican church was established.

By 1700, the English empire in both the Atlantic World and the Indian Ocean Basin was therefore on sound footing. Despite the political and social upheavals of the 17th century, England was poised to become the predominant imperial power at the start of the 18th century. In fact, England emerged stronger as a result of these struggles. The long struggle with Habsburg Spain had been won. As part of the treaty of Utrecht (1713), which ended the War of the Spanish Succession, England legally shared in the lucrative slave trade, or *asiento*, of Spanish America. Thanks to the marriage treaty of 1661 and the Methuen Treaty of 1703, Portugal also had become a trusted ally. As for the Dutch, they had been largely defeated in the Atlantic World; New Amsterdam had become New York. William of Orange was king of England. In Asia, the EIC had survived the crucial period of 1623 to 1674 when the VOC had both the military power and motivation to extinguish the English Company. That opportunity had been missed, and by 1700, the EIC was well positioned for the future. In fact, the English Company had already demonstrated a greater appreciation of the shifting tastes of European consumer society by increasing its share of the textile trade and the importation of tea—crucial commodities of the 18th century. Ironically, the great global warfare of the 18th century for England would not be fought against Spain, the Netherlands, or Portugal. Rather it would take place with another power, which like the English, had been largely excluded from the Iberian-dominated overseas world of the 16th century: France.

THE FRENCH CHALLENGE, ca. 1500–1600

The campaign to win an overseas empire for France began when Francis I (r. 1515–1547) declared his intention to contest the division of the overseas world between the two Iberian powers that was enshrined in the Treaty of Tordesillas. He declared, "The sun shines on me just the same as on the other; and I should like to see the clause in Adam's will that cuts me out of my share in the New World." Francis was perhaps the greatest ruler of the Valois dynasty. A contemporary of Henry VIII and Charles V, this Renaissance king had extensive and expensive distractions both within his kingdom, including disturbances caused by the Reformation, and in Europe, where he fought long-standing wars, especially for dominance in Italy. Yet, Francis I, as a reflection of his power, wanted an overseas empire to compete with his rivals. If his retainers could find an alternative route to Asia, the accompanying wealth would enhance his reputation and provide much-needed cash for his ongoing wars and the extensive building campaign in the Loire valley.

In 1524, Francis I first underwrote an expedition under Giovanni da Verrazano to find the Northwest Passage. Although Verrazano failed in this attempt, he did claim Newfoundland for France, and then explored a good portion of the eastern seaboard of America, which he called *Francesca,* honoring his royal patron. During the next decade, Francis I was too busy warring in Italy to exploit this promising start. The French king, captured at the battle of Pavia (1525), was even held a prisoner by Charles V for more than a year. It was only in 1534 that he financed an expedition under Jacques Cartier in search of a passage to Asia and "certain islands and lands where it is said there are great quantities of gold and other riches."

THE VOYAGES OF JACQUES CARTIER, 1534–1544

On his first voyage, Cartier reached Newfoundland in May 1534. He then explored the region and traded for furs with the local Micmac Indians. From them, he learned of a large river to the west which he thought might offer the passage to Asia he sought. Cartier found the St. Lawrence River and claimed the region for Francis I. Cartier's second voyage began in May 1535 with three ships and more than 100 men. This time, he sailed up the St. Lawrence to the Huron village of Stadacona, today Québec City. Cartier then continued on to Hochelaga, today Montreal, in October. Since it was too late to return to Europe, Cartier and his men spent the winter in Stadacona after building a small fort and stocking it with food. The Frenchmen remained until the following May and survived an outbreak of scurvy thanks to an Indian drink called *annedda* made from the white cedar tree. When Cartier returned to France, he brought the Huron chief Donnacona with him so that he might relate the story of the "Kingdom of Saguenay" farther north, which was supposedly rich in gold and precious stones. His second voyage had revealed the vast extent of the St. Lawrence and the rich potential trade in furs.

Cartier's third voyage began in May 1541. Instead of continuing the elusive search for the Northwest Passage, this expedition of five ships was charged with finding the "Kingdom of Saguenay," and establishing a permanent settlement on the St. Lawrence. Cartier attempted his own settlement some 10 miles upriver from Stadacona at *Cap-Rouge* (Red Cape). He named the settlement Charlesbourg-Royal. There, the colonists and convict-exiles landed along with the cattle brought to assist the colony. As winter approached, the French labored to built cabins surrounded by a palisade. Another small fort was built overlooking the site. Some of the colonists also began searching for precious metals. Quartz cyrstal and iron pyrites were mistaken for diamonds and gold. In early September, Cartier sent these samples home on two ships. Throughout the winter of 1541–1542, conditions deteriorated. The Hurons became increasingly hostile, scurvy broke out, and Cartier waited in vain for the arrival of the *sieur* de Roberval, who had been charged by Francis I with colonizing Canada. In June 1542, the remaining settlers left for home.

Francis I had named Roberval "Lieutenant-general in the Country of Canada." Jean-François de La Roque de Roberval, a well-connected courtier, was expected to build fortified towns and churches and to "spread the Holy Catholic Faith." He received £45,000, as well as convict-exiles, to begin the colony. Roberval re-established the settlement at Charlesbourg-Royal. He also explored the St. Lawrence to the rapids at Montreal as well as the Saguenay River in search of gold. The harsh winter of 1542–1543 took its toll. Extreme cold, a poor diet, and the spread of disease exacerbated grumblings among the convicts, who were already upset over the lack of ready wealth in the new colony. Roberval dealt harshly with these men, hanging six in a single day. From his arrival in Canada, he had misgivings and a ship had returned to France asking the king for help. Francis I sent a rescue mission in 1543 but Roberval and what remained of the expedition had already deserted the colony and sailed for home.

The 16th-century attempts to find a Northwest Passage to Asia and to colonize Canada had been failures. Francis I died in 1547, and for the remainder of the century, France was consumed by the Wars of Religion, which made any government-backed attempt at colonization impossible. Some nobles and merchants did fund private voyages. Many of these expeditions left from the Atlantic ports of Normandy and Brittany where merchant capitalism was developing, especially among the Huguenots. French fishing fleets continued to visit the cod-rich grounds off Canada, and fur trading took place with the Huron, Iroquois, and other tribes. In ports like Rouen and Dieppe, with a strong interest in textiles, the dyeing potential of *pau-brasil* attracted interest. As early as 1503–1504, a French ship had reached the Brazilian coast in search of this valued wood. By far the most important French attempt to establish a presence in Brazil was the France Antarctique scheme of 1555–1560. Nicolas Durand de Villegagnon, a Huguenot, with a fleet of three ships and 600 men, reached the Bay of Guanabara, today Rio de Janeiro, in November 1555. Fort Coligny was established on a deserted island in the bay. For the next five years, the colony held out despite a lack of support from the Crown and Villegagnon's harsh rule. As noted in Chapter 1, only in 1560 when the Portuguese governor-general Mem de Sá arrived with a large military force were the French eventually expelled.

THE FRENCH EMPIRE IN CANADA AND THE CARIBBEAN, 1600–1700

It was only at the beginning of the 17th century, with the new Bourbon dynasty under Henry IV (r. 1589–1610) and Louis XIII (r. 1610–1643), that colonial schemes again received royal support. In 1608, two years before his assassination, Henry IV supported the first successful settlement in Canada, or New France, under the direction of Samuel de Champlain. Champlain was an experienced explorer who had sailed in the Caribbean. He returned to France in 1602 and received a pension from Henry IV and an appointment as royal geographer. The following year he sailed for the first time to New France. Champlain explored the St. Lawrence region and parlayed with local tribes for information on the great inland waterways, including Lakes Erie and Ontario, the Detroit River, and Niagara Falls, before returning to France. In the spring of 1604 he served as historian for the expedition of Pierre Du Gua de Monts to Acadia (today, Nova Scotia), which founded the *habitation* at Port-Royal (1605). In 1605 and 1606 Champlain remained in New France, exploring the Atlantic Coast of North America as far south as Cape Cod. The most tangible result of these early expeditions was his famed 1607 map of these regions.

In early July 1608, Champlain founded his *habitation* at Québec. During his first winter there, 19 of the original 28 colonists died due to scurvy and other diseases. Nevertheless, the settlement took hold thanks to Champlain's determination and his involvement in Indian

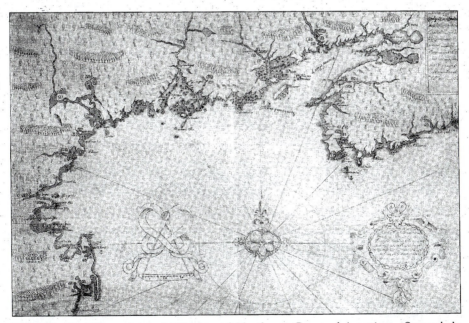

PHOTO 4.2 Champlain's 1607 Map of Northeast Coast of America. Samuel de Champlain's map was based on his personal exploration of this coast from 1603–1607. He intended to present it to his patron, King Henry IV. Champlain's meticulous eye for useful detail includes French coastal settlements as well as Indian villages from Cape Sable to Cape Cod.

warfare. This intervention began in 1609 when he forged an alliance with the Hurons and the Algonquins against the Iroquois. In the ensuing campaign, Champlain explored the Rivière des Iroquois, found the large lake that now bears his name, and defeated a small party of Iroquois in a skirmish in upstate New York near Ticonderoga (July 1609). In this battle, Champlain's skill (or luck?) with an arquebus played a notable role, when he killed two Iroquois chiefs with a single shot. This act impressed his Huron allies but also helped turn the Iroquois into enemies for most of the next century. Flushed with victory, Champlain returned to France and arranged a favorable marriage with Hélène Boullé, then only 12 years old. As part of the marriage contract, she remained with her parents for two years and did not reach Québec until 1620.

By April 1610, Champlain was back in New France. He spent the next two decades extending his knowledge of this vast area and entrenching French power in North America. In 1611, Champlain shot the rapids of Lachine with the Huron and founded La Place Royale, near present-day Montreal. Louis XIII named Henry, Prince of Condé, lieutenant-general of New France, and Champlain his lieutenant. The attraction of Asia, however, still exerted a strong influence, and Champlain was also ordered to find a passage to China and India. This explains his subsequent search for the Great Northern Sea (Hudson Bay). To implant the French presence in Canada, Champlain encouraged young Frenchmen to live with the Hurons and other tribes, and to learn their languages and customs. These men, known as *coureur de bois* (literally, forest runners, or scouts), lived from the fur trade and spread French influence into the Great Lakes area. Champlain also worked for the conversion of the Hurons and other tribes to Roman Catholic Christianity by bringing out five priests from the Augustinian Recollect Order in 1615. Although a shaky alliance was reached with the Iroquois in the mid-1620s, tensions thereafter mounted with the English. Champlain was even forced to surrender Québec to an English fleet in 1629, and the place was recovered only in 1632. Champlain returned to New France as commander of the colony in 1633 at Cardinal Richelieu's behest. He died on Christmas Day 1635, having done much to launch the French empire in North America.

As the 17th century progressed, the Crown took a more active interest in colonial ambitions in the New World. Richelieu supported Champlain's activities by founding the Company of One Hundred

Associates in 1627. This Company enjoyed a monopoly for the fur trade, but experienced difficulties from the outset. Competition from the English, problems with the Iroquois, resentment over the fur monopoly, and the demands of the Thirty Years' War all undermined its activities. In 1663, the Company voluntarily surrendered its charter. Richelieu exported his religious policies to New France as well.

Mirroring his campaign against the Huguenots at home, he stipulated that only Catholics could live in the colony; Protestants were required to convert or leave. Many did, for English settlements. Richelieu also introduced *seigneurialism* to the New World. Lands were divided into *seigneuries*, granted to a *seigneur*, who enjoyed economic and labor obligations from his tenants. In France, *seigneurs* were overwhelmingly noble, but in New France, military officers, the Catholic Church, and local associations were sometimes granted these lands in return for their service to the Crown. Thanks to inheritance laws which allowed women to inherit a husband's property, about half the *seigneuries* of New France were actually controlled by women in 1663.

The minority of Louis XIV (1643–1661) was a period of uncertainty for the colony. Above all, the number of settlers remained very small. The fur trade was also in disarray as a result of the victories of the Iroquois over the Huron. Beginning in the early 1660s, however, this period ended with the policies of Louis XIV's great minister, Jean-Baptiste Colbert. Colbert strove diligently to rationalize and improve France's financial and overseas situation. He was one of the foremost proponents of mercantilism–a bellicose economic theory that postulated a fixed amount of wealth in the world. To increase one's share of this wealth mandated that it be taken from those powers with a larger share, especially the Dutch and the English. Colbert placed New France under the direct control of the Crown in 1663. For better defense against the English and the Iroquois, he despatched a regular regiment to Québec. Adminstratively, the governor-general and a royal intendant were placed under the control of the minister of the Navy (Colbert).

Richeleu's Company was also forced to renounce its monopoly. Colbert then appointed a new royal intendant for justice, police, and finance, Jean Talon. Talon's mission was to extend royal control and to gauge the colony's resources. He conducted a systematic census in 1665–1666, which recorded name, age, occupation, and martial status. Talon also recorded manufacturing and agricultural resources, domestic animals, *seigneuries*, royal buildings, and churches. In the end, Talon estimated that there were 3,215 people of European background in the colony, 2,034 men and 1,181 women. Colbert and Talon then sought to formulate policies based on these data to improve the colony. To assist the economy, new roads and bridges were built. To address the disparity between men and women, some 900 *filles du roi* were sent to New France between 1665 and 1673. As Talon wrote in 1673, "the number of settlers has increased significantly as a result of the King's decision to send young women from France and by the marriage of these women to the soldiers stationed in the colony." There had been 700 births from these marriages in 1671 alone. By 1690, there were over 8,000 settlers in New France. Talon, following Colbert's model in France, also did much to encourage new manufacturing enterprises and sought to reform the *seigneurial* system by requiring the *seigneurs* to reside on their lands or lose them.

The results of Colbert's campaign were mixed. Once Louis XIV's European wars began in the late 1660s, Crown support dwindled for New France. While the population increased, this was due to internal reproduction, not emigration from France. Moreover, the ca. 8,000 subjects in Canada paled in comparison to the ca. 100,000 then in English colonies. Talon's new industries developed slowly and never surpassed the value of the fur trade. More problematically, the English reached Hudson Bay and James Bay, set up the Hudson Bay Company, and broke the long-standing French monopoly in the fur trade. To offset this, the French expanded south around the English colonies on the Atlantic seaboard. In the early 1680s, René Robert Cavelier, *sieur* de La Salle, explored the Ohio and Mississippi River valleys, and claimed this huge territory for France all the way to the Gulf of Mexico. La Salle called this new French colony Louisiana, in honor of his king. To connect these lands with Canada, a string of fortresses was built.

Emulating the imperial policies of its rivals, France also constructed a more profitable empire than its holdings in North America in the Caribbean, West Africa, and South America. In 1635, Richelieu's *Compagnie des Îles de l'Amérique* took the islands of Guadeloupe and Martinique. Pierre Belain, *sieur* d'Esnambu, landed on Martinique with 100 settlers and founded Saint-Pierre. The forests were cleared and tobacco and cotton planted. To facilitate the development of a plantation economy, Louis XIII authorized the importation of black slaves from Africa in 1642. By mid-century, sugarcane had also been introduced. By the chaotic 1650s, the Crown had sold the *seigneurial* rights of the island to Dyel Duparquet. Colbert wanted more effective Crown control. He purchased the rights to the island from Duparquet's heirs in 1664 and placed it under the auspices of his West India Company. In 1674, Martinique became part of the king's royal domain. By 1700, the population was over 6,000 and the sugar economy was flourishing. On Guadeloupe, a similar scenario played out. In the 1630s, French pirates had settled on the island of Tortuga off Hispaniola (Santo Domingo). During the following decades the French began to occupy the western portion of the larger island. By 1664, French influence was such that Colbert included the island in his plans for the West India Company. In 1697, Spain formally granted the western half of the island to Louis XIV. Exploiting slave labor, Saint-Domingue became one of the richest colonies in the world in the following century, producing 40 percent of France's sugar.

To procure slaves for these lucrative Caribbean plantations, the French established a presence on the western coast of Africa at Senegal in the 1620s. In 1659, a French slaving station was rebuilt at the mouth of the Senegal River, and the French captured the island of Gorée from the Dutch in 1677. From these outposts, French trading companies bought slaves to the New World. In South America, the French set up a colony in Guyana, despite the almost constant harassment from the local Amerindian population, as well as the Dutch and the English. The French, like the English, Dutch, and Portuguese, had therefore constructed an Atlantic empire that stretched from Canada to South America, from the Caribbean to West Africa. New France was rich in land and natural resources but very sparsely populated; Martinique and Guadaloupe were short on land but rich in population and sugarcane. As with their rivals, the 'triangular' trade across the Atlantic powered by exploited African labor made the entire system function. The plantation economies of the Caribbean were so lucrative that when forced to make a choice at the end of the Seven Years' War in 1763, the French Crown chose to retain these small Caribbean islands instead of the huge land mass it had carved out in Canada.

THE FRENCH EMPIRE IN THE INDIAN OCEAN BASIN, 1500–1700

French ambitions in the Asian trade began as early as the reign of Louis XII (1498–1515) and Francis I. In 1503, a group of Rouen merchants outfitted two ships for a voyage to India. These ships departed from

Le Havre, but no records exist on their fate. Francis I issued declarations in 1537 and 1543 exhorting his subjects to undertake long ocean voyages, and some enterprising men listened. Portuguese sources record the presence of a French ship on the west coast of India in 1527. The following year, the *Marie de Bons Sécours* was seized by the Portuguese in Asia. In 1530, the two French vessels reached Sumatra. For the remainder of the 16th century, however, the principal involvement of French mariners in the Asian trade was the attempts of corsairs to intercept returning Portuguese carracks richly loaded with Asian goods. These attacks generally took place off the Azores and periodically yielded results. It was only after the societal chaos of the Wars of Religion ended and the reign of Henry IV began that government-backed efforts to break into the monopoly of the Portuguese in the spice trade began in earnest.

In November 1600, the Company of Eastern Seas was formed with a capital pool of some 80,000 *écus*. This Company sent two ships to the East Indies but met with little success. In 1604, Henry IV granted a trading monopoly in Asia to a 'Society for the Voyage to the East Indies,' but this Company was soon undermined by a lack of private investment, Portuguese and Dutch opposition, the continued preeminence of continental foreign policy aims, and the internal strife during Louis XIII's minority. In vain, the Crown attempted to instill new life into the project in July 1619 by transferring monopoly privileges to a reconstituted entity, the Moluccan Company. This Company managed to send the marginally successful expedition of Antoine Beaulieu to Sumatra and Java, but for the next 20 years nothing much was accomplished. Richelieu also tried his hand at creating a viable East India Company. By Letters-Patent of June 1642, monopoly privileges were granted to the *Compagnie d'Orient*. Nevertheless, the cardinal's scheme to colonize Madagascar (Isle-Dauphiné) eventually bankrupted it. Private attempts between 1655 and 1662 under the auspices of the *maréchal* de La Meilleraye and Nicolas Fouquet also failed.

Down to Colbert's time, therefore, French attempts at mercantile expansion to the Indian Ocean were sporadic and unsuccessful. Yet, this unimpressive legacy would be fundamentally altered during the 10 years beginning in 1664. Based on his theory of finite global wealth, Colbert believed it was imperative to challenge Dutch supremacy in world trade for France to prosper economically. In the early 1660s, he was content to do this by waging a 'peaceful' economic war against the United Provinces with a series of tariffs. Colbert believed that the key to Dutch economic power was the huge profits made from the Asian trade. Break the power of the VOC, and the prosperity of Amsterdam would crack. To that end, in September 1664 he founded the Royal East India Company with a projected capital pool of 15 million *livres*. Unlike earlier French attempts, Colbert's Company was initially backed by serious material and monetary support from the Crown. The Company's first fleet sailed for Madagascar in 1665, and the following year a large squadron of 14 ships and 1,700 men also made for the Isle Dauphiné. The capital outlay on these two fleets was substantial: 2,765,300 *livres* out of a pool of 5,415,916 *livres* that the Company possessed by July 1667. Despite Colbert's efforts to raise investment from the middle class, nearly 2 million had come directly from Louis XIV and most of the rest from noble courtiers. Colbert's Asian initiative thus remained dependent on support from a Crown and nobility that continued to view this campaign as merely an extension of Europe's dynastic struggles.

Colbert relied heavily on the advice of the enigmatic merchant adventurer, François Caron. During his long career with the VOC, Caron had amassed knowledge of the Asian trade matched by few Europeans of the age. He was especially well versed in matters relating to Japan, Siam, Ceylon, and Indonesia. Louis XIV's ambassador in the United Provinces exploited Caron's resentment against the VOC, as well as offering financial and honorific inducements, to attract him to Colbert's Company in 1665. Caron's plan for undermining the VOC was simple. The French should exploit the hostility toward the Dutch that existed among various Asian kingdoms to facilitate the foundation of French trading factories from India to Indonesia. Caron also wanted the Company to acquire an exclusive trading entrepôt, where subsequent economic and political operations could be based. From 1665 to 1670, a series of factories was established in Persia and India but administered from Surat. Caron also negotiated with the Zamorin of Calicut, the rajah of Kandy on Ceylon, and the king of Bantam.

Notwithstanding these efforts and the heavy capital investment of the Crown, the new Company was plagued by problems. The French suffered from a lack of familiarity with the quality, prices, and buying seasons for the products in the trade. Caron, for all his experience, was much more in touch with the intricacies of the South China Sea trade than with that of India. His 15-year hiatus in Europe had also weakened his grasp of the changing commercial and political realities in the region. Consequently, the French frequently overpaid for inferior merchandise. The French also had to become acquainted with the subtleties of the sailing routes, anchorages, and alternating monsoons of the Indian Ocean . The Company, moreover, was forced to forge links with indigenous powers in the face of strong opposition from the Dutch, English, and Portuguese. France's rivals had invested much time and money to gain trading concessions throughout Asia. As a result, the French were often forced to pay large gratuities to off-set this influence, expenditures that quickly drained the Company's coffers. By 1669, the future did not appear bright. As Gerald Aungier, the EIC chief in Bombay, wrote, "The French have utterly lost their Creditt as well for Merchants as Souldiers by their great debts and indiscreet management of their affaires." The existence of these prob-lems reached Colbert's ears in January 1669. Colbert responded by writing a long report. He admitted mistakes. In Paris, the directors had erred in sending out fleets that were too large and costly without first possessing adequate information on what awaited them. "These great expenses of the first fleets would have been capable of com-pletely ruining the Company, if it had not been sustained not only by the protection, but also by the great sums of state revenues that the King liberally gave it." On Madagascar and in Surat the problems were "great and considerable," with over 470,000 *livres* wasted. Colbert recommended that the directors should only send a few ships out each year, watch expenditures closely, and sell returning products in prime seasons. As for Asia, he declared that the Crown was searching for a *homme de guerre* who would help solidify the young Company and French ambitions in the trade.

By March 1669, Colbert was convinced that the only way to break Dutch economic power was to wage a military war against them. In Europe, Louis XIV was busily preparing to attack the United Provinces for dynastic and geopolitical reasons. The 'ingrate' Dutch had frustrated Louis's 'just' attempt to grab the Spanish Netherlands (Belgium) in 1667–1668. For the only time in the reign the dynastic priorities of the Sun King and the economic priorities of Colbert matched: the power of the burghers of Amsterdam would have to be destroyed.

The decision to dispatch the Persian Squadron of 1670 was the culmination of Colbert's Asian strategy. It was timed to take advan-tage of, and complement, the approaching continental war against the Dutch. Given the state of affairs in Europe and Asia, Colbert's plans had a real chance of destroying Dutch dominance in the Asian trade while establishing France as a major power in the developing world economy. In May 1669, Colbert informed his cousin and navy inten-dant Colbert de Terron of the king's intention to send a royal fleet to the Indian Ocean together with three *Compagnie* ships. Colbert's esti-mate of one man-of-war of 60 guns, and five of 40 to 50 guns show that it was to be a formidable fighting force. His cousin should select ships "of a quality which will easily make known the grandeur and dignity of our Majesty in those far away countries." Colbert de Terron was instructed to assemble the fleet by early 1670 with as much secrecy as possible. In the meantime, Colbert did his best to facilitate the mission of the squadron by negotiating for a triple anti-Dutch alliance in Asia with the English and the Portuguese.

In March 1670, the Persian Squadron departed, one of the most powerful European fleets to sail to Asia to that time. Five well-armed royal men-of-war, a frigate, and three storeships made the voyage, carrying well over 2000 men, including Colbert's recently formed *regiment royal de la marine*. The expenditures in outfitting this fleet reflect the seriousness of the Crown, at least initially, toward the "eastern enterprise." At departure, the cost was more than 1,000,000 *livres*. An experienced officer, Jacob Blanquet de La Haye, com-manded the fleet with the title of lieutenant-general for Louis's Asian possessions. His instructions empowered La Haye to appoint gover-nors in the lands he occupied, "on the islands or *terre firme*, in Africa and Asia from the Strait of Gibraltar to the Indies." Upon reaching India, La Haye should take the title of viceroy. Significantly, Colbert also instructed La Haye to follow the wishes of the Company direc-tors in Asia, particularly Caron, who was said to have a "profound" knowledge of everything that should be done for the Company's advantage.

The subsequent history of the Persian Squadron did not live up to this promising beginning. Madagascar was reached only in November 1670, long after the sailing season for India had ended. Consequently, the squadron was forced to 'winter' there. La Haye spent the next eight months fighting an ill-conceived war with several Malagasy tribes who refused to submit to French authority. The fleet finally reached Swally Hole, the anchorage for Surat, in early October 1671. After talks with Caron, it was decided to first make for Goa and then to Ceylon, one of the main targets in Colbert's instructions. Negotia-tions in January 1672 with the Portuguese viceroy Luis de Mendonça Furtado, however, proved stillborn. The squadron did reclaim the village of Alicot, expelling a Dutch garrison in the process. But this success was more than offset in an encounter with a VOC fleet under Rijkloff Van Goens, the Dutch governor of Ceylon. Caron, using his powers from the Crown, prevented La Haye from engaging this fleet, an action that caused "much discontent and murmuring from most of the captains and officers of the fleet" who had voted to attack.

The French squadron anchored at the bay of Trincomalee on Ceylon in March 1672, and began to fortify key positions in the bay. Nevertheless, a subsequent blockade by Van Goens and Caron's inexplicable refusal to open hostilities against the Dutch forced La Haye to sail for the Coromandel Coast of India in early July. On 20 July, the fleet anchored before the town of St. Thomé, then under the control of the Qutb Shahi Muslim sultanate of Golconda. La Haye's request for supplies was refused and his envoys treated "disrespectfully." In retaliation, the French captured the town in late July. The storming of St. Thomé was the only triumph for the Persian Squadron. Ironically, it was ill-advised. This act created serious complications for La Haye's fleet. First, it alienated the English and Portuguese. The English were jealous of a French settlement only three miles from Madras, while St. Thomé had been under Portuguese control for more than a century until their expulsion by the sultan of Golconda in 1662. Of more immediate concern was the fact that La Haye had invited retaliation from that same indigenous power. Abul Hasan, the Qutb Shahi ruler, wanted to demonstrate his power to all concerned, including the Mughal emperor Aurangzeb who had expansionist designs in the south. Soon an army of over 8,000 men was sent to reclaim the town.

Caron, sensing the outcome, put his private treasure aboard a ship and departed in October for Europe. This hasty departure proved fatal for the controversial director, as he was lost when his ship went down in the Tagus River near Lisbon in 1673. Meanwhile, La Haye's heavily outnumbered forces fought well during the ensuing siege, which lasted for nearly two years. As long as it was possible to resupply by sea, the French could hold out against the besieging army of Golconda. But in June 1673, Van Goens appeared with a large Dutch fleet, which blockaded the French by sea. La Haye's efforts were also undermined by a lack of support from the EIC in Madras. Despite the fact that Charles II had joined the European war against the Dutch, William Langhorn, governor of Fort St. George, refused to support the French. More damning was a lack of reinforcements from France. Once the European campaign began, Louis XIV's focus shifted almost exclusively to operations there. As a result, the colonial projects of Colbert in Asia, like those in New France, suffered. The huge sums of money, manpower, and sea power that had funded the foundation of the Company and the Persian Squadron ended. La Haye received no reinforcements after departing from Goa in January 1672. Given the overwhelming odds he faced at St. Thomé, this lack of support was the primary factor in his defeat. The French surrendered in September 1674.

The destruction of the Persian Squadron constituted a devastating setback for French economic and political ambitions in the Indian Ocean. The military and financial losses associated with the fleet, the unchallenged primacy of continental foreign policy aims for the remainder of Louis XIV's reign, and Colbert's gradual eclipse from power all ensured that the level of Crown support for colonial projects that had characterized the years 1664–1672 was never repeated during the 17th century. Nevertheless, the French Company attempted to continue operations. Able employees like François Martin based at the settlements granted to the Company from 1664 to 1674 at Surat and Pondicherry did their best. It was difficult, however, to overcome the legacy of La Haye's defeat and the Crown's subsequent neglect. In 1683, the year of Colbert's death, the Company's monopoly privileges were suspended. The rather makeshift semiprivate operation that followed stood little chance of competing in a market system dominated by the entrenched institutional edifices of the Dutch and English and a reforming Portuguese *Estado da India*. During the War of Spanish Succession (1701–1713) French trading activities in Asia came to a virtual halt. Louis XIV's love of dynastic warfare had seriously undermined France's chance for a sizable Asian trade. Only in the years after his death would a revitalized *Compagnie des Indes Orientales* begin to make strides and win the type of economic and political power in Asia that Colbert had hoped to achieve half a century earlier.

SOURCES

■ Huron Society through French Eyes

Samuel Champlain was not only one of the most intrepid and important of the early French explorers in North America, he was also a prolific writer regarding his exploits. There were financial, as well as political, reasons for Champlain's desire to share his experiences through the printed word. Throughout Europe there was a strong interest in reading travel accounts about distant and exotic places. Thanks to the accounts of Marco Polo and others, a general knowledge about the routes and cultures of the Middle East and Asia existed in early-17th-century Europe. But the reading public's fascination with the "New World" was still unfulfilled and thus very strong. Men like Champlain were exploring a terra incognita, and this fact fueled demand for publications on their expeditions. Thus, Champlain could make money from these books, and self-promotion with the Crown was also not a bad thing. Given these realities, Champlain never failed to include his name in the titles of his works. As early as 1598, he had written his *Brief discourse on the many remarkable things that Samuel Champlain from Brouage encountered in the West Indies.* Some of his early published works included *Savages: Or Voyage that the Sieur de Champlain made in the year 1603* (n.d.) and *The Voyages of the Sieur de Champlain Saintangeois, 1604–1613* (1613).

As you read this selection from his 1619 book, how would you rate Champlain's skills as an objective observer? Provide specific examples to support your evaluation. How would the daily existence for the Huron compare to life for the French peasantry of the same period? How would the role of women compare in the two cultures? Would this description encourage the French Crown to underwrite future expeditions? Explain your answer. Compare Champlain's description of the Huron with Columbus's description of the Tainos more than a century earlier. What strikes you as more significant, the similarities or the differences? What do you conclude from your comparative analysis of these two accounts?

Source: Samuel de Champlain *Voyages to New France: Being an Account of the Manners and Customs of the Savages and a Description of the Country, with a History of Many Remarkable Things that Happened in the years 1615 to 1618,* trans. Michael Macklem (Ottawa: Oberan Press 1970), 76–85.

The Huron country lies in latitude 44° 30' and is seven hundred miles from east to west and thirty from north to south. Like Brittany,[1] it is almost completely surrounded by water. The land is fertile and most of it is cleared. There are about eighteen villages, of which six are really fortified towns, with stockades surrounding the living quarters. The stockades are made of wooden stakes set in three rows and lashed together, with galleries behind from which the defenders can throw boulders down on the enemy or pour water on him if he tries to set fire to the defenses.

The population of the country is about thirty thousand, of which two thousand are warriors. They live in lodges made of bark . . . At one end of each lodge there is an open space where they store their Indian corn in large casks made of bark. Mice are everywhere and everything they want to keep safe, such as food or clothing, has to be hung up on wooden pegs. The average lodge will have a dozen fires and two dozen families. The smoke inside is thick and blinding and diseases of the eyes are common, in fact many of the older people have lost their sight altogether. The trouble is that there are no windows and so there is no way for the smoke to escape except through a single hole in the roof. . . .

They are a happy people, even though their life is wretched by comparison with ours. They have never known anything better, so they are content with what they have. The staple of their diet is Indian corn mixed with red beans and cooked in a variety of ways . . . Their clothing is made from skins of all sorts. Some of these they get by skinning their own game; others they get in exchange for corn, meal, beads, and fishnets from the Algonkins and Nipissings who are great hunters . . . . They decorate their clothes with colored bands made out of glue and strips of skin . . . .

For the most part the people are cheerful and good-natured, though some are surly enough. Both men and women are strong and well-built. Many of the women and girls are attractive and have good figures, clear skin, and regular features. Most of the young girls have good breasts. The women do much of the work around the house and in the fields, sowing the corn, gathering the wood, stripping and spinning the hemp, making fishnets. They are expected to harvest the corn and store it, cook the meals and take care of the house. They are in fact no better than beasts of burden. As for the men, they do nothing but go hunting and fishing, build the lodges and fight the wars. When they have nothing else to do, they go trading in other parts of the country. On their return they eat and drink and dance until they can stay awake no longer. This is all they know of work.

---

[1]An Atlantic province of France situated on a peninsula.

■ The Dutch through English Eyes

Sir Josiah Child (1630–1699) came from a prominent London merchant family. After serving an apprenticeship in the family business, he struck out on his own during the Commonwealth by serving as a supplier to the navy. Assisted by Cromwell's aggressive foreign policy, he made a fortune and invested a good portion of it in the English East India Company. Thanks to these heavy investments, Child became a member of the board of directors in 1677, deputy governor, and finally governor. His brother Sir John Child, sent to live with an uncle who was head of the English factory at Rajapur, also worked for the EIC. By 1682, John Child had become head of the Company's operations in Surat and Bombay, while Josiah became governor in London. In the 1660s, Josiah Child began dabbling in economic theory, publishing under the pseudonym "Philopatris." In these works, he strongly advocated the importance of the East India Company and its monopoly.

As you read this selection, why do you think he focused on the Dutch as a model? How do you think English society in the late 1660s compared with the Dutch? What is the most surprising part of the Dutch system in your view? Which of these atributes would you adopt in establishing an ideal social climate for trade? Did these Protestant 'virtues' differ from those in Portugal and Spain?

The prodigious increase of the Netherlanders in their domestick and forreign Trade, Riches, and multitude of Shipping, is the envy of the present, and may be the wonder of all future Generations: And yet the means whereby they have thus advanced themselves, are sufficiently obvious, and in a great measure imitable by most other Nations, but more easily by us of this Kingdom of England, which I shall endeavour to demonstrate in the following discourse.

Some of the said means by which they have advanced their Trade, and thereby improved their Estates, are these following:

First, They have in their greatest Councils of State and War, trading Merchants that have lived abroad in most parts of the World;

Source: Brief Observations Concerning Trade and Interest of Money by Josiah Child (London, Printed for Elizabeth Calvert at the Black-spread Eagle in Barbican, and Henry Mortlock at the Sign of the White-Heart in Westminster Hall, 1668) 1–3. Available on The Avalon Project, Yale University, http://www.yale.edu/lawweb/avalon/econ/trade.htm.

who have not onely the Theoretical Knowledge, but the Practical Experience of Trade, by whom Laws and Orders are contrived, and Peaces with forreign Princes projected, to the great-advantage of their Trade.

Secondly, Their Law of Gavel-kind, whereby all their Children possess an equal share of their Fathers Estates after their decease, and so are not left to wrastle with the world in their youth, with inconsiderable assistance of fortune, as most of our youngest Sons of Gentlemen in England are, who are bound Apprentices to Merchants . . . .

Fourthly, Their giving great incouragement and immunities to the Inventors of New Manufactures, and the Discoverers of any New Mysteries in Trade, and to those that shall bring the Commodities of other Nations first in use and practise amongst them; for which the Author never goes without his due Reward allowed him at the Publique Charge . . . .

Sixthly, Their parsimonious and thrifty Living, which is so extraordinary, that a Merchant of one hundred thousand pound estate with them, will scarce spend so much per annum, as one of fifteen hundred pounds Estate in London.

Seventhly, The education of their Children, as well Daughters as Sons; all which, be they of never so great quality or estate, they always take care to bring up to write perfect good hands, and to have the full knowledge and use of Arithmetick and Merchants Accompts; the well understanding and practice whereof, doth strangely infuse into most that are the owners of that quality, of either Sex, not onely an ability for Commerce of all kinds, but a strong aptitude, love, and delight in it; and in regard the women are as knowing therein as the men, it doth incourage their Husbands to hold on in their Trades to their dying days, knowing the capacity of their Wives to get in their Estates, and carry on their Trades after their Deaths: Whereas if a Merchant in England arrive at any considerable Estate, he commonly withdraws his Estate from Trade, before he comes near the confines of old Age, reckoning that if God should call him out of the World, while the maine of his Estate is engaged abroad in Trade; he must lose one third of it, through the unexperience and unaptness of his Wife to such Affairs, and so it usually falls out.

Besides, It hath been observed in the nature of Arithmetick, that like other parts of the Mathematicks, it doth not onely improve the Rational Faculties, but inclines those that are expert in it to thrifiness and good Husbandry, and prevents both Husbands and Wives in some measure from running out of their Estates, when they have it always ready in their Heads what their expences do amount to, and how soon by that course their ruine must overtake them . . . .

Elevently, Their Toleration of different Opinions in matters of Religion: by reason whereof many industrious People of other Countreys, that dissent from the Established Government of their own Churches, resort to them with their Families and Estates, and after a few years cohabitation with them, become of the same Common interest.

■ Mercantilism through the Eyes of Jean-Baptiste Colbert

Jean-Baptiste Colbert was one of Louis XIV's most powerful ministers from 1661 until his death in 1683. During these years, he reformed French finances and for a time succeeded in doubling the king's income. Colbert was one of the foremost proponents of the economic theory of mercantilism, which included the establishment of overseas colonies. As minister of the navy and colonies, he was instrumental in seeking a French empire in both the Atlantic World and the Indian Ocean Basin during the 17th century. Louis XIV's continental wars, however, eventually undermined Colbert's reforms and his power at court. The following selections come from his *Memorandums on Commerce* of 1664 and 1669.

As you read the texts, try to define mercantilsm as he envisioned it. For example, did mercantilists like Colbert believe in a fixed or unlimited amount of wealth in the world? What methods were acceptable in seeking more economic power? How would an increase in trade benefit the king and his people?

Memorandum of 1664

Sire, it pleases Your Majesty to give some hours of his attention to the establishment, or rather the re-establishment of trade in his kingdom. This is a matter that purely concerns the welfare of his subjects but that cannot procure Your Majesty any advantage except for the future, after it has brought abundance and riches among his people . . . it will be well to examine in detail the condition to which trade was reduced when His Majesty took the government into his own hands [1661]. As for internal trade and trade between [French] ports: The manufacture

Source: Lettres, Instructions et Mémoires de Colbert, ed. Pierre Clément (7 vols, Paris: Imprimerie Impériale 1861–1882) II: 263, 268–271; VI: 263–264.

of cloths and serges[2] and other textiles of this kind, paper goods, iron-ware, silks, linens, soaps, and generally all other manufactures were and are almost entirely ruined. The Dutch have inhibited them all and bring us these same manufactures, drawing from us in exchange the commodities they want for their own consumption and re-export. If these manufactures were well re-established, not only would we have enough for our own needs, so that the Dutch would have to pay us in cash for the commodities they desire, but we would even have enough to send abroad, which would also bring us returns in money-and that, in one word, is the only aim of trade and the sole means of increasing the greatness and power of this State.

As for trade by sea, whether among French ports or with foreign countries, it is certain that, even for the former, since in all French ports together only two hundred to three hundred ships belong to the subjects of the King, the Dutch draw from the kingdom every year, according to an exact accounting that has been made, four million *livres* for this carrying trade, which they take away in commodities. Since they absolutely need these commodities, they would be obliged to pay us this money in cash if we had enough ships for our own carrying trade. As for foreign trade: It is certain that except for a few ships from Marseilles that go to the Levant, maritime trade in the kingdom does not exist, to the point that for the French West Indies one-hundred-fifty Dutch vessels take care of all the trade, carry there the foodstuffs that grow in Germany and the goods manufactured by themselves, and carry back sugar, tobacco, dyestuffs, which they [the Dutch] take home, where they pay customs duty on entry, have [the commodities] processed, pay export duties, and bring them back to us; and 'the value of these goods amounts to two million *livres* every year, in return for which they take away what they need of our manufactures. Instead, if we ran our own West Indies trade, they would be obliged to bring us these two million in hard cash. Having summarized the condition of domestic and foreign trade, it will perhaps not be inappropriate to say a few words about the advantages of trade.

I believe everyone will easily agree to this principle, that only the abundance of money in a State makes the difference in its greatness and power . . . . Aside from the advantages that the entry of a greater quantity of cash into the kingdom will produce, it is certain that, thanks to the manufactures, a million people who now languish in idleness will be able to earn a living. An equally considerable number will earn their living by navigation and in the seaports.

---

[2]Worsted wools.

Memorandum of 1669

> One can advance with certainty that the commerce of all Europe is carried on by ships of every size to the number of 20,000, and it is perfectly clear that this number cannot be increased, since the people are always equal in number in all of these states, and that consumption is likewise equal, and of this number of 20,000 ships, the Dutch have 15 to 16,000, the English about 3 to 4,000, and the French 5 to 600 . . . . Commerce causes perpetual combat in peace and in war among the nations of Europe, as to who shall win most of it . . . . [T]hese last two[3] cannot improve their commerce save by increasing the number of their ships, and they cannot increase this number, save from the 20,000 which carry all this commerce, and consequently by making inroads on the 15 to 16,000 of the Dutch.

■ New England through Puritan Eyes: John Winthrop's *City upon a Hill Sermon*, 1630

John Winthrop (1588–1649) was born in Suffolk, England, and studied at Trinity College, Cambridge, and law at Gray's Inn. In the 1620s, he worked as a lawyer in London. Like many of his generation, Winthrop became a fervent Puritan, who believed that the Church of England (Anglican Church) had to be 'purified' of Catholic rituals and dogma. Moreover, he believed that God would punish England for this heresy. He and other Puritans therefore sought shelter and a new life. Winthrop was elected governor of the Massachusetts Bay Colony in 1629, and in April 1630 he commanded a large fleet of ships and 700 colonists that sailed for the New World. Although Winthrop labored diligently to entrench this new Puritan colony over the next two decades, he is best known for his "A Modell of Christian Charity" sermon, more popularly known as the "City upon a Hill" sermon, delivered at the outset of the expedition.

As you read this selection, what does it tell you about the relationship between the secular and the divine in the 17th century? For Winthrop, did the Puritans enjoy a special relationship with God?

---

[3]England and France.

Source: Collections of the Massachusetts Historical Society, 3rd Series (10 vols, Boston: Little, Broan 1838), VII: 46–48.

Would God bless and assist their new colony? What was the price of this support? How do you think English Anglicans would have reacted to this sermon in 1630? How about in 1650?

Now the only way to avoid this shipwreck and to provide for our posterity is to follow the Council of Micah,[4] to do Justly, to love mercy, to walk humbly with our God, for this end, we must be knit together in this work as one man, we must entertain each other in brotherly Affection, we must be willing to abridge our selves of our superfluities, for the supply of others necessities, we must uphold a familiar Commerce together in all meekness, gentleness, patience and liberality, we must delight in each other; make other's Conditions our own; rejoice together, mourn together, labor, and suffer together, always having before our eyes our Commission and Community in the work, our Community as members of the same body, so shall wee keep the unity of the spirit in the bond of peace, the Lord will be our God and delight to dwell among us, as his own people and will command a blessing upon us in all our ways, so that wee shall see much more of his wisdom power goodness and truth then formerly we have been acquainted with, we shall find that the God of Israel is among us, when ten of us shall be able to resist a thousand of our enemies, when he shall make us a praise and glory, that men shall say of succeeding plantations: the lord make it like that of New England: for we must Consider that we shall be as a City upon a Hill,[5] the eyes of all people are upon us; so that if wee shall deal falsely with our god in this work we have undertaken and so cause him to withdraw his present help from us, we shall be made a story and a byword through the world, we shall open the mouths of enemies to speak evil of the ways of god and all professors for Gods sake; we shall shame the faces of many of gods worthy servants, and cause their prayers to be turned into Curses upon us till we be consumed out of the good land whether we are going: And to shut up this discourse with that exhortation of Moses that faithful servant of the Lord in his last farewell to Israel Deut. 30.[6] Beloved there is now set before us life, and good, death and evil in that we are Commanded this day to love the Lord our God, and to love one another to walk in his ways and to keep his Commandments and his Ordinance, and his laws, and the Articles of

---

[4] An ancient Jewish prophet.
[5] The image is that of Jerusalem on Mount Zion.
[6] The rest of this selection is a paraphrase of Deuteronomy 30:15–20.

our Covenant with him that we may live and be multiplied, and that the Lord our God may bless us in the land whether we go to possess it: But if our hearts shall turn away so that we will not obey, but shall be seduced and worship other Gods our pleasures, and profits, and serve them, it is propounded unto us this day, wee shall surely perish out of the good Land whether we pass over this vast Sea to possess it; Therefore let us choose life, that we, and our Seed, may live; by obeying his voice, and cleaveing to him, for he is our life, and our prosperity.

Epilogue: Making Connections

By the end of these two centuries of discovery and expansion, the globe had not only been encompassed, but a good deal of it had been carved up into empires by the major Western European powers. In Asia, the Portuguese found a complex trading system already in existence upon their arrival. First, they ruthlessly defeated the Arab traders and Muslim states that hitherto had dominated the oceanic trade with their naval might. Then, they disrupted the traditional Levantine trade through the Red Sea and Persian Gulf using this same military superiority, and reoriented the spice trade around the Cape of Good Hope to Lisbon. In the process, Portugal obtained wealth and power far in excess of what the country's size and resources would have portended in 1500. In Asia, however, the Portuguese also confronted the powerful land empires of Persia, Mughal India, Japan, and China, states that Portugal's relatively paltry armies could never hope to defeat. Thus, from the beginning to the end of these centuries, the Portuguese had been restricted to coastal enclaves from which they sought to dominate the oceanic trade. In the Americas, on the other hand, the Portuguese and the Spaniards obtained colonies where their military technology and the ravages of Old World diseases gave them the ability to expand inland, which they willingly did in search of gold and other resources. Of course, the effective control over these vast territories was somewhat tenuous. The resilience of indigenous structures and the development of maroon societies of escaped slaves limited the power of these Iberian empires during this period.

Into these overseas empires, the Portuguese and Spaniards exported the dominant features of their societies. Administratively, viceroys, captains-general, and councils dominated by the nobility and clergy ruled for the king. Economically, a monarchical monopolism was established that sought to extract precious metals, customs revenues, and profits from mercantile exchange for the Crown. The king claimed ultimate power over all this overseas trade, just as he claimed ultimate authority over his kingdom, but he was willing to share it with nobles, merchants, bankers, and even the New Christians, if the price was right or necessity demanded. Socially, the dominance of the nobility was also entrenched thanks to huge land grants and the need for military service. But loyal, if humble-born soldiers could also share in this bounty overseas, something that was much more difficult to obtain at home. With regard to religion, the Catholic faith was spread throughout these empires and the power of the Roman Church, as in Portugal and Spain, was formidable. Mass conversions were made, while the Inquisition was exported as well, as a means of religious and social control. The clergy, however, found itself in an ambiguous position between perpetuating the dominant culture and religious dogma of Iberia while increasingly drawn to the spiritual and material needs of indigenous converts. As defenders of their flocks, these priests were frequently the targets of derision and resentment by landowning colonists. Finally, in the Atlantic empires of Portugal and Spain, slavery constituted a vital component of the imperial system, which by definition resulted in suffering and death for millions of Africans during these two centuries. As had traditionally been the case in medieval Europe, the wealth and power of the imperial elite was produced by the forced labor of the exploited masses.

The entrance of the Protestant powers of the Netherlands and England into this imperial competition has traditionally been viewed as constituting a definitive break with the Iberian Century of 1500–1600. In some ways this was undoubtedly true. But upon closer examination, especially in Asia, the view that the entrepreneurial structures of the Protestant trading companies gave them inherent and insurmountable advantages in their struggle with the monarchical monopolism of the Portuguese Crown has been overstated. The attempt to portray the VOC and the EIC as vanguards for pristine proto-capitalist structures, while attractive, is flawed. One fundamental problem with advancing the strict dichotomy of proto-capitalist versus monarchical monopolism, which lies at the base of this model for the commercial struggle between the Atlantic economies (and Asian companies) of these Protestant and Catholic powers, is that it assumes largely static and unchanging structures and priorities for these rivals during the course of the entire 17th century. This was far from the case, as Dutch policies in Indonesia, India, and Ceylon well illustrate. At the time of the amalgamation by the States-General of the United Company there was general agreement in the Netherlands that this new commercial entity should at all costs avoid what was perceived as the fatal error of the Portuguese in Asia: unnecessary and prohibitively expensive territorial expansion, in favor of pursuing a profitable trade that would avoid burdensome military expenses. Yet, from the time of Coen onward, this pristine entrepreneurialism, if indeed it ever existed, was jettisoned in favor of a quest for monopoly that by definition entailed huge military and administrative expenses.

The Dutch built and maintained fortresses, kept large numbers of troops both European and Asian on the payroll, and adopted the pass system of the Portuguese wherever possible. In Asia, the Dutch system became a virtual mirror image of the *Estado da India* more than a capitalist rejection of it. Proto-capitalism had been abandoned for what might be called 'vulturine' mercantilism. As a result, warfare was endemic for the remainder of the 17th century. By the mid-1670s, the far-flung empire of the Dutch was firmly wedded to the warfare and military expenses that had initially characterized the *Estado da India*. Decisions in Amsterdam and Batavia were adopted based not so much on the transparency of markets, but by their relationship to the geopolitical equation of power politics. These policies placed the VOC on the verge of overextending its resources as it prepared to defend its widely dispersed possessions against Asian and European rivals. These rivals were either bent on revenge (like the reforming *Estado da India*), committed to winning a larger share of the trade (like the French and English), or merely defending themselves against

Dutch territorial intrusions (like Rajah Sinha II). Rather than avoiding the costly mistakes of the Portuguese, the Dutch had come to embrace them: overextension, huge military and administrative costs, almost constant warfare, an obsessive desire to monopolize key commodities in the trade, and a growing primacy of imperial geopolitical priorities over sound proto-capitalist practices.

In the end, however, whether this overseas rivalry conformed to the strict dichotomy of proto-capitalist versus monarchical monopolism or a more symbiotic model whereby all of the imperial powers gradually came to resemble and adopt the tactics and methods of their rivals, the key factor is that the construction of these overseas global empires constituted a fundamental revolution in the history of humankind. The interchange of trading goods, disease pools, and ideologies that took place from 1500 to 1700 created the foundations for the world we inhabit today. As early as the 18th century, in the midst of the Enlightenment, leading thinkers had already appreciated this fact. In 1776, Adam Smith in his *Wealth of Nations* noted, "the discovery of America, and that of a passage to the East Indies by the Cape of Good Hope, are the two greatest and most important events recorded in the history of mankind." Since that time, the empires forged by the Europeans have come and gone, and technology, political systems, and even the role of religion have all changed, but the elemental cultural and economic links forged during the Age of Discovery still remain at the basis of human interaction on this globe. In many parts of the world today, the languages that are spoken, the foods that are eaten, and the beverages that are consumed are all direct legacies of this process. Economically, the development of insurance companies, large-scale banking, world markets, and mass consumer societies are all outgrowths of the linkages established during this Age of Discovery. Moreover, the ethnic and racial interaction that followed in the wake of the arrival of the Europeans quickly produced mixed populations and new ethnicities which today form significant demographic groups worldwide. Religiously, this age began the process of globalizing not only Christianity, but Hinduism, Islam, and Buddhism as well.

That said, there are still many questions to ponder about this cross-cultural process from ca. 1500 to 1700. How was it that a small, arid, and relatively poor country like Portugal managed to create the first global empire and not her more powerful rivals? How did the strategy of the Protestant Dutch and English differ from that of the Iberians? And did religious differences among the Europeans really matter in this process of empire-building around the globe? To what degree did the Europeans have an impact on and even change the structures they encountered, and to what degree were they changed by them? Where was life more markedly different in 1700 than it had been in 1450: Lisbon, Seville, London, and Amsterdam, or Aden, Agra, Melaka, and Bantam? What was the major impact of the Europeans on Amerindian and Asian cultures during this period? In the New World, were the Europeans assisted more by their technological advantages or their diseases? In Asia and Africa, why was it only in the 18th and 19th centuries that the Europeans were able to create large land empires? When, if ever, during this period did the Atlantic World and global empires of the Europeans become more important to them than their position in the Asian trade? And finally, did European structures or individuals play the more important role in the Age of Discovery? In essence, how important were the lives and careers of Vasco da Gama and Christopher Columbus for world history? How did their accomplishments help establish the basis for the economic, religious, and cultural structures for the world we live in today?

Bibliography

Useful Works on the Age of Expansion and World Trade

Traditional works on the background and advances that led to the Age of Discovery include J.H. Parry, *The Age of Reconnaissance: Discovery, Exploration and Settlement* 1450 to 1650 (1963, 1981), and his concise *The Establishment of European Hegemony: 1415–1715: Trade and Exploration in the Age of the Renaissance* (1959, 1966). Both books have been standard fare on syllabi for undergraduate courses on European expansion for decades. *See also* Felipe Fernández-Armesto's *Before Columbus: Exploration and Colonization from the Mediterranean to the Atlantic, 1229–1492* (1987) and *Pathfinders: A Global History of Exploration* (2006). For the development of the spirit of discovery and intellectual trends that facilitated it, readers should consult Daniel J. Boorstin's engaging work *The Discoverers: A History of Man's Search to Know His World and Himself* (1983). The advances in military science that assisted the Europeans in their quest for empire are detailed in Carlo Cipolla's *Guns, Sails and Empires: Technological Innovation and the Early Phases of European Expansion, 1400–1700* (1965) and Geoffrey

Parker's *The Military Revolution: Military Innovation and the Rise of the West* (1988, 1996). For an overview of trade in the major regions of the globe, see Philip Curtin, *Cross-Cultural Trade in World History* (1984), Fernand Braudel, *The Mediterranean and the Mediterranean World in the Age of Philip II* (2 vols, 1972), *The Wheels of Commerce: Civilization and Capitalism, 15th–18th Century* (3 vols, 1984), K.N. Chauduri, *Asia before Europe* (1991), and most recently Erik Gilbert and Jonathan Reynolds, *Trading Tastes: Commodity and Cultural Exchange to 1750* (2006). Anthony Pagden's *Lords of all the World: Ideologies of Empire in Spain, Britain and France c.1500–c.1800* (1998) and *Peoples and Empires: A Short History of European Migration, Exploration, and Conquest, from Greece to the Present* (2003) are interesting studies on the intellectual underpinnings of empire.

Useful Works on the Portuguese Overseas Empire

Charles R. Boxer was the most prolific scholar on the Portuguese overseas world. During his long and distinguished career, Boxer published hundreds of books and articles. Among his best were the classic *The Portuguese Seaborne Empire, 1415–1825* (1969), *The Church Militant and Iberian Expansion* (1978), *Race Relations in the Portuguese Colonial Empire, 1415–1825* (1963), and *Salvador de Sá and the Struggle for Brazil and Angola, 1602–1686* (1952). Standard 19th-century accounts on the Portuguese empire include F.C. Danvers, *The Portuguese in India* (2 vols, 1894), R.S. Whiteway, *The Rise of Portuguese Power in India, 1497–1550* (1899), and Edgar Prestage, *The Portuguese Pioneers*. More recent studies on the Portuguese overseas world include George D. Winius and B.W. Diffie, *Foundations of Portuguese Empire, 1415–1825* (1977), Sanjay Subrahmanyam, *The Portuguese Empire in Asia, 1500–1700* (1993), M.N. Pearson, *The Portuguese in India* (1987) and *World of the Indian Ocean, 1500–1800: Studies in Economic, Social and Cultural History* (2005), R.J. Barendse, *The Arabian Seas: The Indian Ocean World of the Seventeenth Century* (1998) and A.J.R. Russell-Wood, *A World on the Move: The Portuguese in Africa, Asia, and America, 1415–1808* (1993). Recent biographical works include Peter Russell, *Prince Henry the 'Navigator'* (2001), Sanjay Subrahmanyam, *The Career and Legend of Vasco da Gama* (1998), and Glenn J. Ames, *Vasco da Gama: Renaissance Crusader* (2005). On the early development of Brazil, see C.H. Haring, *Empire in Brazil: A New World Experiment with Monarchy* (1958), B.W. Diffie, *A History of Colonial*

Brazil (1987), Stuart B. Schwartz, *Sugar Plantations in the Formation of the Brazilian Society: Bahia, 1550–1835* (1985) and Russell-Wood's *Fidalgos and Philanthropists: The Santa Casa da Misericórdia of Bahia, 1550–1755* (1968). A provocative attempt to reexamine the *Estado da India* from the Indian perspective can be found in M.N. Pearson's *Merchants and Rulers in Gujarat: The Response to the Portuguese in the Sixteenth Century* (1975) and *Coastal Western India* (1981). For the rehabilitation of Portuguese Asia after 1663, see Glenn J. Ames, *Renascent Empire?: The House of Braganza and the Quest for Stability in Portuguese Monsoon Asia, ca. 1640–1683* (2000).

Useful Works on the Spanish Overseas Empire

For an overview on internal developments in Spain and the development of the empire, the best place to start is with J.H. Elliot's *Imperial Spain, 1469–1716* (1963). Henry Kamen's more recent *Spain's Road to Empire: The Making of a World Empire* (2002) and *Empire: How Spain Became a World Power, 1492–1763* (2003) are also of interest. Traditional works from the vast historical literature on this topic include Samuel Eliot Morison's classic biography of Columbus, *Admiral of the Ocean Sea* (1942) and W.H. Prescott's standard 19th-century works, *The Conquest of Mexico* (1843), *The Conquest of Peru* (1847), and *History of the Reign of Ferdinand and Isabella* (1837) which are still impressive for both their erudition and their historiographical significance. Other standard accounts on the development of the imperial system include J.H. Parry, *The Spanish Theory of Empire in the Sixteenth Century* (1940) and *The Spanish Seaborne Empire* (1966), C.H. Haring, *The Spanish Empire in America* (1947), Charles Gibson, *Spain in America* (1967), and R.B. Merriman, *The Rise of the Spanish Empire* (4 vols, 1934). Recent works generally tend to examine the structures of the empire more from the indigenous perspective. These studies include James Lockhart, *The Nahuas after the Conquest: A Social and Cultural History of the Indians of Central Mexico, Sixteenth through Eighteenth Centuries* (1992), D.A. Brading, *The First America: The Spanish Monarchy, Creole Patriots and the Liberal State, 1492–1866* (1991), Inga Clendinnen, *Ambivalent Conquests Maya and Spaniard in Yucatan, 1517–1570* (1988), Patricia Seed, *Ceremonies of Possession in Europe's Conquest of the New World, 1492–1640* (1995), and Matthew Restall, *The Maya World: Yucatec Culture and Society, 1550–1850* (1997) and *Maya Conquistador* (1998). For an interesting study on the development of piracy as a weapon against Spain's empire, see Kris Lane, *Pillaging the Empire: Piracy in the Americas, 1500–1750* (1998).

Useful Works on the Dutch Overseas Empire

The classic study in this field remains C.R. Boxer's *The Dutch Seaborne Empire, 1600–1800* (1965). Boxer later wrote *Jan Compagnie in War and Peace, 1602–1799: A Short History of the Dutch East-India Company* (1979). On the VOC, two important works that emphasize the relationship between indigenous structures and the Dutch Asian empire are J.C. van Leur's sociologically based *Indonesian Trade and Society: Essays in Asian Social and Economic History* (1955) and M.A.P. Meilink-Roelofsz's *Asian Trade and European Influence in the Indonesian Archipelago between 1500 and about 1630* (1962). Other works on Dutch power in Asia include Tapan Raychaudhuri's *Jan Company in Coromandel, 1605–1690: A Study in the Interrelations of European Commerce and Traditional Economies* (1962), Dianne Lewis, *Jan Compagnie in the Straits of Malacca, 1641–1795* (1995), R.G. Anthonisz, *The Dutch in Ceylon* (1929), Sinnappah Arasaratnam, *Dutch Power in Ceylon, 1658–1687* (1958), and Om Prakash, *The Dutch East India Company and the Economy of Bengal, 1630–1720* (1985). On the structural advantages of the Dutch Company and their impact on the trade, see Niels Steensgaard, *The Asian Trade Revolution of the Seventeenth Century* (1974).

For additional information on the Dutch West India Company, see Jaap Jacobs, *New Netherland: A Dutch Colony in Seventeenth-Century America* (2005) and Russell Shorto's popular history *The Island at the Center of the World: The Epic Story of Dutch Manhattan, the Forgotten Colony that Shaped America* (2004). On the Dutch in Brazil, Boxer's earlier work *The Dutch in Brazil, 1624–1654* (1957) is informative. Willie F. Page, *The Dutch Triangle: The Netherlands and the Atlantic Slave Trade, 1621–1664* (1997) examines the overall trading system in the Atlantic. Jonathan I. Israel also has several important books in this field—*The Dutch Republic and the Hispanic World, 1606–1661* (1982), *Dutch Primacy in World Trade, 1585–1740* (1989), and *The Dutch Republic: Its Rise, Greatness, and Fall 1477–1806* (1995). For an interesting take on the societal forces that shaped the Dutch during this period, see Simon Schama, *The Embarrassment of Riches: An Interpretation of Dutch Culture in the Golden Age* (1987). Finally, there are several edited works on empire with valuable chapters on the Dutch experience overseas. These include James D. Tracy, *The Rise of Merchant*

Empires: Long Distance Trade in the Early Modern World 1350–1750 (1993) and *The Political Economy of Merchant Empires: State Power and World Trade, 1350–1750* (1997) and Johannes Postma and Victor Enthoven, *Riches from Atlantic Commerce: Dutch Transatlantic Trade and Shipping, 1585–1817* (2003).

Useful Works on the English Overseas Empire

The early English voyages to America have been authoritatively examined by Samuel Eliot Morison in his work *The European Discovery of America: The Northern Voyages A.D. 500–1600* (1971). For a more 'fanciful' take, see Bernard Bailyn, *The Peopling of British North America: An Introduction* (1986). Standard works on the early colonization schemes usually presented from the view of the colonizers include David B. Quinn, *The Failure of Raleigh's American Colonies* (1949) and *England and the Discovery of America, 1481–1621* (1974), Kenneth R. Andrews, *Elizabethan Privateering: English Privateering during the Spanish War 1585–1603* (1966), and Julian S. Corbett, *Drake and the Tudor Navy* (2 vols, 1899).

More recent studies providing a wider perspective include James Axtell, *The Invasion Within: The Contest of Cultures in Colonial North America* (1985), Denys Delage, *Bitter Feast: Amerindians and Europeans in Northeastern North America* (1993), Jack P. Greene, *Pursuits of Happiness: The Social Development of Early Modern British Colonies and the Formation of American Culture* (1988), Karen Ordahl Kupperman, *Indians and English Facing off in Early America* (2000), Peter E. Pope, *Fish into Wine: The Newfoundland Plantation in the Seventeenth Century* (2004), and Giles Milton, *Big Chief Elizabeth: The Adventures and Fate of the First English Colonists in America* (2000). Eric Handeraker and Peter C. Mancall, *At the Edge of Empire: The Backcountry in British North America* (2003) provides an interesting revisionist take on the importance of the shifting frontier areas for the empire. Perhaps the best overviews of the rapidly developing field of Atlantic history are given in Bernard Bailyn's *Atlantic History: Concepts and Contours* (2005) and David Armitage and Michael J. Braddick, *The British Atlantic World, 1500–1800* (2002). For a provocative Marxist analysis of traditionally ignored groups in the Atlantic, see Peter Linebaugh and Marcus Rediker, *The Many-Headed Hydra: The Hidden History of the Revolutionary Atlantic* (2001).

On the English East India Company, the standard works include Holden Furber, *John Company at Work: A Study of European Expansion in India in the Late Eighteenth Century* (1951), K.N. Chaudhuri, *The English East India Company: The Study of an Early Joint-Stock Company 1600–1640* (1965) and *The Trading World of Asia and the English East India Company* (1978), William J. Barber, *British Economic Thought and India, 1600–1858* (1975), and William Foster, *The East India House: Its History and Associations* (1924). For a good overview of the struggle for empire in Asia, see Furber's *Rival Empires of Trade in the Orient, 1600–1800* (1976). Giles Milton's *Nathaniel's Nutmeg: Or, The True and Incredible Adventures of the Spice Trader Who Changed the Course of History* (1999) is a popular account of the early struggle in Indonesia between the English and the Dutch.

Useful Works on the French Overseas Empire

It is significant that in the 1960s a companion 'seaborne' empire volume on the French never appeared to complement those of Boxer and Parry on the Portuguese, Dutch, and Spaniards. Nevertheless, there are several standard works beginning with the 19th-century studies of Francis Parkman. Parkman's studies included *The Pioneers of France in the New World* (1865), *The Jesuits in North America in the Seventeenth Century* (1867), and *Count Frontenac and New France under Louis XIV* (1877). Other traditional accounts include Thomas Chapais, *The Great Intendant: A Chronicle of Jean Talon in Canada, 1665–1672* (1914), Samuel Eliot Morison, *Samuel de Champlain, Father of New France* (1972), John Fiske, *New France and New England* (1902), W.J. Eccles, *France in America* (1972) which covers Canada, Louisiana, and the Caribbean islands, Ramsay Cook, *The Voyages of Jacques Cartier* (1993) and Cornelius Jaenen, *The Role of the Church in New France* (1976) and *Friend and Foe: Aspects of French-Amerindian Cultural Contact in the Sixteenth and Seventeenth Centuries* (1976). Also of interest is Jacob M. Price's *France and the Chesapeake: A History of the French Tobacco Monopoly* (1973).

The classic study on the overseas projects of Jean-Baptiste Colbert remains C.W. Cole's *Colbert and a Century of French Mercantilism* (2 vols, 1939). For additional background on the development of mercantilism, Cole's earlier work *French Mercantilism before Colbert* (1931) is still valuable. Interesting recent works on the French empire in Canada and the Caribbean include Daniel H. Usner, *Indians, Settlers, and Slaves in a Frontier Exchange Economy: The Lower Mississippi Valley*

Before 1783 (1992), Peter Moogk, *La Nouvelle France: The Making of French Canada* (2000), and James Pritchard, *In Search of Empire: The French in the Americas, 1670–1730* (2004).

Studies on the French East India companies, especially in English, are far less numerous than on the French presence in the Atlantic region. This is one field relating to European expansion that still requires more scholarly attention. That said, the existing studies include George B. Malleson, *History of the French in India* (1909), S.P. Sen, *The French in India: First Establishment and Settlement* (1947), Glenn J. Ames, *Colbert, Mercantilism and the French Quest for Asian Trade* (1996), and for a slightly later period, Catherine Manning's *Fortunes a Faire: The French in Asian Trade, 1719–48* (1996).

Index